THE COUNTRY LIFE COLLECTOR'S
POCKET BOOK
OF SILVER

THE COUNTRY LIFE COLLECTOR'S

POCKET BOOK
OF SILVER

JUDITH BANISTER

COUNTRY LIFE BOOKS

Published by Country Life Books
and distributed for them by
The Hamlyn Publishing Group Limited
London · New York · Sydney · Toronto
Astronaut House, Feltham, Middlesex, England

© Copyright Country Life Books 1982

All rights reserved. No part of this publication
may be reproduced, stored in a retrieval system
or transmitted, in any form or by any means, electronic,
mechanical, photocopying, recording or otherwise, without
the permission of the copyright owner.

First published 1982

ISBN 0 600 38271 0

Printed in England by
Hazell Watson & Viney Ltd.
Aylesbury, Bucks.

Contents

I	A Brief Survey of Styles	7
II	A. The Craft of the Silversmith	67
	B. Decorative Techniques	78
III	Objects	86
IV	Glossary of Terms	204
V	The Marks of Silver	233
VI	Notes and Hints for the Collector	252
	A. Fakes, Forgeries and Furbishing	253
	B. The Care and Cleaning of Silver and Silver-Gilt	261
Appendices: A. Some Useful Dates		268
	B. Weights and Measures	272
	C. The Patent Office Design Registry	273
A Short Critical Bibliography		275
Index		278

CHAPTER ONE

A Brief Survey of Styles

Despite popular usage, the habit of naming styles of silver (or of any other of the applied arts) by the reigns of monarchs is to be deplored. Generally speaking, one style did not come to an end with the death of one sovereign and another leap into prominence on the accession of the next. The illogicality of the habit, perpetuated by many dealers and writers, can best be exposed by considering the much overworked term 'Georgian' – intended to cover the reigns of the first four Georges – though often not qualified by their proper name. The Hanoverian Georges reigned from the death of Queen Anne in 1714 until that of George IV in 1830. During that century, styles changed, sometimes subtly, sometimes abruptly. As inconsistent is suggesting that 'Victorian' means a homogeneous style from 1837 to 1901 – an era that ranged from revivalist Gothicism to art nouveau and from naturalism to the aesthetic, not to mention innumerable excursions into rococoism, neoclassicism, japonaiseries and the Arts and Crafts Movement. Indeed, the only excuse for such terms is that dealers want their goods to be 'in date', based on the premise that up to 1830 they are truly to be called antique, on the assumption that subsequently machine, rather than hand, craftsmanship dominated. Similarly, eighty years on, Victorian now has a nice antiquated ring about it, and many countries accept as 'antique' pieces that can be shown to be a century old.

THE END OF THE MIDDLE AGES

Although the extremely rare survivals of English silver dating from the 15th century and earlier are mostly in permanent museum captivity and so beyond the scope of even the most opulent collector, it is salutary to glance at the style and character of medieval plate, if only to discover the origins of later form and ornament.

Silver in the Middle Ages was primarily for the rich, though the well-to-do household generally had at least one cup or bowl of silver and enough spoons for each member of the family to have one apiece. Wills and inventories reveal that both professional men and craftsmen were often able to afford quite extensive collections of silver, some of it parcel (or part) gilt for greater show as well as for durability. To possess silver was a token of standing. As a storehouse it had the advantage that it could be turned into money should war, taxation or other necessity arise. The greater the house, the more extensive and varied the display of plate, though it must be pointed out that the 'gold plate' so frequently mentioned was seldom anything other than silver-gilt, except in royal collections. Nonetheless, every man of substance, commoner or noble, was eager to put on a fair show and indulge in the love of ceremony. The etiquette of the table has lingered on – the placing of the chief guests has its origins in the great ceremony of the salt, for instance. This time-honoured tradition both in England as well as abroad produced some of the most splendid of all known pieces from the later Middle Ages until the war-torn years of the 17th century, and gradually transformed the great house from feudal hall to domestic palace.

Wills and inventories cast a faint light on what the average household might possess. In 1436 Thomas Damett, a canon of St Paul's, left his Mother 'I silver cup chaced and covered with writing . . . 1 dozen of silver spoons and a silver salt with gilt edges (quoted by John Harvey in *Gothic England*). The cup must have been rather like the famous Studley Bowl and cover, now in the Victoria and Albert Museum, which is decorated with a Gothic alphabet.

When a rich householder of Paris in 1392 set down the order of a feast for the guidance of his young wife (*Le Ménagier de*

Paris, Traité de Morale et d'Economie Domestique, translated by Eileen Power) he noted that two *maîtres d'hôtel* would be needed. Among other duties, they would set out 'the silver salts for the high table, the four great gilded goblets, the four dozen hanaps, the four dozen silver spoons, the ewers and alms mugs and sweetmeat dishes. . . .' A hundred years later, the old order had little changed. Even 200 years later, as Queen Elizabeth I made her progresses from one nobleman's great house to the next, emptying the purses of her hosts as she did so, she sat at high table furnished with a great salt and gilded goblets, spoons and standing cups, ewers and basins filled with rosewater in which to dip the fingers. The latter, at least until the end of her reign, were still the best tools for eating in a forkless age.

It is virtually impossible to compile a clear and detailed historical survey of medieval English silver. Little remains, much is unmarked. Secular silver is so scarce that one can only record that most surviving cups and salts, for instance, show a kinship with contemporary architecture in their fine crestings and meticulous flower-and-foliage ornament and their use of armorial finials. Examples are the Foundress's Cup at Christ's College, Cambridge, bequeathed by Lady Margaret Beaufort to her foundation in 1509, or the lobed thistle-like cup and cover belonging to the Armourers' and Brasiers' Company presented to them by John Richmond in 1547, but probably made some forty years earlier.

At that time, the font-shaped bowl was much in favour, as the Cressener Cup of 1503 shows, a plain cup enriched only by an enamelled print (medallion) in the finial of the cover, that remained in family possession until purchased by the Goldsmiths' Company in 1908. Contemporary with these Gothic cups were the simple silver and silver-gilt mounted mazers, shallow maplewood bowls that had been in use, especially in monasteries, for many hundreds of years. One of the most famous, the Saffron Walden mazer of 1507, was kept in the almshouses there until 1929, and from which, on a visit in 1659, the diarist Samuel Pepys drank off 'a draft of their drink in a brown bowl, tipt with silver, .. and at the bottom was a picture of the Virgin and the Child in her arms, done in silver'. It was sold at Christies twice, in 1929 and in 1971.

More ornate were the great standing salts, of which several remain in the treasured collections of Colleges and City Companies. By the end of the 15th century, an hourglass shape came into fashion, with hexagonal panelled or lobed sides, the precious salt contained in a small hemispherical well in the centre of the upper section.

More English silver survives from the reigns of King Henry VIII and his children than from the previous two centuries together. Still it is tantalisingly rare. The reign of Henry VIII was one of the most destructive of any in the history of English silver and gold. The King, inheriting the Kingdom that had at last been unified by his father's efforts, saw himself as a monarch in the European style, though his empire consisted of only some three million souls. And their souls were ruled by a Church, rich, powerful and foreign. The Reformation of 1536 'down-razed' the abbeys and monasteries, which were looted of their treasures. The King's seemingly inexhaustible demand for money sent the greater part to the melting-pot, but even that was not enough to prevent the debasement of the currency. From that time the Lion Passant standard mark acquired a crown, to signify that the sterling standard was that laid down by the King, not the Goldsmiths. Now royal and personal wealth began to replace the wealth formerly held by the Church, and the King and his Court sought to outshine every other in Europe.

In Europe, new ideas were astir. Spreading gradually from Italy northwards into France and Germany, the Low Countries and England, and finally into Scandinavia, the rebirth of learning brought with it a new awareness of form, of the classical orders and classical ornament that was soon to oust the Gothic and put an end to the Middle Ages. With a universal appeal the Renaissance blazed through Europe bringing a new refinement to art, architecture and artefacts of every kind.

Henry VIII's Court became a magnet for artists and craftsmen, among them the Swiss-born Hans Holbein the Younger who arrived in England in 1526 and who executed both paintings and goldsmiths' work for the King. After a late start – the earliest surviving piece of truly Renaissance style bearing English hallmarks is the Boleyn Cup of 1535 at Cirencester, though others of earlier date no doubt met their fate in Charles I's melting-pots a century later – the new fashion quickly became established. This was fostered both by foreign goldsmiths from Germany and the Netherlands and by the elegant pattern-books of engravings, showing form and decoration in the new manner. These were styles that the English craftsmen imitated as best they could, though usually with less skill than the continentals.

Nonetheless, inventories, reports and occasional survivals tell a story of silver-gilt splendour not only in palace and castle but also in well-to-do households throughout the land. A good deal of medieval plate probably made way for flagons, tankards, goblets, salts, dishes and standing cups in Renaissance taste. The cups had deep bowls supported on high stems ringed with cast brackets. The salts often were of architectural design, and the great ewers and tankards of globular form. Only the ubiquitous spoon, with its fig-shaped bowl and decorative finial – diamond, acorn, Apostle, maidenhead or seal-top – changed hardly at all from its medieval counterpart.

Decoration of the basic Renaissance style required considerable skill on the part of the chaser and the engraver and a proper sense of form – not always evident – on the part of the silversmith. Finials, often of exaggerated proportions, surmounted by warriors bearing spears and shields, scrollwork at every corner, urns and mouldings, foliage and flowers were used lavishly, and sometimes indiscriminately, to produce as much intrinsic splendour as the piece could bear.

A BRIEF SURVEY OF STYLES

The mounting of rock crystal, serpentine and other hardstones, as well as of rare Chinese porcelain, ivory, ostrich eggs, coconuts and even glass accorded very well with the 16th-century taste for richness. Fortunately for posterity, a fair number of such mounted wares survive, avoiding destruction, perhaps, because the amount of gold or silver used did not warrant it. From the middle of the century onwards, huge quantities of Rhenish stoneware were imported, the most common being the speckled brown ware known as tigerware, and these were almost always mounted in silver or silver-gilt. William Harrison, recording the customs of the English in the 1580s, noted that all sorts and conditions of people drank from 'potts of earth of sundry colours, and moulds, whereof many are garnished with silver'. Besides tigerware, there was a pipe-grey stoneware associated with Siegburg, as well as various slip-dash types of pottery. The shape of these pots, on spreading foot, with bellied body, tall neck and D-shaped handle made them very suitable for mounting. The chased or engraved neck mounts included a domed cover, usually chased with swags of fruit and with a baluster or sometimes a disc finial, and box hinge; the mount sometimes also extended down the handle. The foot was also protected with a mount decorated with simple stamped borders, while three straps sometimes extended to a rib round the waist of the tankard or jug. More rarely, the whole jug was encased in a cagework of pierced silver. It is interesting to note that the straight unlipped mount of these jugs pours extremely well.

All-silver tankards (livery pots) were also globular in form – the earliest appears to date from 1556 – but the straight-sided tapered style of flagon form was by far the most popular, richly chased with strapwork and foliage or, for those with simpler tastes and smaller purses, engraved with similar designs. Plainer still were the new Communion cups and paten covers in an almost standard form ordered by Queen Elizabeth in 1570. During the next five or six years they replaced the old chalices in every parish throughout the land: many by provincial silversmiths reveal local variations, such as almost conical instead of deep flared bowls made in Sussex. Near the centre of the bowl a girdle of engraved strapwork enclosing arabesques or an inscription was usual. Of similar form, but with the strapwork engraved near the rim were beakers, in the late 16th to early 17th century with slightly flared bowls, stamped rim feet and about 6 in. high. Smaller similar beakers are chiefly of 17th-century date, and very popular from 1660 onwards.

Plain functional goblets, sometimes with a cover, on a tall stem and a low spreading foot were sometimes delicately engraved with trailing flowers and foliage, with small cast scroll brackets applied near the top of the stem to make them into 'grace cups'; at their most elaborate at the turn of the century, they were sometimes given panelled and richly chased bowls. An extension of this type of cup with a cover was fashionable between 1599 and the 1640s: the steeple cup, so called from its pyramid finial. 'Pattern-book' decoration included lilies of the valley, strapwork, vines and sea monsters either chased or engraved.

The medieval mazer bowl seems to have inspired the taste for standing mazers (a fashionable Renaissance development especially in Scotland) and closely akin to them were shallow standing bowls. Usually mis-called tazze, they were not in fact cups but stands for fruit, sweetmeats or simply as decoration at the table. Many featured repouss´-chased scenes from the Bible or classical literature within the bowls, or sometimes profile heads.

Standing salts during the later 16th century remained a central feature of ceremonial at table. They were now of architectural form, with four or more columns enclosing the main feature, the salt in a small well at the top, and with a high domed cover surmounted by one of the ubiquitous warrior finials. Rock crystal or glass remained a popular material for mounting into these great salts, as in the Gibbon Salt of 1576 with a figure of

Neptune enclosed in the rock crystal (now in the Goldsmiths' Company collection) or the glass and enamelled Vyvian Salt of 1592 (in the Victoria and Albert Museum).

The prosperity engendered by exploration and trade during Elizabeth's reign brought wealth to a huge new merchant class, and, paradoxically, this brought a rather less opulent approach to plate: the new rich required well-stocked cupboards full of silver, but often aspired to less grandiose trappings of feudal origin. Many items gradually assumed a more domestic appearance, rather than the massive display plate used in the great halls where the higher nobility still dined in public splendour.

The salt as yet remained a focus of table setting, but in the last decade of the 16th century a new smaller style came in: the tiered three-piece bell salt, the lowest section of skirt form, on three or four feet, containing a well, with another tier above, and on top a small spice caster. That remained in fashion until about 1620, alongside the plain cylindrical type with a steeple top. Small trencher salts, placed by each guest, were really miniatures of the 16th-century standing salt. These continued to be made, and at the same time suggested the form for a new style of standing salt: the capstan or spool shape, surmounted with three or four cast scroll brackets, on which, it is thought, a plain dish, cover, or napkin was laid to cover the salt.

Silver and parcel-gilt dishes and plates must once have been fairly plentiful, though few have survived. One notable collection is a set of twenty-two dishes and plates of varying sizes, from $8\frac{3}{4}$ in. to just over 15 in. in diameter that were recovered many years ago after having been buried on Dartmoor about 1645 during the Civil War. Called the Armada service, because it was supposedly made from silver taken from the Spanish ships (although some dishes date from 1581, seven years earlier), it was made for Sir Christopher Harris between 1581 and 1601, and weighs no less than 480 oz. 12 dwt.

Several sets of highly exceptional plates and bowls include a

A BRIEF SURVEY OF STYLES

1 Standing salts TOP ROW, FROM LEFT *c.* 1570, *c.* 1600, *c.* 1670.
Trencher salts CLOCKWISE FROM CENTRE *c.* 1720, *c.* 1735, *c.* 1690,
c. 1745, *c.* 1810, *c.* 1790, *c.* 1770, *c.* 1760.

dozen of 1567 engraved with the Labours of Hercules within parcel-gilt borders and another twelve made in 1568 and 1569 engraved with the parable of the Prodigal Son. Six bowls with Old Testament subjects have also survived, and so have a ewer and basin with portraits of English sovereigns and another with Biblical scenes, all by the same but as yet unidentified engraver, some of the work signed P over M. Their survival no doubt was due to the quality of the decoration.

The ewer and basin was, of course, an important dining-room accessory, for even at the end of the 16th century forks were a dandified, foreign custom really only appropriate for fishing out preserved fruits and other suckets from their containers. It took another hundred years for such affected manners to be acceptable at the Englishman's table. Tall bellied ewers and great broad-rimmed basins kept many a silversmith busy – though of course there must have been as many or more made in latten (brass) and in pewter for less wealthy households.

But even the not-so-rich had a collection of spoons to bring to table, and Apostle and other Saintly finials continued to be made even after the suppression of the monasteries and the general removal of statues and of other Roman Catholic plate from the churches. A few exceptional and famous sets include a series of warrior finials and, the most notable of all, the Tichborne set of twelve figures of history and legend, led by Queen Elizabeth herself. They were made in 1592 by the most prolific of the London spoonmakers of the period, William Cawdell. Other finials included the charming Lions Sejant, and a wide variety of seal tops, with a decorative shaped and chased baluster terminal surmounted by a seal-like disc on which the owner's initials or, more rarely, crest could be engraved.

In an age not noted for cleanliness, apothecaries were firm in pointing out the advantages of silver saucepans and porringers for serving invalid foods, and a number of these have survived. Other smaller pieces of domestic silver first made in the 16th and early 17th centuries include shallow dishes for sweetmeats, small bowls possibly used for wine-tasting, and baskets for cakes (or cates) and for fruit, always much esteemed in summertime and successfully preserved in the still room for use in winter. Small shallow dishes, known as 'saucers' were in fact originally probably used for just that: the sauces and garnishes that improved the salty or overstrong taste of fish and meat before the days of refrigeration.

Silver was also used for all kinds of toilet pots, for perfume, small boxes and caskets, and for candlesticks, though none all of silver has survived until the beginning of the 17th century, the finest being a pair of 1624 preserved in the Kremlin in Moscow.

The enormous quantities of plate amassed by Henry VIII and his daughter Elizabeth I recorded in the inventories published by the British Museum in 1955 make tantalising reading. There are accounts, some scanty, some detailed, of treasures great and small. There are depressing little notes recording how some were made into new plate, some appeared damaged, some stolen, some presented to distinguished recipients. But more than all those, quantities were 'sent to the Mint', first in 1600, when Elizabeth ordered old and unused plate and jewels to be eliminated and a great new recoinage instituted. This also occurred throughout the reigns of James I and Charles I. Both were lavish in their raids upon the Jewel House to raise money and to bestow gifts – many of them presented by embassies to foreign courts, among them that of Russia which still retains in the Kremlin an extremely fine collection of 16th- and 17th-century English silver.

While James I was generous is his dispersal of the treasures and wholly unsuccessful in his efforts to restore the finances of the monarchy, Charles I sought both to be patron and to profit from further dispersal of old treasures. By 1626 he had pawned his country's gold plate in the Low Countries, and the following year, in a desperate effort to replenish the Exchequer, he levied the Forced Loan. So his subjects' savings as well as the treasures of the Jewel House vanished into the melting-pot, but his needs still seemed insatiable. When in 1640 he attempted to seize the bullion kept at the Mint, his overtaxed and often frankly hostile subjects turned to the goldsmiths for safe-keeping their valuables and providing necessary 'running cashes' – the origins of the modern banking system.

A BRIEF SURVEY OF STYLES

Yet Charles I remained personally interested in the work of fine goldsmiths, and in 1635 persuaded Christian van Vianen of Utrecht, son of Adam, to come to London. Exponent of the sinuous mannerist style known as 'auricular', van Vianen's work in England continued the manner of his father: rich with chased grotesque masks, scrolls, wave ornament, serpents and chased scenes. One of his early pieces made in England survives: the large dolphin-decorated dish in the Victoria and Albert Museum. His great service of plate made for the King at Windsor survived only a few years before it went, with so much more of the nation's plate, into the melting-pot to pay for the Civil War.

The War virtually annihilated the plate that had survived the 16th-century taste for refashioning old into new. Old and new together went to pay for men and arms. The silversmiths suffered the worst recession they had ever experienced. Few apprentices were taken, for there was hardly any silver to make more than the occasional spoon, beaker, cup or shallow bowl, usually of very thin gauge decorated with embossed or punched ornament.

Under the Commonwealth, things were little better. Puritanism decried such unnecessary luxuries, and what had survived the depredations of both sides was considered outdated or, more often, meet only for the new tax-gatherer Cromwell. Yet, strangely, one or two silversmiths did manage to produce really fine plate during the War and the Interregnum. The most notable was the maker using the mark of a Hound Sejant, who made such superb flagons as the pair of 1646 formerly at Thirkleby Church (one now at Temple Newsam, Leeds, the other in the Victoria and Albert Museum) or the pair now in the Irwin Untermyer collection in New York. Occasionally there are fine skirt tankards surviving, a few small globular covered mugs, and one or two decorative dishes, but for the most part the work of the silversmith was at a standstill. The Restoration of Charles II in 1660 was to restore more than a monarch to his throne. It heralded a revival of the art of living.

A BRIEF SURVEY OF STYLES

FROM THE RESTORATION TO THE HIGH STANDARD:
1660 to 1696

So welcome and significant did the goldsmiths of England consider the day that 'the King came into his own again' that, in celebration, they decided to make May 29th, which was also the King's birthday and Oak-apple Day, the day on which they would in future change the annual date letter, which, since 1478, had been changed every St Dunstan's Day, May 19th. And so it remained in London until altered to January 1st in 1975.

The goldsmiths were right to celebrate, for the restoration of the Monarchy and the return of the Court from exile on the Continent, where they had been able to indulge their taste for rich plate, brought immediate business. State and civic pomp had to be engendered, while houses and estates bestowed on those who had remained loyal to the King's cause were in need of rich furnishings. Trade, too, began to prosper again, and the silversmiths soon found their order books full with commissions from the growing band of wealthy merchants trading overseas in both East and West.

The craftsmen whose skills at first seemed in abeyance, unable to handle more than the flimsiest gauge metals and hard-pressed to emulate the robust baroque ornament fashionable abroad, soon learned to raise and chase the cups, salts, salvers, dishes, and other silver that the newly rich and the restored nobility so ardently desired to make a proper show. Silver itself, however, remained in short supply, though huge quantities were ordered by Charles II, not only for the royal regalia but also for gifts at home and abroad. Thus a good many of the tankards and mugs, beakers and bowls, dishes and salvers, cups and even spoons of the 1660s remained relatively thin until patrons were able to amass a good storeroom of plate. With this, in due course, they could replenish their stocks by exchanging for heavier and better pieces: supplies very essential for many a goldsmith after the

'Stop of the Exchequer' by the King in 1672 which ruined many of those who had acted as bankers on his behalf.

Stylistically, there was at first little change. Old patterns were revived, and lost plate made anew without much recourse to fashion. A few patrons still hankered after the tall standing cups and great salts that had gone into the melting-pot, but the age of the high table had died. Though the nobility put a good deal of silver on display, for most people it was a question of having domestic pieces to serve their needs at table: tankards and mugs, plates and dishes, spoons, a few rare forks, candlesticks, cups and jugs. The three new beverages – tea, coffee and chocolate – all demanded new vessels, while manners learned abroad brought a new lavishness with great toilet services and even silver-mounted furniture that seemed to emulate the halls of Versailles rather than be suited to the English town or country house. The famous bed made for Nell Gwyn by John Coqus as a gift of the King was not unparalleled in other rich families; silver sconces graced the walls; there were candlesticks to reflect light on the beautiful marquetry tables and in the great Venetian mirrors; vases and flasks were placed on the stepped mantelpieces, silver-mounted firedogs and andirons and finials on the hearth gleamed 'like winking Cupids'.

The dressing-room became a breakfast-time reception room and the richness of toilet services continued throughout the period. A long and illuminating list was presented by the author of *Mundus Muliebris, or the ladies dressing room unlock'd* probably written by John Evelyn and published in 1690:

> implements
> Of toilet plate gold and emboss'd
> And several other things of cost
> The Table Miroir, one Glue Pot
> One for Pomatum and What Not?
> Of washes, unguents and cosmeticks;
> A pair of silver candlesticks;

A BRIEF SURVEY OF STYLES

> Snuffers and snuff dish, boxes more,
> For powders, patches, waters store,
> In silver flasks, or bottles, cups
> Cover'd or open to wash chaps . . .

The poor groom 'who will needs to Marry-land venture' is to provide all this and much, much more: 'She's a poor miss can count her store'. Toilet sets comprising as many as twenty or thirty pieces were not uncommon, often made up by several different silversmiths, and in a variety of styles – the baroque Dutch designs with naturalistic chasing vying with those decorated with the exotic, usually flat-chased, sometimes engraved, oriental motifs known as chinoiserie.

For display, these baroque styles, with the emphasis on naturalistic flowers, fruit, scrolling foliage, birds, animals, monsters and mythological figures, imparted that degree of richness which for many recalled the last days of Renaissance mannerism at the beginning of the century. This appealed, too, to the stonemasons and woodcarvers, the weavers and architects who were rebuilding an England growing increasingly rich on overseas trade.

Perhaps the most typical of all mid-17th-century domestic wares were the two-handled cups variously known as porringers or caudle cups and used, it appears, for all sorts of food and drink. They were made in every size, from tiny dram cups to great covered examples with a capacity of a pint or more. In Commonwealth days they had often been mounted on a skirt foot, with rather spindly cast handles and with simple panels of matted and embossed stylised ornament. After the Restoration, many were of bombé shape, the bodies chased richly with often rather coarse, though sometimes well-chased, naturalistic motifs below a plain everted neck and with scroll handles, some cast, some of bolder scroll form. A favourite subject for the repoussé chasing was a lion and a unicorn amid foliage, though goats, cupids, camels and other subjects were sometimes included.

Occasionally, between about 1670 and 1685, the background was cut away from these repoussé-chased designs and the pierced-out pattern fitted with a plain gilt liner, usually cylindrical. It was a most effective technique, chiefly used for covered cups, but occasionally for tankards and for one rare standing cup, that given by Samuel Pepys to the Clothworkers' Company. Rather fewer than thirty such cagework cups and tankards are recorded, most of them unmarked. A few have been noted with the marks of Thomas Jenkins and of Jacob Bodendick, two of the most eminent silversmiths of the second half of the century.

Naturalistic themes were also used for finials, feet and other small parts, usually cast and chased to represent pomegranates, acanthus buds, clusters of foliage, or as contrasting masks of comedy and tragedy. Less happy were the rather emaciated cast handles of scroll form, often with such stylised terminal heads that they look little better than blobs. Coats of arms engraved on cups, plates, dishes, ewers and so on were often enclosed within plumed or scroll mantling, the arms themselves depicted in the simplest style, usually without use of heraldic colours.

Not all silver of the period was highly ornamental. The so-called 'puritan' tastes that had made their first impact on English silver at the beginning of the century were much favoured, especially for everyday silver. This included beakers (now usually about 4 in. high) small bellied mugs with reeded necks, tankards (made in huge numbers), dishes and plates, helmet-shaped ewers, cylindrical flagons, wine goblets, saucepans, the new silver pots used for tea, coffee and chocolate and, another newcomer to the range of domestic silver, the monteith. The skirt foot used on earlier tankards disappeared in favour of a narrow rim foot, and the flat lid turned into a low-domed cover with a peak at the front. Otherwise the tankard changed little during the second half of the century. Larger flagons often, in fact, retained the skirt foot even into the 18th century.

Halfway between the plain and the decorative were pieces

featuring the rather naïve but very charming flat-chased chinoiseries, which appear to be an entirely English conceit fashionable from about 1670 to 1690. The designs were mostly of oriental scenes of gardens, bridges, temples and other buildings peopled with warriors, long-robed mandarins, and others carrying parasols or with coolie-type hats. Curious gnarled trees, exotic plants, marigolds and strange birds appear here and there among them. Perhaps originating from the silks and porcelains that came to Europe with the tea and spices, they were adopted by the English decorators for many items, though not, curiously, for the pots from which to serve the tea and coffee that came from those eastern regions.

Another restrainedly decorative technique first used about the middle of the century was cut-card work. Usually at this period of very simple foliate outline, the decoration had the added effect of strengthening the body of the piece to which it was applied. Occasionally, a rib of beading was applied to the centre of a leaf shape; more often, until the arrival of new techniques from France towards the end of the century, the cut-card work of the period was refreshingly simple.

For mounts to strengthen the foot, rim or cover of a piece, gadrooning was the most popular – almost identical in style to the carving undertaken for the cabinetmaker, just as chinoiseries corresponded to the designs of the japanner. Moulded ribs on tankards and flagons helped also to strengthen them, while repoussé chasing, often worked in patterns based on the acanthus leaf, served the same purpose.

Casting was used for handles, knops, feet and thumbpieces. For tankards, handles were usually of scroll form, made in two halves soldered along the back seam and applied to the body in two places. A hole had to be cut in the underside or near the lower terminal to allow the steam to escape when being soldered – hence the old story of a whistle with which to call the potboy. The lid was hinged above the handle and fitted with a cast thumbpiece –

2 Tankards and Livery pot TOP ROW Livery pot, *c.* 1550; tankards, *c.* 1570, *c.* 1655; BOTTOM ROW *c.* 1670 to 1690, *c.* 1760, *c.* 1790.

sometimes so roughly used that the top of the hollow handle has become dented. The most popular late-17th-century thumbpieces were of simple scroll form, sometimes known as bifurcated, or of corkscrew pattern. More important flagons and tankards had more elaborate details, sometimes pomegranates or even birds, in which case the tankard was usually supported on matching feet in the Scandinavian manner. These too were cast and then chased up to bring out the detail.

On cups and covers, handles were often more spindly, stylised foliate designs with terminals formed as female busts which often betray a paucity of design-consciousness among the English silversmiths. Others were bolder, scroll-pattern sometimes with a graduated spine of beading. The finials to the covers were also cast and usually transcended the quality of the handles. Among the most effective were open acanthus buds or other flower designs, or Janus masks of Tragedy and Comedy facing in opposite directions. More formally, others were of baluster or vase shape.

The rather untidy swirl-fluting and naturalistic, stylised flower designs of the baroque and the limited appeal of chinoiseries give much English silver of the second half of the 17th century a rather provincial or, at best, naïve appearance. But at the time of 'the Glorious Revolution' that brought Dutch William and his Stuart Queen to the throne in 1688, there was something of a revolution taking place in the world of the silversmith. An inevitable change in style was accelerated by the influx of hundreds of French-born Protestant craftsmen. The refugees, often from the provinces rather than from Paris, included not only silversmiths but members of almost every trade and skill in the country unable to endure Louis XIV's Revocation of the Edict of Nantes which, for almost a century until 1685, had allowed them religious toleration. In London, as elsewhere, hostility to the newcomers was fierce, not least among the most skilled crafts. Many formerly successful Frenchmen were forced into poverty or had merely to work as journeymen for the masters who, while opposed to competition, were only too willing to accept their techniques and styles.

Their techniques included extensive use of casting; their styles brought in the curvaceous baluster form and formal ornament, regularising the baroque which for so long had held showy sway. Their English opponents managed to complain about their workmanship even while they emulated it. They suggested, for instance, that the Huguenots made too much use of solder and that they, being denied the Freedom of working in the City of London, used to send their work to be assayed and marked at the Hall through registered workers. But gradually the Huguenots established themselves, were admitted to citizenship and to the Freedom of the Goldsmiths' Company. They could in no small measure claim to be responsible for the supreme craftsmanship and elegant design of English silver for the next sixty or seventy years.

As it turned out, the native silversmiths had good cause to bless the newcomers. For the first time in history (except when lower standards were common in the reign of Henry VIII or when goldsmiths had themselves contravened the sterling standard) the craftsman had to work with silver that was softer than sterling, known, from the newly prescribed marks, as the Britannia standard. For many years, goldsmiths and their patrons alike had contravened the law, clipping or even melting down the coinage to make up for the dearth of silver bullion. In March 1697 the tables were finally turned on the goldsmiths by the Government who had the previous year introduced the Great Recoinage and had further passed 'an Act for Encouraging the bringing in of wrought plate to be coined'. No longer was sterling to be the metal of silverwares, but a costlier and finer alloy of 11 oz. 10 dwt. to the 12 oz. pound Troy: 8 pennyweights per pound purer and therefore softer and heavier than sterling. It was, in fact, close to the standard of wrought silver in France, and, despite occasional later inaccurate statements to the contrary, took decoration well and was excellent for casting.

THE AGE OF THE HIGHER STANDARD: 1697 to 1720

In itself, the higher Britannia standard of silver had no effect on English silver design. It was imposed in March 1697 at a time when the influence of the immigrant French Huguenot craftsmen was becoming fully felt. Their work was much admired by patrons and acknowledged, even if rather sullenly and secretly, by the traditionally minded silversmiths who were slowest to adapt and loudest in their condemnation of the foreigners in their midst. It was a period when the graceful baluster curve, an elegant application of what was to become Hogarth's 'Line of Beauty', became fully established and remained the underlying form of

English domestic silver for a century and more. Everything, from candlesticks to coffee pots and beer jugs, tankards and mugs to the feet of salvers and the branches of candelabra and chandeliers, conformed to the new curved outline that had first made its appearance about 1685. This counteracted the florid baroque and the remnants of Renaissance styles that had somehow survived and been revived at the Restoration.

Some formalisation had been bound to come, if only as a reaction to the baroque. Already there had been an equivalent to the William-and-Mary style in furniture and architecture in the vertical flat-fluting used for punch bowls, monteiths, and the bases of coffee and chocolate pots. Just as acanthus and other foliate chasing was given some formality and gadrooning, a slantwise fluting borrowed from the cabinetmaker, formalised the borders of salvers and candlesticks. The latter gradually, and soon entirely, were made in the new baluster pattern, with circular, square and, most of all, octagonal bases. These emphasised the style that has come, however mistakenly, to be called Queen Anne: a style that came in with her predecessors Mary II and her Dutch husband William and which continued well into the reign of her Hanoverian successor George I.

The Huguenots taught the English goldsmiths how to use silver of good gauge; to cast it and to use that most attractive method of applying mouldings, cut-card ornament and other details, to pierce caster tops and bread baskets with superb finesse. They sharpened chisels so that they could achieve minute cuts even better than those to be achieved sixty years or so later with the saw-piercing frame, and accentuated that delicate piercing with engraving. They were also masters of that elegant simplicity which appealed to the English patrons, often unadorned except for a simple flirtation with cut-card ornament and the use of the baroque cartouche of architectural scrolls and foliage to contain engraved armorials.

Nor was all Queen Anne silver plain. Throughout history, of

course, many of the most functional of domestic silverwares have been relatively plain, or at least with decoration restricted to less expensive techniques. So much the metal, so much the fashion, remained the standard method of charging well into the 19th century. The price of silver was relatively stable from 1660 to 1800 but the cost of making it varied (at so much per ounce) according to the amount of work lavished upon it. Many patrons liked plain tankards and mugs, coffee pots and teapots, dishes and plates, and salvers that would stand up to fair wear and tear without the risk of having engraved or chased ornament ruined by constant use. But for greatest display, and particularly for the range of new domestic silverwares first made during the Queen's reign, the wealthy liked the French-style richness of design with its applied detail and superb cast ornament. Decoration was used extravagantly in such rarities as wine coolers about 1710, in a few unusually fine cups and covers, in sideboard dishes, ewers and footed salvers. These items were chiefly made for ambassadorial use and issued by the Jewel House, the plate later becoming the perquisite of the Ambassador, an unofficial proceeding but often with ingenious reasons offered for its retention, especially when no fee for the service appeared.

With few exceptions, these more ornamental pieces were commissioned from Huguenot goldsmiths such as Philip Rollos, David Willaume, and Pierre Harache, though some of their fiercest critics such as Benjamin Pyne and John Bache did produce some extremely fine pieces in their workshops. The first decade of the new century saw the Huguenot influence establish itself and prosper, as, indeed, trade in England was prospering – though the complaint to the Company in 1711 of no fewer than 53 London goldsmiths sounded a sour note. They called the Huguenots 'Necessitous strangers' yet almost at once contradicted themselves by stating that to compete with them they had to put 'much more time and labour into working up' their silver and without extra cost. And they were still unhappy about the

A BRIEF SURVEY OF STYLES

enforced higher standard though in fact many of their French-born competitors found it expedient as the standard alloy in France approximated to the Britannia standard.

The first two decades of the 18th century heralded a greater domesticity. It was then that all kinds of new tablewares made their first appearance. In the dining-room, silver dishes and plates were supplemented by pretty fluted dessert dishes (often called strawberry dishes), the first sauceboats made their appearance and a two-handled bowl, believed to be a soup tureen, was made in 1716 by Pierre Platel. Spoons were now more graceful, with 'dognose' terminals replacing the trefid, the backs of the oval bowls strengthened and enhanced with a tapering rat-tail. Three-pronged forks of similar sturdy style were often provided to match, and silver-handled knives graced the most opulent dining-tables. Capacious oval bread baskets, usually with fixed handles, imitated wickerwork in their pierced sides, while footed salvers were used for dessert and for cheese – and, incidentally, in the confectioners' shops just as silver tankards were used for serving beer and ale in the taverns.

It was, however, 'Coffee, tea and chocolate' that had 'become capital branches of the nation's commerce' as Defoe noted in 1713, fully established both in the home and in the coffee-houses that became the ancestors of the London clubs. Tall tapering coffee pots, often with side-handles for ease of pouring, and similar chocolate pots, indistinguishable except for the aperture in the high-domed cover through which the molinet or stirrer could be inserted to froth up the beverage, were used both at home and in the coffee-houses, those for domestic use different only in that they often bore the owner's coat of arms.

At the tea-table, delicate porcelain from China was more practical than silver for the little handleless cups which guests placed upside down on a salver when empty. The tea-table itself was a silver oblong salver placed on the table top, usually of similar area. Interestingly, when the Roman silver Corbridge

A BRIEF SURVEY OF STYLES

3 **Coffee pots** LEFT 1702, RIGHT 1719.

lanx was found in Northumbria later in the century it was described in *The Gentleman's Magazine* as 'a tea board'. Another newcomer to the tea-table was the kettle and stand, and a new fashion introduced the taking of cream or milk with tea. Some perferred it cold, when it was served from a small bellied ewer with scroll handle and short lip – like a miniature beer or wine jug. Others liked their cream warmed, and for this an egg-shaped covered pot, usually on three legs and with an insulated wood handle, made its appearance. Sugar was served from plain covered bowls, and teaspoons, since there were no saucers, placed on an oval or oblong fluted dish or spoon tray. The teapot itself was of pear-shape, and sometimes supported on a spirit-lamp stand, like a miniature kettle.

About 1712, the tapering cylinder and the plain vase shape that had typified so much silver for the past twenty years was often replaced by what is technically a more difficult form: the octagonal. Casters, small salts, coffee and chocolate pots, candlesticks, salvers and waiters, sugar bowls, coffee-pot stands and kettles, even toilet caskets and two-handled cups appeared in the new octagonal shape. The panelled theme ran from the stepped moulded foot right up to the small finial on the cover. Its vertical emphasis whether on plain tapering pieces or used in conjunction with the baluster curve endowed the silver of the period with the elegance that has, for the modern collector at least, always been considered the most desirable. For the patrons and householders of the age, it was but an introduction to a new era that was to burgeon and bloom into a whole century of exquisite English silver.

FROM FORMAL ORNAMENT TO ROCOCO:
1720 to 1765

The emphasis on form rather than ornament during the second decade of the century changed little when sterling was restored in 1720. This was something of a rebuff for those silversmiths who had complained that the Britannia standard was unsuited to ornament (a patently inaccurate suggestion, since the most skilled craftsmen, and most notably of all, the eminent Paul de Lamerie, continued to use the higher standard even when it was no longer obligatory). But silver design, like that of furniture and architecture, never stayed still for long, and the leaders of society were forever insistent on new styles to titillate their palates and to arouse the envy and admiration of their friends.

Basically, the baluster form remained, and for candlesticks, jugs, casters, tankards and mugs was almost uniform. The high domed cover of the coffee and chocolate pots looked wrong with curved bodies with a 'tuck-in' base, so a flatter bun-like cover, usually with an acorn or baluster finial, and a curved spout opposite instead of at right angles to the handle were introduced. Curves also typified two newcomers to the dining-table: the soup tureen and the sauceboat, their shapes usually oval, and of somewhat compressed form. Sauceboats (the earliest known date from 1717) were at first made of oval boat shape, or an oval or octagonal foot, with two scroll handles on either side and pouring lips at either end. Also of basically curved form were the small bellied salts, on a stepped foot or on three or four scroll or hoof feet, that began to replace the plain trencher salt. Sets of casters, usually with a larger sugar caster and a smaller matching pair for pepper and dry mustard were sometimes fitted in ring frames known as Warwick cruets. Even the ink and pounce pots on standishes, or inkstands, were of baluster shape.

The baluster was an ideal basis on which to build a decorative style. As so often, even when at war, the English found their best inspiration in the arts of France. By 1720 the formal, low relief ornament of the Régence that followed Louis XIV's death in 1715, provided an opulent style that was put to use by the leading Huguenots, such as Paul Crespin and his contemporary Paul de Lamerie and, to a lesser degree, hinted at in the panelled stems of candlesticks, the borders of salvers and waiters, and in the decoration of the now ubiquitous two-handled cups.

Gradually, ornamental borders of scrolls, shells, foliage and scalework began to appear, a sort of extension of the formal baroque cartouches which for the past twenty years had contained the arms, crest or monogrammed initials of the owner. Sometimes these were engraved, but by about 1720 fine flat chasing was usually favoured, while more and more detail was added to the strapwork and other applied mouldings round the bases of two-handled cups, ewers and even, on rare occasions, tea and coffee pots. Elegant little lion masks grew out of paw feet, palmers' (pilgrims') shells adorned the gadrooned rims of salts and waiters, or were incorporated into the shoulders of candlesticks. Gradually the rims of salvers became more ornamental, and the scrolling outlines of Chippendale and Bath borders replaced the plain gadrooned and moulded patterns. From there it was but a small step to introduce shell or foliate motifs at intervals.

Tea-table silver continued to be relatively plain. The pear-shaped teapot gave way to the bullet shape, almost globular, on a spreading foot with a small plain drop-in lid (occasionally hinged, though it will be found that not a few exterior, as opposed to concealed, hinges are modern). The tea kettle with its accompanying spirit-lamp stand allowed for some decoration in the apron of the stand, usually at this period pierced with formal scrolls and diaper patterns, in the manner of the cake and bread baskets.

Plainest of all were spoons, forks and knife handles. The rounded end, the oval bowl, sturdy prongs (usually three) for forks, pistol-type grips for the otherwise rather cumbersome steel-bladed knives typified the so-called Hanoverian pattern. It was usually crested on the reverse, since the flatware was generally laid bowl or prongs downwards. Though few have survived in their entirety, this is the age of the first tableware services with matching tablespoons, knives, forks, dessert spoons and forks and even teaspoons, soup ladle, gravy spoons and other serving flatware *en suite*.

The coming of tea, coffee and chocolate more or less ousted the need for tankards, though mugs continued to be made for children's use, while the growth of a substantial glass industry banished the silver goblet for wine and other alcoholic drinks. Punch, however, stayed in constant fashion throughout the 18th century; by the 1720s this was generally served from capacious but plain bowls, a few of them supplied with elaborate cast scroll drop-handles. Some, of special merit, were engraved with scrolls and scalework.

By 1730 the stage was set for a revival of ornament. The shells and scrolls, foliage and strapwork once used so reticently were now interpreted with a profusion of detail chased in relief, often freely in the style that the rather severe and conformist design critics of the 1830s mockingly dubbed 'rococo'. This denigrated the style, but unintentionally coined a felicitous term for the rocky shells and marine motifs, the seaweed and coral, the wave ornament and asymmetrical fantasies that dominated design and produced some of the finest tours de force ever created in English silver.

France was the progenitor of the style, largely disseminated by Juste-Aurèle Meissonier, designer to the King of France, who in the mid-1730s published a book of designs, and furthered by Hubert Francois Gravelot who settled in England in 1732.

The London silversmiths, and most of all the best Huguenot craftsmen, achieved a subtle blend of the dignified and the fanciful, marginally less extravagant than the rococo of the French Court. English rococo gratified the rich man's desire for display, yet the underlying clarity of line was seldom lost beneath the swirling scrolls and foliage that turned simple silver vessels into encrusted virtuosity.

Instead of the great salt of former days, the soup tureen and the many-branched épergne took their place as the centrepiece of the dining-table, while sideboard and mantelpiece gleamed with two-handled standing cups and great sideboard dishes. The subtle lustre of silver rather than the glint of gold meant that relatively little silver of the 1730s was gilded, though a certain amount was later so treated during the Regency period.

Not all buyers of silver could afford, nor all silversmiths had the special skills to create, silver in the high rococo style. Even the most prestigious goldsmiths made mistakes, particularly in design, with ewers that do not pour well, sauceboats that are hard to hold, tureens with such small handles that spillage of hot soup must sometimes have been inevitable. But generally speaking, all the London silversmiths maintained a high standard of workmanship; whether making a pair of plain cast candlesticks, a small waiter or a bun-top pepper, there was the same attention to detail and to finish.

By the 1730s more and more silversmiths were beginning to specialise in certain trades. Casters were often the work of Samuel Wood who had been apprenticed to specialist maker Thomas Bamford, in a line that went back to Jacob Harris in the 1660s.

Candlestick-making, too, became a specialist craft, with the Cafes and the Goulds making cast 'sticks and presumably often selling them to retailer-manufacturers. Edward Wood and his apprentice David Hennell dominated salt-making, and for salvers there was first of all Edward Cornock, who also made tobacco boxes, John Tuite, Robert Abercromby and George Hindmarsh. It was a trend that was to continue and expand during the coming decades.

The leading goldsmiths did not restrict themselves in this way, though a certain amount of overstriking of other makers' marks suggests a growing retail trade. There was also a great deal of tax evasion. The 6d. an ounce duty imposed as the price of the return to sterling apparently irked even the most prestigious. So began the practice of 'duty-dodging'. Even in an age little concerned with the antique, and often using secondhand silver as so much bullion to be exchanged for new, the goldsmiths realised that marks were expected, even if they did not fall under the eye of the Company's Wardens. So they sometimes cut out the marks from an old piece and inserted them into the new, giving rise to such anomalies as an early-17th-century coffee pot. Sometimes they sent a small and insignificant piece for assay, and then transposed the marks, saving themselves and their customers quite massive duty on large wares. And for special orders, they sometimes risked all, and merely struck their own maker's mark four or five times. All these methods had become so prevalent by the 1750s that at last, in 1758, the duty was removed.

The middle years of the century also saw a growth, albeit slow, in mechanisation. Methods of rolling silver to achieve thinner gauge, the assembly of candlesticks from stamped parts and giving them stability by filling them, the development of the saw-piercing frame, and the invention of fused or Sheffield plating were all soon to have tremendous effect, especially on the medium-price trade.

These developments helped to spread the highest fashions,

which were soon copied in relatively modest versions, especially for tea-table silver. Rococo tea-table silver relied heavily for inspiration on a new version of oriental fantasy. As has been seen, the earliest chinoiseries of the period from about 1675 to 1690, were charming, but naïve, scenes interpreted in engraving or flat-chasing. At the turn of the century, a few rare pieces of silver bearing London marks – or none at all – have been recorded decorated in the manner of Chinese lacquer-carving. The mid-18th century gave the Chinese themes a new dimension by repoussé-chasing and by casting, often mixing oriental and European, with very English-looking ladies seated at tea-tables but with pagodas and Chinese umbrellas in the background, and coolie or tea-plant finials. This decoration was much favoured for sets of tea caddies, usually contained in safely locked wooden, tortoiseshell or ivory chests, and from which the lady of the house blended her own favourite teas, 'the Black, the Green and Gunpowder the Strong'. For those who could not open their purses to the exotic caddies and other tea wares made in the highest rococo style, there were plenty of more modest examples from which to choose. There were caddies decorated with swirl-fluting, plain teapots that hint at the rococo with scroll-work below the curved spout, and a plentiful variety of pretty teaspoons, some stamped with Apollo or satyr masks at the terminal, others with 'picture-backs' which ranged from scrolls or foliage to ships, teapots, roses, the Prince of Wales's Feathers (the future George IV was born in 1762) to a caged bird and the motto 'I love Liberty' dating from the political fracas over Wilkes's *North Briton*, which firmly established the freedom of the press.

Salvers and waiters of all sizes, and candlesticks, both simple and branched, were probably the most plentiful of all mid-18th-century silverwares, and were made in as many styles as there were sizes, with more or less decoration as purse and fashion dictated. Epergnes, table baskets and smaller baskets and dishes for sweetmeats, pickles and other delicacies (scallop-shaped

4 Tureens LEFT 1728, RIGHT 1744.

dishes, for instance, were actually specified as being 'scallops for oysters' though we now tend to call them butter-shells) were likewise made in all sizes and qualities. By the late 1730s the doublelipped sauceboat had generally given way to the oval boat-shape with a scroll or flying-scroll handle at one end and a broader pouring lip. Soup tureens, sometimes made in pairs and supported on large meat-dish-like stands, were possibly the most important of all dining-table wares and much expense was lavished on their chasing. Few, however, were as impressive as those made in 1740 by Paul Crespin, one in the Royal Collection, the other now at Minneapolis – huge centrepieces the design of which has been generally accredited to Nicholas Sprimont, soon to be involved with the Chelsea Porcelain factory. Epergnes, often as much as 16 in. high and with a spread of 18 or 20 in.; held baskets, dishes and even incorporated candle-holders in their branches. These centrepieces were evidence of the piercer's skills and, like other pierced work such as wine coasters, were often made by specialist makers such as the Norwegian-born Emmick Romer, Thomas Pitts, by the highly competent firm run by Elizabeth Godfrey, and by Archambo and Meure, whose partnership supplied all sorts of silver in a light and delicate style.

The lesser silversmiths, who had watered down the styles of the masters and who were quick to make use of the new lighter-gauge silver and mechanical aids, in their own way hastened the end of the rococo. It began to lose its freshness, and to acquire a tawdry tiredness. The leading craftsmen, such as Edward Wakelin and Thomas Heming, looked across the Channel to France again, but the rather compressed fluted styles being made there had little immediate appeal or impact in England. For once the impetus came from farther afield, brought home by the elegant young men who were sent on grand tours of Europe and who had ventured with their notebooks and sketch-pads among the classical ruins of Italy, Greece and Asia Minor.

THE NEW CLASSICISM: 1765 to 1800

The rise of neoclassicism was as revolutionary in mid-18th-century Europe as it was inevitable. Sixty years is not long in the development of silver styles, and the century had seen them change from the formal to the rococo, with its marine fantasies and its parallel development, the 'gaudy gout of the Chinese'. Horace Walpole, perhaps the foremost art critic of the century, began to castigate the ornamental frivolity of the rococo. He himself turned to the equally fantastic Gothic, though few patrons followed suit and very little silver in the Gothic revival style was made. England's traditional source of inspiration, France, had been greatly weakened by almost a century of incessant wars and her goldsmiths, even though they produced superb and massive designs for grand occasions, had little appeal in Britain. In fact, it was the British who became the progenitors of the new fashion that swept Europe during the next half-century.

The social structure of British society, especially in the great cities of London, Edinburgh and Dublin, was an ideal nursery for novelty. Talk and travel were the chief pastimes of those who lived in the towns and who did not always follow the country sports of the squire and his relations. The Grand Tour was as vital – often more vital – a part of education as the University and the schoolroom. For some years young men and their tutors as well as older connoisseurs had been bringing back reports of the classical sites being excavated in Italy, Greece and Asia Minor. One of the most enthusiastic, who put his knowledge and vision to practical use, and who gave his name to the new style, was a young Scots architect, Robert Adam.

He was not the first to see, study and sketch the ruins of Herculaneum and Pompeii, Athens and Palmyra. These had been published during the 1750s and early 1760s in a series of publications, which were soon followed by others that in turn had immense effect on the applied arts. Every aspect of the classical world was adopted as the source for pottery and furniture, carpets, woodwork, plasterwork and textiles, not forgetting silver and its lesser but nonetheless fashion-conscious cousin, fused plate. There was often confusion among the manufacturers, craftsmen and entrepreneurs about which culture a pattern derived from. To many, it was all one, the pure classicism of the ancients: Wedgwood's new works, where so many Greek vases were emulated, was mistakenly called Etruria, but the resultant neoclassicism with its formalising of antique shapes and patterns was all that mattered in this new pan-European movement. It had begun in Britain, but soon held sway in Paris and in Hanover, Berlin and Vienna, Rome and Lisbon, Stockholm and St Petersburg and across the ocean in New York and Philadelphia.

By 1762, the year of the birth of the young Prince who was to give his name to the next major English style – the Regency –

Robert Adam was the most fashionable and sought-after architect-designer of the day. He had already made his mark with the Admiralty Screen in London, the plans for remodelling the interior of the Duke of Northumberland's Syon House in Middlesex, and nearby Osterley was in process of construction. Inside and out, the architect was arbiter of taste, commissioning work from all the crafts so that the result would be a harmonious whole. This standard 18th-century practice was often to have disastrous results half a century or so later when men trained in one medium tried to interpret their work in half a dozen other media without fully understanding the limitations (or the capabilities) of the machine. Even in the second half of the 18th century, when contacts between architect and designer, builder and craftsmen, were still relatively close, there could be unhappy errors of judgment in foisting the form or ornament of one object on another. This was a particularly prevalent habit in silver which did not easily assimilate, say, the relief carving of marble or the shapes of pottery vessels, which, however elegant, were not necessarily practical. Such were the round-based oval teapots made in the neoclassical style by the Swede, Andrew Fogelburg, who had settled in London about 1770; they required a cradle for support.

Because many of Adam's designs in other materials had a delicacy and lightness, there is a popular misconception that neoclassical silver is plain rather than richly decorated. This is, in fact, due to its immediate and widespread popularity. Only when the new classicism became watered down for a wider market was the original richness of the style replaced by simpler forms and engraved rather than chased or applied ornament. The original designs for silver by Adam and his contemporaries, notably Wyatt, were as impressive and splendid as any of the less formal rococo or the Romanised Regency to come. Applied detail, good repoussé chasing and cast details, such as ram's-head terminals, paterae and festoons, typified the new style, of which the chief distinction from the outworn rococo was a return to formality and the use, wherever possible, of classical forms such as the urn and the vase.

In Wedgwood himself there is a hint of the new commercial instincts of the age, the idea of disseminating to a larger public the lastest fashions once available only to the nobility and gentry. In the world of silver, his counterpart was his friend Matthew Boulton. He had taken over his father's business making buttons, buckles and other smallwares in silver, fused plate and cut steel, but his ambition was to be accounted the leading silversmith of Birmingham. The new classicism appealed to him both because it was in the highest fashion and, using a certain amount of machinery, was feasible to make whereas the rococo was too complex. Boulton took a lively interest in all aspects of art and science. He was a leading member of the Lunar Society which numbered such distinguished men as Dr Joseph Priestley, Dr Erasmus Darwin, Wedgwood and James Watt among its founders in 1766. He visited the seats of noblemen, not only to become known to the owners but also to collect ideas and designs for his silverwares, a practice that stood him in good stead when it came to the political business of establishing an assay office in Birmingham in the teeth of bitter opposition from the London Goldsmiths' Company. His ambition in that field was realised when the Act of 1773 set up assay offices in Birmingham and in Sheffield, the first provincial offices established since Norwich, Newcastle, York, Exeter and Chester had been confirmed in the years 1700 to 1701.

With the perilous and time-consuming journey to Chester or London to have his silver assayed and marked no longer necessary, Boulton's Soho factory began to replace his fine ormolu business – a far from paying proposition – with silver. Though Robert Adam is often credited with designs for Soho, it appears that in fact drawings were made for Boulton by another London architect, James Wyatt, and he may well have used others. It must

A BRIEF SURVEY OF STYLES

be said, however, that the more day-to-day wares Boulton was later constrained to make (often to compete with his own Sheffield plated wares) needed virtually no designer at all.

In Sheffield, where the platers were certainly as aware of the neoclassical fashion as Boulton or the London silversmiths, the establishment of the assay office there was of less immediate importance, although the leading firms of platers were glad to diversify, offering similar patterns of candlesticks, sugar baskets and teapots in either fused plate or silver. Not that the London retailers (and some manufacturers there) were any too pleased, and with the connivance of the London Assay Office not infrequently overstruck the Sheffield makers' marks and hallmarks. This was a backhanded tribute to the superb finish of the loaded silver candlesticks made in Yorkshire.

5 Adam-style coffee urn *c.* 1780.

A BRIEF SURVEY OF STYLES

As the neoclassical taste swept the country from Exeter to Edinburgh, the long-established baluster shape gave way for the first time to the classical urn for jugs, coffee pots, cups and tea-urns, while there was a natural revival of the column candlestick, now based upon the Corinthian column. More refined taste gradually banished that in favour of the elongated vase shape on square or circular base. The chief details, at first richly cast, chased and applied, were the ram's head, the long-established lion mask, the laurel festoon, applied classical medallions in the manner of Tassie gems, Vitruvian scrolls, beading (or pearling as it was more attractively known), trails of pendant husks, anthemion and formal foliage borders, and circular or oval flowerheads or paterae.

Formality was the keynote, but it was usually formality with a light touch, like the low relief delicacy of Adam plasterwork or a Wedgwood portrait medallion. In silver it was soon to be interpreted by engraving rather than chasing, most effectively by the technique known as bright-cut which added a distinctive brilliance to what would otherwise have appeared rather pedestrian. The art of engraving had, except for armorials, been much in abeyance since the onset of the rococo. One or two exceptionally fine engraved pieces showed the art to be far from dormant by 1759, when several individual tea caddies began to appear engraved overall with 'damask' designs. By the early 1770s there were artist-engravers capable of such exquisite tours de force as the tea-vases made by Courtauld and Cowles in 1771 with their classical Flaxman scenes engraved against a satin-finished ground, or the teapot of 1772 made by Francis Crump, a simple drum made into a work of art with fine engraved scenes from *The Decameron*.

Such engraving was, of course, little less costly than expensive relief chasing and the best applied detail; however, the revival of the craft and the simple but effective borders developed for bright-cut work soon made it the chief ornament of the great corpus of moderately priced tea-table and other wares that were competing with the popular and inexpensive fused plate. New production techniques were everywhere welcomed; the flatting mill, steam power, the fly press and the specialisation of manufacturers in making parts for assembly and even entire unfinished stampings and castings for trade use may not have contributed greatly to the prestige of the silversmith, but it did help to sell his wares to a huge new market at home and abroad. The metal might be of lighter gauge, the designs less individual, the decoration more pedestrian, but the volume of business continued to increase, and London, Newcastle, Edinburgh, Chester and Exeter Assay Offices became increasingly busy: even York, which had scarcely opened its doors since about 1720 began to test and mark silver again about 1780. It was as though the thriving industry in Sheffield plating had helped to revive the silver trade. A dozen years later in 1784 this revival suggested once again to Government that the silversmiths were ripe for picking, and their wares should once more be subject to duty.

This re-imposition of 6d. an ounce tax did nothing to improve the gauge of silver used. In fact, it probably most helped the Sheffield silversmiths who were so skilled at stamping and assembling parts, especially for candlesticks, which they loaded with resin or plaster to give them stability. A good many of the less competent London craftsmen, unable to afford new machinery or even to change their methods of working, went bankrupt. The more far-sighted, such as the firm of Bateman & Co., headed by the redoubtable Hester, but probably largely operated by her sons Peter and Jonathan, produced a good wide range of everyday wares eschewing expensive decoration, which they limited to bead and thread edges and generally rather less elaborate engraving. But the idea worked, and by the early years of the 19th century the firm of Bateman & Co. were a force to be reckoned with and supplied goods to retailers and agents throughout the country.

The popular acceptance of simpler shapes and styles meant that in general the plain vase and the oval tended to dominate form, touched only with a few lines of bright-cut engraving, itself often arranged as oval medallions to enclose armorials or, more often for this wide market, with a monogram of initials. Piercing, often done with a fly-press, sometimes with the vertically held saw in a frame, added to this light and pretty look. This was echoed in the simplicity of satinwood furniture, likewise inlaid with ovals and flower motifs. It was a trend that irritated many of Adam's contemporaries, notably Wyatt, Henry Holland and Sir William Chambers, all of whom had a more Palladian approach. They, like Walpole and the much maligned but no means inconsiderable patron of the arts, King George III, 'abhorred filigraine toy work.' Indeed, it could be said that it was the King rather than his son who introduced the so-called Regency style. With as keen an eye as his extravagant son, the King had found a new magnificence and the goldsmiths who could carry it out with aplomb.

THE AGE OF GILDED GRANDEUR: 1800 to 1830

So far as the applied arts are concerned, the era usually described as Regency in fact began about 1795 and lasted at least until the death of the King who, in the interim, from 1811 to 1820, had acted as Regent for his ailing father. George, Prince of Wales did, of course, have an enormous influence on every aspect of the arts, from architecture down to the smallest detail of furnishings for the lavish houses he and the courtly patrons of the day required. Gradually a Roman splendour began to overlay the restrained Grecian forms; once again the chaser and the modeller began their ascendancy, as they had in the early rococo period, over the engraver and the proponent of simplicity.

In the sculptors of the day they found immediate support. 'Massiveness', boomed Charles Heathcote Tatham, 'is the principal characteristic of good Plate'. He further enjoined the silversmith to 'consider Chasing ... as a branch of Sculpture'. Whether one likes it or not, this precept was to find adherents in silversmithing, especially in the making of presentation plate, throughout the rest of the century. It is a trait that has, in some measure, been revived today. No one, whether artist, sculptor, architect or silversmith, seems to have stopped to consider whether such sculptural themes were wholly appropriate to silver or silver-gilt.

The first requirement in producing plate of such magnificence was a body of craftsmen competent to make up the lavish designs. Matthew Boulton's chief difficulty, besides cash flow, in creating the great silver trade that he hoped to emanate from Soho was the fact that Birmingham had no tradition of silversmithing other than in the fields of smallwares. The one truly expert silversmith he employed was Benjamin Smith, an irascible man who understandably left the firm and went to London, to be joined later by his brother James, in Lime Kiln Lane, Greenwich. There Benjamin was first in partnership with Digby Scott, who possibly also hailed from Birmingham. The two seem soon to have been among the foremost exponents of the new grander classicism, undertaking several important commissions for the Royal Goldsmiths, Rundell and Bridge, who had come to the notice of King George III by 1797. Of equal stature as a craftsman, though with admittedly a much less happy sense of form and proportion, was Paul Storr, who from 1807 until 1819 was manager/partner in Rundell's Dean Street factory in Soho, London. Both firms tackled the daunting task of reproducing in silver the massive and sculptural designs for banqueting services and presentation silver provided by John Flaxman, E. H. Baily, Piranesi and others in which the ability to model and cast silver became almost a first principle in its manufacture.

Though Rundell's had the lion's share of Court business, many patrons still remained faithful to other firms, notably that of Wakelin and Garrard, in Panton Street, Haymarket, successors through several generations of that other Goldsmith to a Prince of Wales, George Wickes, patronised by George III's father. The firm of Bateman & Co., and Emes and Barnard of Amen Corner near St Paul's, inheritors of the business of Henry Chawner and his predecessors, both saw the new trend for heavier and more decorative silver as ripe for exploitation. Both being suppliers on a nationwide basis to the thriving retail trade, the new fashion quickly spread. The silver retailers of Manchester and York, Chester and Edinburgh, Exeter and Bristol were soon supplied with silver and silver-gilt that would stand comparison with most of the products said to be specially designed, but more often adapted from originals, for their clients at Rundell's and at Garrard's.

The basic elements of this new grand classical idea were much the same as those that had been expounded by Adam and his contemporaries thirty years earlier. The chief inspiration remained classical architecture and statuary with the vase and the urn dominating. Plinths, often of triangular incurved form, supported vases, candelabra, dessert dishes and centrepieces, the sides overlaid with festoons and swags of flowers and foliage. The covers and, in the case of candelabra, the centres had finials in the form of Lions Passant, eagles or other grandiose insignia. Great paterae and bold scrolling foliage added a ponderous dignity to handles of cups and branches of candlesticks.

Besides the tapering classical vase that had been fashionable in the late 18th century there was now the campana shape widely used for cups and for wine coolers. Compressed circular shapes began to appear for matched tea and coffee services, often with deep and finely cast and chased borders of anthemion and foliage, or basketwork, berried foliage or, more plainly, vertical fluting. For the dining-table, the vine fruited over coasters, wine coolers, table centrepieces and dessert stands, often interspersed with classical putti peering from among the foliage or grasping bunches of grapes. Following Tatham's dictum, massiveness was characteristic of everything from centrepieces and soup tureens

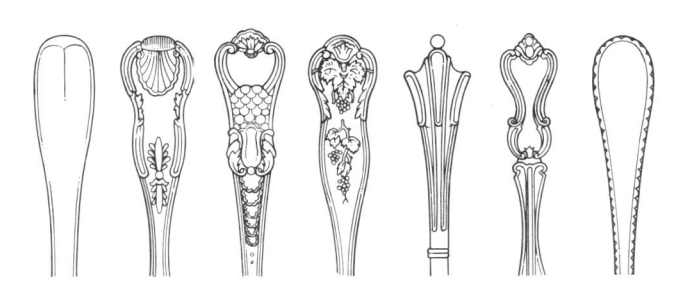

6 Flatware FROM LEFT Old English, *c.* 1760; Kings, *c.* 1820; Coburg, *c.* 1812; Bright Vine, *c.* 1820; Albany, *c.* 1860; Albert, *c.* 1840; Feather-Edge, *c.* 1765.

to entrée dishes, tea trays and even teapots, now made to hold perhaps two pints or more. Even tableware was much heavier than during the 18th century, with a host of ornamental patterns such as Kings, Queens, Hourglass and Coburg, usually doublestruck (i.e., with the pattern on both sides) weighing perhaps twice that usual for Old English, Hanoverian, feather-edge and the like.

Silversmithing skills among the leading craftsmen of the day were of a very high order. Raising such massive plate was in itself no mean achievement, and the huge trays and salvers, meat dishes and sideboard dishes required careful workmanship. This ensured that they were truly flat and would not warp with the application of fashionable mounts of heavy gauge, some richly cast, chased and pierced. If not cast and chased, pieces would usually be decorated with borders of chased foliage, shells or basketwork. Such work had, of course, been at least as well executed during the rococo period, but never before had silversmiths in England achieved such distinction as modellers on so great a scale. The silver trophies and testimonials born of the long Napoleonic Wars introduced whole series of allegorical figures to challenge the silver modellers, all despite a huge increase in the duty on silver, which rose in 1797 to 1s. an ounce, 1s. 3d. in 1804 and a penal 1s. 6d. in 1815. This was no mean figure when one realises that a good many candelabrum-centrepieces weighed well over 500 oz. apiece.

For about the first fifteen years of the new-style classicism, Graeco-Roman styles predominated, with an abundance of heavy cast and chased borders and a taste for boldly half-fluted bodies. A variation during the first decade of the century, albeit a short-lived one, was the Egyptian style, with sphinxes and lotus plants replacing the more conventional lion masks, anthemion borders and acanthus foliage. It was a style inspired by the major excavations being undertaken in Egypt during the first years of the new century; but the Roman, rather than the Graeco-Egyptian, seems to have been more to the English grandee's taste, whether in great cups, tea urns or ewers or in small objects such as cigar lighters in the form of Roman lamps.

For the more modest user, fused plate and thinner gauge silver were, of course, much less costly, and the workshops of London, Sheffield and Birmingham turned out a vast range, especially of candlesticks and tea-table wares which ranged from the starkly plain to passable imitations of the grand manner. Decoration was, however, admired as the symbol of good taste in all classes of society, and there was also some retrospection. As early as 1807, Robert Garrard, successor to Wakelin's, was beginning to revive the rococo, at first with flat-chased ornament in the manner of Paul de Lamerie, later with cast and chased rococo details. The swirl-fluting, cast dolphin feet and supports, and craggy marine motifs by the 1820s seemed a refreshing change for the heavier and much-gilded styles still emanating from Rundell's on Ludgate Hill.

There was also a fashion for naturalism – even the dignified tables of the firmest adherents of Regency splendour found room for honey pots formed as straw skeps, honey-gold with gilding and surmounted by finials formed as a bee, though a disc-finial actually proved more practical. First made in the late 1790s, these beehive honey pots remained popular and were still being made as late as the 1850s. Flowers and leaves were also used to create charming ideas for chamber candlesticks and tapersticks, inkstands and sweetmeant baskets. Tea and coffee services were sometimes covered with a profusion of flowers and foliage that extended from leafy feet to flowery finial. A version of these naturalistic themes was the 'Union' border, incorporating the English Rose with the Thistle, Daffodil and Shamrock, a national theme that was especially popular from 1820 onwards.

Indeed, by the 1820s, the seeds had already been sown for the enormous variety of styles that crammed one upon the other throughout Queen Victoria's reign. The rococo revival, for instance, led many owners to send plain pieces such as coffee-pots and bowls of the early 18th century to be 'improved' by additional chased or engraved ornament. Some of this chasing up, though perhaps without as much refinement as the originals, was of much better standard than that done to plain pieces some fifty or sixty years later; but as with most copies, something of the freshness of the originals was inevitably lost.

Another backward look, superbly interpreted by Edward Farrell (who worked frequently for one of the most colourful retail silversmiths of the day, Kensington Lewis), was cast and chased silver decorated with high relief scenes in the manner of David Teniers the Younger. Farrell also put his chasing and modelling skills to use with enormous tankards and flagons repoussé-chased in high relief with complex classical scenes, in the manner of north German tankards of the 1670s.

Many manufacturers were well aware of the fact that some of the designs they made were 'of a mixt style' as Emes and Barnard noted when commissioned to make a candelabrum in 1828 incorporating details 'from an old Engravg. of an ancient fragment in India' alongside ornament 'in the Greek and Gothic style'. In 1820, Philip Rundell struck his sponsor's mark to a great tankard that copied the wooden 'Glastonbury Cup', its drum with an arcade of Saints above 'carved' swans and formal flowerheads.

Replicas and reproductions of subjects in other materials seem not to have deterred the silversmiths or their patrons. The Warwick Vase, a replica in miniature of the marble vase from Hadrian's Villa (now in Glasgow City Museum) was tackled with more or less success by craftsmen from Paul Storr downwards. It continued to challenge makers, usually with much less exactness than Storr, until about 1910. There was also a busy trade in reproductions of earlier silver, a trade no doubt much encouraged when Rundell and Bridge purchased much old plate from the Royal Collections. Supposed to have it melted down, they instead fostered interest in past silver. Besides apparently disposing of many of the Royal pieces to more discerning customers, they made copies of many of them bringing Gothic and medieval, baroque and Palladian, rococo and neoclassical – and mixtures of them all – to the notice of a new public and a new generation of manufacturers. The latter, without a true understanding of design principles, tended to mix one with another in their efforts to woo a growing public with novelty.

THE AGE OF DIVERSITY: 1830 to 1870

The year 1830 was once considered a terminal date for the truly antique, after which it was believed that virtually nothing of any importance was hand-made. The fallacy of this argument has already been seen in the extensive development of machinery during the last quarter of the 18th century, especially in Birmingham and Sheffield. Also, the craft of the silversmith by no means vanished in the era of technical advances – especially at the times of the great trade exhibitions in 1851 and 1862. It must be admitted that the period did its utmost to involve the machine in the production of decorative wares of all kinds, sometimes with great success, as modern collectors have proved, sometimes with a large measure of banality.

A BRIEF SURVEY OF STYLES

In the silver trade, 1830 is as arbitrary as any other date in ending or defining a style. The accession of William IV on the death of his brother had no special impact, and the taste for reviving past styles remained unabated. 'Taste' was perhaps the key factor and for the past thirty years that had meant a mixture of massiveness and decoration not always wholly concomitant with domestic silver. The work of the designers of the 1830s in reproducing originals was as often as not inspired, not by a paucity of artists, but by a desire to produce anything made a hundred, two hundred or even two thousand years earlier, and to make it as well as, if not better than, the original. The result, with some exceptions, was inevitably out of period, lacking the freshness and impact of the goldsmiths and others (for copying marble, bronze and other materials, even carved wood or ivory was not frowned upon) who had first created the object.

Where the early 19th-century silversmiths succeeded was in their real ability to model, cast and chase metal. The generally highly ornate designs that had been made high fashion by Rundell & Bridge at the turn of the century were perpetuated in the rococo revival that followed the great Romanising of the earlier period. Rococo in turn gave way to a taste for naturalism; here good modelling and chasing remained an essential skill. Overlapping foliage in low relief was transformed into dishes and bowls supported on cast shell or flower feet, water-lilies were turned into inkwells and tapersticks and flowers and foliage trailed over the sides of cups and mugs. Many silversmiths adapted the suggestions for naturalistic foliate stems, figures and other embellishments from Knight's *Vases and Ornaments designed for the use of Architects, Silversmiths, Jewellers &c*. So candlesticks and candelabra, dessert stands and great centrepieces, presentation cups and vases were enriched with scrolling foliage and basketwork, flowers and, most of all, with graceful allegorical figures representing virtues, industry, science, justice, plenty, the arts and other 19th-century favoured attributes.

7 Candelabra *c.* 1810.

On a more domestic scale, the garden themes were used in relief on the popular melon-shaped tea and coffee services, on children's mugs and cups, on small dishes, inkstands and toilet silver, sweetmeat baskets and table snuff boxes. Finials put these naturalistic themes in the round, with flowers, buds, and even bird models. The expert stamping that had been developed in Sheffield during the later 18th century was extended to Birmingham by the 1830s. Low relief cast, stamped and chased detail, usually of very good definition, became a speciality of the Birmingham smallworkers and boxmakers, such as Joseph Willmore, Nathaniel Mills, the Linwoods and many others.

The rise of Sheffield and Birmingham had helped to revolutionise the trade, a factor accelerated by the improved communications by road, rail and canal; retailers in distant parts of the country could buy their hand-made silver in London, their Sheffield-plated wares in Sheffield, or from Boulton's in Birmingham, and toys and other smallwares in Birmingham. Now a new process meant that almost everyone could afford to buy made its impact. In 1840 G. R. Elkington patented silver-plating by electro-deposition, and for the next few years began buying up the patents of all the technical improvements devised by his contemporaries. He then proceeded to license the process – in 1843 Barnard Brothers of London, one of the largest firms also making silver there, paid 'upwards of 1500£ including some tools &c.' This included 'new large Stamp, fitting up of Cellar Shop & Gilding and Plating Shops, Vats, Boilers &c.&c. New Casting patterns & Iron Dies for blocking &c.' for the 'Electro Process'.

One obvious result of this greatly increased trade was the danger of plagiarism of designs. This had greatly exercised designers, including silversmiths, ever since the late 18th century. An Act of 1798 was implemented in 1814, rather curiously entitled 'for encouraging the art of making Models and Casts of Busts and other Things . . . and for giving further Encouragement to such Arts'. This accounts for many centrepieces and other objects signed 'Published as the Act Directs'. Even so, design piracy continued. In 1842 a Design Registry (*see* p. 273) was inaugurated, patented designs being struck with a special diamond-shaped mark. This began to appear on all kinds of wares from tea services to pencils. It was especially applied to all kinds of Victorian trivia and 'table toys' such as novelty condiment sets, fruit ladles, inkpots and claret jugs, often formed as birds, animals, monsters and the like.

Though the taste for natural subjects never completely deserted the Victorians, fashions for different period styles rose and fell. By 1840 medievalism was in vogue again and this time attracted silversmiths who had virtually ignored Horace Walpole's Strawberry Hill Gothic some ninety years earlier. The chief architect of the new gothic style was A. W. N. Pugin, who as a young man had been spotted by John Gawler Bridge of Rundell, Bridge & Rundell in the Print Room at the British Museum. He made several designs for the firm in medieval style as early as 1827. The firm's flagon of 1830 for York Minster hints at the pinnacles of gothic design, but it was after they had closed down in 1842 that the fashion for the gothic really flowered. Much of it was designed by Pugin for the Birmingham firm of John Hardman & Co., who chiefly produced ecclesiastical metalwork.

A slight divergence from the pinnacled gothic of Pugin was to be found in the medieval style of figure groups and centrepieces designed by Edmund Cotterill for Garrard's, successors to Wakelin & Taylor. Here Scott's novels and Byron's poetry played their part in promoting the fashion. In furniture, draperies, textiles and interior design generally, it was the gothic, with its rich colours, that appealed. This appeal was only endowed on silver by the use of gilding and, in small measure, by enamelling, a skill essayed at the huge Elkington factory which so dominated trade for a century from 1840 onwards.

'The Select Committee on Arts and Manufactures' appointed by Parliament in 1835 helped to forge links between the crafts and industry, but in many ways it was almost too late to weld the two together. The Prince Consort a few years later leant his active support to all the arts, encouraging exhibitions at which individual craftsmen could display their virtuosity. These exhibitions in 1851 culminated in the biggest and most ambitious of all, the Great Exhibition at the Crystal Palace, the setting itself an embodiment of technical advancement.

Designing for exhibitions had, in effect, the result of striving for variety for its own sake. It did, however, encourage the craftsmanship that veered between the grandiose and the portentous and the charming.

Of all Victorian silver (and that from the middle of the century also included plated wares) the tea service was the most important item, the all-essential wedding present along with the canteen of tablewares. Sculptural ability was used for small silver as well as for huge testimonial pieces. Where the latter would be a massive agglomeration of figures, usually allegorical or historical, the former used them with a nursery-tale prettiness: milkmaids and young swains holding little trays for visiting cards, or carrying baskets for salt or pierced for posies. Nearly everything was of a sturdy gauge, making it more functional an acquisition for the modern collector than many of the flimsier semi-machine-made wares of the later 18th century.

If anything, the 1862 Exhibition produced even more extravagant and pretentious designs than had been offered in 1851. 'Exhibitionitis' had indeed swept the world from Paris and New York to Munich and Manchester. Such fairs were open to all the world, and a feature of English silver manufacture was the employment of foreign designers – Morel Ladeuil, for instance, who worked for Elkington & Co., and whose great table entitled Sleep was their prize exhibit. By then Elkington's had perfected the technique of electro-typing, introduced by 1845. This technique allowed any material of any form, in low or high relief, metal, wood or ivory, to be reproduced in every detail. So successful were they that in 1870 the firm were commissioned to go to Russia to electro-type the early English silver in the Czar's possession. This included the great Elizabethan and early Jacobean flasks, cups, flagons and perfume burners of which those now in the Kremlin are virtually the only surviving examples, and the treasures of the Hermitage, such as the great Kandler wine cistern of 1735. These electro-types are now in the study collection of the Victoria and Albert Museum.

Besides electrodeposition, Elkington's sought to extend their ranges with enamelled wares. Cloisonné enamels were an attractive way of bringing the Victorian love of colour to silver and to electroplated wares. It was, however, almost a last attempt to revive an ailing trade. The era of exhibitions probably did more harm to domestic silver design than it brought business to the firms who showed there. Many were not geared to the policy of expansion, which was anyway seldom commercially justifiable.

The trade needed fresh ideas and a new human-size approach. For that they had to wait until the 1870s.

FROM COMPLACENCY TO THE CRAFTS MOVEMENTS: 1870 to 1914

In 1853 the American Commodore Perry and his 'black' ships arrived off Japan, and at once began to open up trade with the islands that had for so long been isolated from the West. By 1867 the last *shogun* was ousted and the Emperor restored, with a new capital, Tokyo, replacing Kyoto. The arts of Japan, so long hidden, were by no means stagnant. For the European artist they provided an exciting new inspiration, and a weapon with which they could finally demolish the pompous and ponderous taste of the 1850s and 1860s. Soon the world of fashion talked of nothing but 'high art' and the 'aesthetic taste', in every aspect of furnishing and the applied arts.

Among the first to take advantage of the new style were the silversmiths of London, Birmingham and Sheffield. G. R. Elkington in Birmingham and Barnard Bros. in London are the two firms that stand out as promoters of the new Japanese style – curiously called 'Chinese' despite the fans, butterflies and cloud shapes which provided a pot-pourri of Japanese ideas. There appears to have been considerable interchange of ideas and pieces, and Elkingtons unashamedly appear to have overstruck Barnard's marks, especially for their overseas business. As a rule, Elkington's own japonaiseries were flat-chased or in relief, often imitating the intricate *komai* work though they could not, under British hallmarking laws, inlay base in precious metal. Barnard's more often used engraved designs, sometimes parcel-gilt, and these were used by both firms for electro-plated wares.

The new refinement of taste was furthered by J. W. Hukin and J. T. Heath, who registered their mark at Birmingham Assay Office in November 1875. Their speciality was mounting glass in silver. They firmly embraced the aesthetic taste, even commis-

8 Japonaiserie tea service *c.* 1875 to 1885.

sioning designs from the avant-garde Dr Christopher Dresser recently returned from Japan. Dresser also designed for James Dixon of Sheffield and, perhaps even more surprisingly, for Elkingtons during the late 1880s.

'Movements' of all kinds were a feature of the second half of the century: movements towards better conditions in factories, for better housing, better standards of morality, education and, in the context of the applied arts, better design. One of these was the Arts and Crafts Movement, which aimed to establish a fresh nationwide approach to design while also advocating a new life for the craftsman. He was to be essentially a hand craftsman. In the words of William Morris, his works were to be 'a message of honesty and joy to the possessor and a cause of growth and joy to the worker'. The Christian-socialist ideals of the progenitors of the movement were much too unworldly to make commercial success complete. But the various communities of craftsmen up and down the country did help to shed, in a limited way, some light on the importance of the hand-made in a world that had been overtaken by shoddiness and repetitiveness.

The trouble with the movement was that it was fragmented. In Birmingham in 1890 about twenty silversmiths and other metalworkers came together at the instigation of the twenty-five-year-old Arthur Dixon to form a Guild of Handicraft. Two years earlier, in London, C. R. Ashbee had founded another Guild which managed to remain a viable business until 1907; he and his fellow artists travelled and lectured extensively, spreading their word and works throughout Europe and America. Not all their work concerned silver, or even metalwork. Pottery, furniture, glass, textiles and architecture all came under the spell of the various schools of design. Indeed, silversmithing was in a very depressed state from about 1890 onwards. At the end of that year Barnard & Co. recorded that 'Business has suffered a sudden pull up at the time of Prince Albert Victor's death, this and the influenza epidemic produced a general stagnation. . . .' Later they were able to report that 'things are waking up a little'. Soon after it was the old story of depression again, with 'the price of the metal . . . beyond calculation'. Fortunately, the Government removed the duty in 1890 and within a few years business improved.

The coldly ascetic designs of the Arts and Crafts Movement, with their insistence on function and their avoidance of anything that smacked of the machine (so that clumsy rivets replaced concealed hinges and hammer marks banished the smooth surfaces left by the planishing hammer) had less appeal for the buying public than for the young students who sat at the feet of William Morris, William Lethaby and Walter Crane. Art and industry appeared gradually to be drifting apart again, though in Sheffield Mappins and Dixons both made valiant efforts to include at least some 'modern' designs in their ranges. Also, Elkingtons persevered with a few designs by Dresser and others, but were apt to fall back on the more ponderous and elaborate pieces at which for so long they had excelled.

But it was to Birmingham that Arthur Lasenby Liberty turned when in 1898 he established the firm's new Cymric range designed by W. H. Haseler. This project for silver and jewellery was soon to be followed by Liberty's even better-known Tudric pewter. Liberty had opened his famous emporium for oriental silks in

A BRIEF SURVEY OF STYLES

1875 in London's Regent Street, and was quick to adopt all the new vogues, bringing over Japanese products and commissioning others. As japonaiserie faded, he turned to the Arts and Crafts style, but by the last decade of the century had found an amelioration of that stark style in the *art nouveau*. Art nouveau, basically simple, added that touch of fluidity and floweriness to the cold ascetic shapes that went before it. Best of all, it appealed to the public, and was emulated, copied and miscopied.

There were many people unable or unwilling to appreciate the modern styles. Between the grandiose and the artistically aesthetic there was a ready market for reproductions or, more often, for approximations vaguely in an old style, for many were assembled without any real knowledge or proper appreciation of the originals. Silver collecting as we now know it was in its infancy. The manufacturers of silver and plated goods started the still prevalent naming of unlikely patterns as Queen Anne, Lamerie, Adam, Louis Quinze and dozens of others, paying lip service to the new pursuit of collecting antique silver. It gave rise not only to the first real studies of silver in England (often with the initial emphasis on medieval and Tudor rather than more recent treasures), but also to a spate of fakes and forgeries, most of which, happily, would not now deceive any but the merest novice; however in their time they were often greatly valued and are often only discovered when submitted for valuation or sent for sale.

Not all reproductions and replicas were inaccurate; several firms, especially in London, even used old patterns and dies to create authentic copies. Among these were Garrard & Co., successors to the firm started by George Wickes, who from the mid-1850s had excelled at fine candelabra, salvers and other silver in the manner of Lamerie, Wakelin and other 18th-century masters. By the end of the century they were rivalled by Richard Comyns, Henry Lambert, Hunt & Roskell and D. & J. Wellby in London, and by Thomas Bradbury and Martin Hall & Co., in Sheffield. Replicas of fine early silver in the collections of the City

A BRIEF SURVEY OF STYLES

Livery Companies, in museums and in private collections included both domestic pieces and ceremonial silver. Examples are the famous Gold Cup of about 1660 from Exeter College, Oxford, the Bacon Cup given to the British Museum in 1913, the Mercers' Company cups copied to celebrate Queen Victoria's Golden Jubilee in 1887 and innumerable copies of the Anointing Spoon made at the time of Edward VII's Coronation in 1911.

Nor were all reproductions confined to early English silver. The archaeological finds in Greece and Asia Minor, especially those of Schliemann at Troy and Mycenae, fired the imagination. The Birmingham firm of Nathan and Hayes, who usually marked their work in Chester, did a lively business in very credible silver and silver-gilt replicas of the famous gold Vaphio cups.

On a more modest scale, there were imports of all sorts of stamped and embossed knick-knacks, chiefly from Germany and Holland, ranging from wager cups formed as skirted 16th-century figures to little trinket boxes. This trade was otherwise very much in the hands of Birmingham stampers and smallworkers, who turned out seemingly endless toilet pieces, étuis, boxes and pin trays, dishes and ash trays. All were often of rather flimsy stamped silver for a public who preferred a bit of showy silver to the latest creation of the new art. When war came, the silver trade was poised between past and present. In Sheffield enormous factories were turning out flatware, cutlery and hollow-ware, both silver and electro-plated, on a huge scale, much of it exported to the far-flung empire. In Birmingham, hundreds of small factories and workshops, often employing only a few men and women, perhaps only the family, produced quantities of small silver and plated goods. Dominating the jewellery quarter were the great factories of Elkington's, one for silver, the other for 'steam goods'. In London, the emphasis remained chiefly on hand-made silver, the bias rather towards the reproduction than the modern. New silver was relatively cheap, old silver even cheaper. The clouds of war gathered, and the thunder of the guns obliterated the thunder of the stamping press. When the silver trade picked up the pieces, the old world had changed beyond all recognition.

SINCE 1914

The two World Wars have, in retrospect, had a disastrous effect on the silver trade. The first banished the world where everything seemed secure. The second so accelerated changes in attitudes and techniques that silver has in many instances become virtually divorced from everyday domestic life and many craftsmen are now constrained to create chiefly for ceremonial and Church.

Between 1914 and 1918, many of the larger companies struggled along, but smaller firms, with the master away perhaps never to return, often went to the wall. When the war was over, the natural and inevitable reaction was to try to start where night had fallen in 1914, often a vain hope. During the war things had seemed almost better. In October 1917, for instance, it was reported in one of the trade papers that 'It is a striking fact that the demand for genuine silverwares is greater than in the best pre-war days.... A surprising number of people at home seem to be anxious to become possessed of some of the "genuine article".' Such hopes were hardly fulfilled. There were not the men to make silver or to train apprentices. Inflation was rampant and within a few months of the armistice, the price of silver had risen to an unprecedented $89\frac{1}{2}$d. per ounce, nearly twice its fixed price during the war. Add to that growing unemployment and disillusion, and there was but poor business and little encouragement for young men to enter the trade.

Throughout the 1920s, things gradually got worse. By 1931 the price of silver had slumped to the lowest ever at a mere shilling an ounce. Nonetheless, there was a brave attempt to create a new modern style, based on the simple shapes first introduced by the Arts and Crafts Movement. Two gleams of light illuminated an otherwise dark stage: the fluid line promoted by the greatest of all modern Danish silversmiths, Georg Jensen, and the hand-made look of the Omar Ramsden atelier. The latter style encouraged the revival of the old skill of enamelling, a discipline superbly executed by men such as Arthur Gaskin in Birmingham. This was taken up by smallworkers for a multitude of pocketwares such as cigarette cases and powder compacts, as well as for presentation caskets and for dressing-table sets. The latter is a speciality with which the name of Albert Carter of Birmingham must always be associated.

Gradually new names were heard – John Paul Cooper and his son Francis, H. G. Murphy and R. M. Y. Gleadowe, Harold Stabler and the engraver G. T. Friend – men who set new standards of craftsmanship and design and who contributed so extensively to the teaching of silversmithing in London and Birmingham during the 1920s and 1930s. There remained, unhappily, a dichotomy between the artist-craftsman and the industrial firms from which the trade has even now failed to recover. A few of the silver firms, especially in London, such as Wakely & Wheeler, Padgett & Braham and Nayler Brothers, did make a point of commissioning designs from contemporary craftsmen-designers, while others maintain a high standard of accurate reproduction silver. Among them were Garrard & Co., William Comyns and Edward Barnard & Sons.

By about 1935 the great influence on design was the cinema. The halls used for showing films were often specially built in a style that blended function with a sense of romantic luxury, aptly termed picture palaces. It was a style to be extended to the new stations being constructed for the underground railway, for large department stores, for factories, banks, office buildings, bridges and hotels. So silver, both domestic and ceremonial, adopted this new stark angularity, often devoid of ornament except perhaps for a few lines of engraving, a series of parallel flutes or pendant stepped detail. Squares, octagons and simple cylinders dominated form. The role of the modeller was often relegated to the making of finials or for pierced and applied crests, armorials or other special details for ceremonial cups, bowls and caskets. Flat chasing and engraving in this new art deco style was a combination of the sinuous and the ascetic. The broad flanges of dishes, for instance, were panelled and decorated with alternating figures and foliage in a development of the Pre-Raphaelite style. Lettering, much influenced or sometimes actually designed by Eric Gill, set a style of legibility that has continued supreme ever since. Chasing was often confined to fluting, either straight, tapered or in wavy patterns, the latter very much favoured by Gleadowe for bowls, vases and cups.

If anything, the Second World War took an even greater toll of the already diminished world of silver. No young men could be apprenticed, established firms turned over almost entirely to war work, while others had to close for lack of workmen or, after the bombing, of premises and tools.

After the war, the need for useful objects brought some work back to the vast antiquated and sometimes dilapidated factories and workshops of Birmingham and Sheffield. Ships and aircraft were being fitted out, the most luxurious with silver, others with silver-plated wares. At the same time the wartime experience of working stainless steel heralded its arrival on the domestic scene. To stimulate demand, competitions were held to encourage craftsmen; students were sponsored at the trade schools; and, there was a new era of exhibitions. The revived British Industries Fair, aimed to promote the export trade at a time when purchase tax at home was at a penal rate, was held annually. Then in 1951 was staged the finest encouragement of all, the Festival of Britain which at last seemed to banish the 'utility' syndrome from the silversmiths' shops. The private patron was, however, almost extinct, though individual businessmen and others were urged to commission silver designers for presentation pieces for the universities, Church, corporations and so on. Leading this new style of patronage was the ancient Worshipful Company of Goldsmiths, who organised craft competitions, and set up a register of craftsmen with specimen illustrations of their work as well as inaugurating an extensive modern collection of their own. Some of the larger manufacturers began to see the advantage of well-designed silver for their mass-produced wares. The Design Council and some of the larger individual retailers all helped to create a better climate for the silver designer.

Some of the best designers of the 1940s and 1950s had made their masterpieces in the late 1930s, only to have their continuity of thought and development interrupted for six bitter years. But in some ways, the war also helped them to develop. When C. J. Shiner and R. G. Baxendale, Robert Stone and Leslie Durbin, Reginald Hill and Robert Goodden took up their pencils and hammers again in 1945, they returned with fresh eyes to create a new post-war style. Their task was daunting, and most had to supplement their output by teaching. They were faced with shortages and restrictions and a crippling tax (to some small extent ameliorated by a special scheme for craft-made commissions), and perhaps even more by a generally hidebound trade. That they succeeded can be measured by the upsurge of interest in modern silver design since the war and the fact that many of the most successful post-war designer-craftsmen have become household names throughout the world.

The immediate post-war years did not see great changes in style. It was perhaps hard enough to convince people that they wanted silver, without making them understand the finer points of modern design. Leslie Durbin put to good use his skills at modelling as in the suite of pelican salts and peppers for Corpus Christi College, Cambridge, made in 1947. His skill was by no means unabated thirty years later in his exquisite silver rose made to celebrate the Queen's Jubilee in 1977 and the fine touch of his specially commissioned hallmarking punch for the same occasion.

Royal occasions have, in fact, been instrumental in producing much of the best silver of recent years. The Silver Jubilee in 1935 showed a firm beginning, to be followed by the Coronation in 1953 and the 1977 Jubilee. Some, such as Goodden's fluted globular-bodied cup and cover of 1953 harked back to the most avant-garde of the pre-war designs made by his uncle, R. M. Y. Gleadowe, as did Baxendale and Reginald Hill, whose superb mastery of symbolism made his work especially effective in ceremonial and Church pieces. The younger generation accentuated the fluid line of Scandinavian silver, pioneered in this country by Eric Clements, with David Mellor and Robert Welch close on his heels. One of the most innovatory of techniques was texturing, introduced by Gerald Benney in the mid-1960s, and since used most effectively for both handmade and mass-produced silverwares. At its best it contrasted with polished surfaces on gently curved silverwares. Another successful technique used with great aplomb by Anthony Elson and by Alex Styles is electro-forming. This was a far cry from the copying of other materials and objects at which Elkington's so excelled more than a century ago. It was used to create, on a commercial scale, handwork specially designed for the method.

There has been growing interest in the revival of piercing, chasing and engraving as well as in old and new production methods. Rare techniques, such as the inlaying of gold, lacy patterns of filigree effect have been skilfully used by Welch, Jocelyn Burton and Stuart Devlin, to name but a few of the young men and women who are developing their own highly individual styles in a tradition that goes back through the centuries to St Dunstan and beyond.

CHAPTER TWO

A. The Craft of the Silversmith

A proper understanding of how silver was – and still mostly is – made in workshop and factory, and the different techniques of decoration add immeasurably to the pleasure of studying and owning silver. Allied with a knowledge of the history of style, the appreciation of the methods used also provides a safeguard against the activities of fakers, forgers and re-furbishers who are seldom able or willing to spend costly time to produce even passable imitations of the antique.

THE MINING AND PREPARATION OF SILVER

From ancient times, when most of the silver worked in the Near East, China and Europe was won from galena (lead sulphide), the metal was extracted from the ore by 'leaching' with nitric acid. The process was used even after the finds of the rich silver mines of Mexico, Peru and Bolivia in the 16th and 17th centuries; but by the time new sources were being unearthed in North America and Australia in the second half of the 19th century, new refining techniques were being developed using hot sulphuric acid. By 1871 they were being used on a commercial scale by the London bullion refiners Johnson, Matthey. The old leaching process dissolved all the base metals out from the ore, leaving only the silver and any gold, so that silver made before the electrolytic process developed in 1884 is seldom entirely free of particles of gold.

Pure silver is much too soft to be durable enough for everyday use, and from the earliest times it has been alloyed with a small proportion of other metal, usually copper. Copper gives it both hardness and malleability (literally, easy to hammer) so that it

THE CRAFT OF THE SILVERSMITH

can be shaped or drawn into wires, without destroying the lustrous grey colour of the metal. By trial and experiment, silversmiths almost everywhere discovered that about $7\frac{1}{2}$ per cent copper produced a workable and durable alloy, changing the soft pure metal so that it becomes more than twice as hard and with almost double the tensile strength.

In England the Anglo-Saxon kings established a silver coinage – the name 'penny' is said to derive from the name of King Penda of Mercia. It is interesting to ponder that most Saxon and Norman silver coins are between 920 and 940 parts fine, many actually of the sterling 925 standard. This name also derives from the coinage, for it is said that it was given to the silver coins made by the Saxon moneyers, the Easterlings, whom Henry II brought over to improve the English coinage. Certainly since 1300, the sterling standard has been the lowest permitted standard of silver in England, containing 925 parts per 1000 of pure silver or, expressed in terms of weight, 11 oz. 2 dwt. pure to the 12-ounce pound Troy. In ordaining that all wrought silver should be of the same standard as the coinage, Edward I acknowledged that the coinage and the bullion used by the silversmith were one and the same. Incidentally, he was responsible for inaugurating the hallmarking system in this country by stipulating that all wares should be struck with the Leopard's Head mark to denote that they had been tested and were of the correct standard.

The bullion, usually in the form of ingots but sometimes worn-out or perhaps old-fashioned plate for remaking, had to be prepared for working by the silversmith himself. Until the early 18th century, when the first rolling mills were established, he had to reduce the ingot to a workable sheet by hammering (or battery) or to billets for making spoons, drawing wire, and the like. A series of hammers of different weights laboriously flattened the metal into sheets as even as eye and patience could make them; when during the lean years of the Commonwealth in the mid-17th century silver was in desperately short supply, the thin sheets must have taken many hours to produce. Today, of course, the refiners and bullion dealers not only prepare sheet, even cutting it into circles and other much-required shapes, but also market wire, castings and solders for the silversmith.

THE TOOLS OF THE SILVERSMITH

Despite modern technical aids, the tools of the silversmith and even his workshop look very much as they must have looked centuries – even millenia – ago. A hollowed out tree-trunk for sinking, a raising stake, shears and calipers, a series of hammers, gravers and punches, and an annealing hearth; even the scales and weights used by the silversmith are little different essentially from those used by Paul Revere or Paul de Lamerie, Cellini or Theophilus or the craftsmen depicted on the walls on ancient Egyptian tombs nearly four thousand years ago. A gas-jet replaces the boy with the bellows over the charcoal furnace, in the factory great presses squeeze patterns on to flatware and knife handles, some simple shapes being deep-drawn, but with few exceptions the craft of the silversmith is still one of hammer and hand, of patience and a wary eye, a labour of skill to bring out the soft lustre while adding durability and function to the form and decorative quality of the metal.

THE CATEGORIES OF SILVER

The work of the silversmith is generally divided into several distinct categories: hollow-ware, flatware and smallwares. Hollow-ware, despite its name, includes trays and salvers as well as cups and bowls, jugs, pots, casters, tureens and even candlesticks. It can be raised, spun or stamped. It is also a term extended to include such other wares that cannot easily be included among flatware (spoons, forks and other flat tableware) or smallwares. Among objects in this group, therefore, are boxes and cases of all kinds, wine labels, pocket silver and the 'toys' of the 18th- and 19-century smallworkers.

SINKING AND RAISING

The first stage in making hollow-wares is to cut a sheet of flat silver, of the required thickness or gauge, to an appropriate size and shape for the piece in hand. Clear and accurate scale drawings, with details in plan and elevation of all the parts – the spout, handle sockets, cover, finial and foot of a coffee pot, for instance – are as essential as clean and undamaged tools. A bowl, for example, is usually made from a circle of silver of good gauge, the size being calculated by adding the average diameter of the body to the height from the base of the piece to the rim.

Over one of the shallow depressions in the wooden steady block – still often a trimmed tree trunk – the silversmith uses a ball-faced blocking hammer to work blow by blow, patiently round the outer edge of the circle, and so on, row upon row working in concentric circles, until the sheet is a shallow inverted dome. Each hammer blow distorts the crystallographic structure of the metal, hardening it. Before cracking-point is reached, it must be made malleable again by annealing it.

Annealing is done by placing the silver in a special pan, known as a hearth, which is rotated in the flame. The silver is brought to a red heat – a dull red that by long experience must be rightly judged, hence the positioning of the furnace in a dark corner so that the colour can best be seen. Then it is quenched, usually in water, occasionally in a bath of oil, and it is ready for further hammering. A piece may have to be annealed many times during its manufacture, and care must be taken to avoid firestain. This is due to the copper in the alloy becoming oxidised just below the surface, leaving a stain that cannot be removed except by stoning down the surface – and so thinning the gauge – or by pickling in acid to dissolve out the copper oxide formed.

Shallow bowls and saucers are further shaped up with the sinking hammer over a sand-filled leather saddle, but deeper wares must be worked over the raising stake. According to the

9 Sinking and raising

size of the piece, this iron stake with a polished face is fixed either in the steady block or the bench vice. With the work tilted over the stake, the silversmith again works row by row round the piece, but this time starts not from the edge but from the centre of the base, until gradually it becomes deeper and narrower. Every time the craftsman reaches the top edge, he hammers it down firmly, a process known as caulking or corking, to give a firm rim that will not readily split. The exception to this is in the making of tumbler cups, in which the weight is hammered back towards the base to give them their characteristic heavy round base. Each time the rows are completed, the piece must be annealed again; for the next row the work must be tilted at a different angle. The hammer blows must be evenly struck, so that the thickness of the silver remains constant; this is especially important when a tall narrow pot is being drawn in or swaged to a baluster shape, or the sides of a pot are being formed into panels. An average sized jug or coffee pot will take about a day to raise by this method.

TURNING UP FROM A CONE

Many simpler silverwares, such as straight-sided tankards, mugs and coffee pots have for long been turned up from a cone of silver, seamed along one edge, then hammered to shape over the stake as with hand-raised work. Faint seam lines can sometimes be detected inside tankards and coffee-pots, usually along the line of the handle. The process means that a mouth-wire has to be soldered to the rim as the metal, obviously, cannot be caulked, and the base and foot must also be soldered in separately. Though turning up was known in the later 17th century, applied mouth-wires were not usual on coffee pots and other jugs before the middle of the 18th century. Once the top edge has been filed smooth in line with the sprung-in mouth-wire, the rim can be hammered into line with the gradual curve of the body.

SPINNING

A technique that appears modern yet is in fact of very ancient origin is spinning, the shaping of hollow-wares of all sorts over a former or chuck in the lathe. It was used for bowls by the Egyptians, but recent advances in the design of chucks and the very careful attention to the gauge of spinning silver – between 0.9 and 1.1 m.m. – have brought the process up to date. The silver is coated with tallow and held in the lathe. As it rotates, the spinner presses a steel-headed tool with a long arm steadied by the craftsman's body under his armpit, starting in the centre of the silver sheet and gradually working towards the edge. The chuck, usually of an easily turned wood such as box or lignum vitae

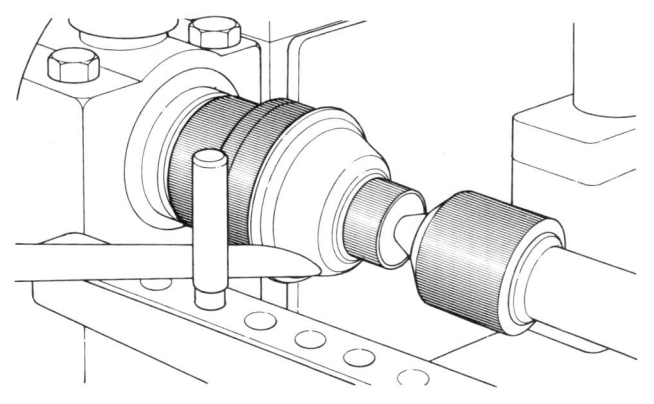

10 Spinning

(occasionally of beech or even of steel) gradually shapes the silver. For jugs, tankards, mugs and so on, the chuck is usually made in sections so that it can be slid out from a semi-enclosed shape without difficulty. As with all other ways of making silver, the ware must be annealed from time to time, if necessary planished, and polished and finished in the same way as hand-raised or stamped silverwares.

STAMPING AND PRESSING

Originally a development of the use of dies for striking coins and medals, the first patents for making small objects of gold and silver by stamping were taken out in the mid-18th century. It was soon adopted for the mass-production of borders, candlestick parts, buckles, boxes and smallwares, especially in Birmingham and in Sheffield's growing fused-plate trade. Soon improved hardened steel dies were in use, and in Sheffield particularly, die-struck work of exceptionally high quality was the rule. Subsequently, however, largely because of the high cost of producing dies, stamping became a token of repetitive and rather soulless silversmithing, with variations often achieved by using a spout from one set of patterns, a handle from another, a body from another adorned with mounts or other decorative details from yet another, so that stamping gradually became concomitant with cheaper and poorly designed wares. At its best, die-stamping was, however, a viable technique that deserved its place in competition with the more traditional methods of making silver.

WIRE DRAWING

The drawing of wires was introduced into England during the 16th century, the wire being produced by drawing a length of silver, tapered at one end for easier manipulation, through the holes in the drawplate, gradually reducing it in thickness until the required size and shape is achieved. Though ductile, the silver must nonetheless be tempered from time to time during the process by annealing it. More complicated shapes than tubular or hemispherical wire must be made in the draw-swage, forming the pattern by using a die held in a clamp and drawing the silver first one way, then back again, over the die. Wires can further be enhanced with the use of the punch, to produce domed effects, by hammering them with punches over an intaglio-cut die, producing stamped decoration such as that often found on medieval and Tudor pieces, or simply by twisting fine wires to give a corded or plaited effect. Even more elaborate mounts can be made by casting.

CASTING

Many spouts, handles, handle sockets, feet and finials in silver are made by casting. The bodies of entire objects such as mugs, parts of candlesticks, and even larger items can be made by casting, the result as a rule being of a heavier gauge than silver made by raising, stamping or spinning.

A pattern of the piece to be cast must first be modelled, exact in every detail, in wood, metal, plaster or modelling wax. Old models, such as have survived, appear mostly to have been in wood or metal. Quite complex designs can be made using the sand-casting method, the moulds being held between two iron cases filled with sand of a special texture, which hardens into the pattern of the mould, itself prepared with a parting substance so that the grains will not adhere to it and mar the outline. The metal must be of good quality, free of impurities and of the correct temperature, or pitting occurs.

Today many smaller parts are made by the lost-wax casting method, using a centrifugal casting machine, the model being made in a special wax and then impressed in a vulcanised rubber mould. Only small parts can be made by this method, which is relatively expensive to instal, but it has the advantage that there is less time spent on finishing than with the older sand-casting or gravity casting.

ASSEMBLY

The spout, handle sockets, foot ring and foot, finial and any applied ornament, such as cut-card work or applied strapwork, must be carefully cleaned up and then soldered to the body of the vessel with a special silver solder. Soldering is a much more skilled operation than it appears to the layman. Neat joints are essential – and most craftsmen pride themselves on a well-concealed joint on the exterior and very little evidence on the inside or underside, though in the 17th century and earlier, and even later in the provinces, excess solder under the foot of say, a tankard or a mug, was often not turned away.

The solder used today has to be at least of the sterling standard in order to conform to the hallmarking laws; zinc today has generally superseded brass in producing a hard silver solder that has a relatively low melting point, so that the material can be used sparingly and precisely. The brass-silver alloy used in the past, over a charcoal flame, gives old silver solders a yellowish tinge not found in modern work: at times a useful guide to whether modern repairers, restorers or even forgers have been at work. A recent development, especially on the Continent, for mass-produced wares is spot-welding.

FINISHING

During manufacture, besides ensuring that the silver remains malleable (by frequent annealing), tremendous care is taken to ensure that the surface is smooth and free from firestain, scratches, file marks and other blemishes acquired during raising, soldering and general handling.

Planishing When the body has been shaped by hand-raising, the silversmith uses a heavy flat-faced hammer to planish, or smooth out the ridges inevitably left by the raising hammers. Planishing is a skilled and especially important aspect of the best hand-made silver, particularly in the making of trays, salvers and waiters. The work to be planished is held over a flat surface plate, removing every trace of the row upon row of hammer-marks that have made the silver not only flat but strong as well. Planishing is a hand-process that, as yet, no machine has replaced satisfactorily.

Polishing Initial polishing to remove scratches, file marks, ridges and minor surface firestain is usually done with finely ground pumice paste on a buffing mop, and then finished with Trent sand and oil. Polishing is a highly skilled occupation, but also a rather dirty one, since the Trent sand tend to fly about and is oily. It also requires infinite patience and knowledge of the processes used in manufacture to ensure that ridges and grooves are not exaggerated by the process that is intended to eliminate them.

After initial polishing, further finishing is effected by using rouge (powdered ferric oxide), occasionally softened with paraffin or white spirit, and a swan's-down or soft woollen mop. But throughout the process great care must be taken to see that no traces of abrasive, acid, specks of steel or other rough materials have been picked up and remain in crevices, chased details, piercing or other parts of the silver, marring its lustre and soft surface polish.

Burnishing The very high polish on silver, known as mirror-finish, is not usually considered suitable for antique silver, and pieces that have had to undergo minor repairs may have to be 'taken down' in tone to try to restore something of the patinated surface naturally acquired by long usage and by years of tarnishing restored by hand-polishing.

A rather different type of high finish, that does not have the glare of mirror polishing, is burnishing. This is a long and meticulous process done by smoothing the surface with agate-tipped or steel-tipped tools known as burnishers. Absolute cleanliness of tool and surface is essential to produce an even and clean surface; it is a technique much used for highly chased wares and for getting into awkward corners not easily cleaned out by normal polishing. It also greatly improves the appearance of gilded wares.

Gilding Formerly the terms 'gold' or 'gilt', as opposed to 'white' or ungilded silver, were commonly applied to large quantities of plate gilded both for show and to reduce the necessity for frequent cleaning. Gilding should never be polished with any abrasive substance, simply washed in warm soapy water and dried with a soft cloth. Hence it is likely to last well; this is all the more so with antique gilding, since it was often applied more thickly than is common with the electrolytic methods of today.

Old gilding was applied using an amalgam of gold and mercury, the gold being added to a pan of boiling mercury. Any area not to be gilded was 'stopped off' with an impervious substance such as varnish. The mercury-gold amalgam was then pasted on, the piece heated and the mercury thus driven off, leaving a layer of gold, of a thickness commensurate with the gold-richness of the amalgam. Obviously the fumes were highly poisonous, and many gilders in the past died young from its effects. Today, fire-gilding is forbidden by law in Britain, though it must be said that modern electrolytic gilding lacks something of the richness of its prohibited antecedent. Some of the special appeal of mercury or fire-gilding was in fact really due to the after-care of burnishing, as well as to the high degree of finish bestowed on pieces to be gilded before the amalgam was applied. Fire-gilding, often rather paler in appearance than electro-gilding, does, however, darken if kept in a closed condition, though in use it has a most attractive lemon tone.

Electro-gilding was a development of the plating processes developed in the 19th century by Elkington & Co. in Birmingham. By 1860 to 1870, it had largely superseded the old process, being acclaimed for its economy of use as much as for its protection of workers' health. It should be pointed out that, though most modern gilding is of reddish hue, colours can be controlled, and lighter shades closer to fire-gilding can with care be obtained.

B. Decorative Techniques

While modern taste frequently puts simplicity first, allowing old silver's chief attraction to be its grey lustre and soft patina rather than the virtuosity of the decorator, even in those periods most often associated with plainness, such as the early years of the 18th century, ornamented silver was still held in high esteem and was charged at a much higher rate because of the additional work of the chaser and engraver. Each age had its own preferences, as in the mid-18th century, when cast and applied detail and superb repoussé chasing were in fashion.

There are basically three types of surface decoration available to the silversmith: that in which no metal is removed, as in all types of chasing; that in which metal is actually added, as in cut-card work; and that in which metal is removed, as in piercing and engraving. Often one or more of these techniques is combined with considerable effect, as in the pierced table baskets of the 18th century with cast and applied details often setting off intricately pierced patterns themselves further enriched with engraving.

CHASING

The term chasing comprises all those forms of decoration achieved without loss of metal. It does not, as the *Oxford English Dictionary* states in one of its rare erroneous entries, mean 'work embossed or engraved in relief' since engraving *per se* entails removal of metal. Using hammer and punch, the chaser coaxes the metal into the design, either in high relief (embossing from the back, and then given further detail from the front by the repoussé technique) or with scarcely noticeable relief, as in flat chasing.

Hundreds of differently shaped tools, often made specifically for a certain design, are needed to achieve different effects, from simple lobing to the detailed definition of, say, a rococo shell; from matted panels to a border of strapwork, scrolls and masks, so like drawing that it is sometimes confused with engraving; from tooling fur or feathers on a model, giving definition to the shapes of the caster who cannot alone achieve the fine detail required and whose sand-pitted surfaces must often be tidied up by the chaser. The latter, of all silver craftsmen, can justifiably consider his work the most important in bringing well-made silver to its finish.

EMBOSSING

The raising of domes and other simple shapes such as lobes, palmate leaves and five-petalled flowers has been practised since men first began to work metals. These usually consisted of domes or other simple tear-drop shapes embossed both on silver and gold bowls. The work is done from the back using domed punches of various sizes which are hammered so that the relief bosses are bumped up, the face of the work being supported on a bed of wax, soft wood or pitch.

For enclosed shapes, such as tankards and pots, the embossing has to be done by 'remote control' using a long iron called a snarling-iron which has a domed head. Fixed in the vice, the end is tapped with the hammer so that the punch bosses the metal of the vessel from inside, the chaser having carefully to follow the pattern traced on the outside of the pot.

REPOUSSE CHASING

Embossing alone gives only very simple shapes, which look primitive unless further worked from the exterior. Almost all embossed chasing is further refined by the technique known as repoussé. The work must be supported on a bed of pitch. Then the design is carefully worked over by the chaser using a wide variety of different punches. Dozens, even hundreds, of them may be needed to complete an intricate pattern, to give highlights, effects of light and shade and other fine details. Again, no metal is removed, though sometimes repoussé chasing is used in conjunction with engraving.

FLAT CHASING

For the collector unused to examining the different types of decoration very closely, the difference between flat chasing and engraving is sometimes difficult to distinguish, especially when long usage has blurred the edges of engraved details. As with all chasing, however, no metal is removed, though flat chasing is akin to engraving in that the designs are often linear rather than in the round. The work is done from the front, using hammer and punches. As before, the silver has to be supported on a bed of pitch to keep it firm – hollow shapes are filled with pitch, which can easily be melted out when the work is completed. As with most decorative techniques, the work is brought to the tool rather than the tool to the work (which would result in patchy uneven surfaces). The silver is further supported on a leather ring which allows the work to be tilted to the required angle, or, if filled, on a sandbag that supports the piece. The pattern is lightly marked out using a chisel-like tracer and hammer. (On rare occasions, the occasional dot mark and guideline can be detected beneath the decoration.) Then, using punches of various shapes and sizes, the chaser works the detail of the pattern, sometimes having to make special tools for the job in hand. A variant of flat chasing is matting, the chaser having to take great care to ensure that the dot-effects are regular and even.

CAST CHASING

This rather loose trade term refers to the process of sharpening up and giving definition to cast ornament, adding details that are more definite than can be achieved in the casting mould. It is really a form of repoussé chasing, worked from the front – truing up flutes, for instance and defining outlines.

APPLIED DECORATION

Applied shapes cut from sheet silver, wires and other decorative mounts serve the double purpose of strengthening rims, handle junctions, spouts and the bases of bowls as well as providing impressive and often very ornate decoration.

Ornamental wires Wires of circular, semi-circular, square or other simple shapes are made in the draw-plate in the same way as the strengthening wires used for rims of vessels and as foot-wires. More elaborate patterns are produced by a process called swaging, hammering strips of silver into a block or die, into which the pattern has been cut, by stamping or by casting. Cast wires used in the rich and intricate designs of the rococo period were introduced during the 18th century. They had, like all castings, to be enhanced by further chasing after being soldered on to the ware.

Cut-card ornament One of the most attractive of all decorative techniques used from about the middle of the 17th century onwards was that known as cut-card work. The cards are very thin sheets of silver, hammered out flat and cut into silhouettes of leaf

DECORATIVE TECHNIQUES

11 Cut-card work on inkstand, 1669.

or scrolling outline and then soldered so flat against the body of the ware that they appear to be integral with it. Originally these foliate and scroll shapes were cut from the sheet using hammer and chisel; but, since the mid-1700s they have been produced, like all pierced work since then, using the saw-frame.

Cut-card ornament was often further enhanced with other details, such as tapering beaded ribs to suggest veining and stems.

12 Applied strap-work on base of cup, 1735.

In the hands of the Huguenot craftsmen a few years later, it was developed into applied strapwork, at first of rather simple pal-

82

mate form, but gradually becoming more and more elaborate in conception, with pierced and chased motifs, medallion heads and other intricacies applied layer upon layer or, latterly, cast and applied to achieve rich confections in the rococo taste.

ENGRAVING, PIERCING AND ETCHING

All these processes entail removal of metal and can be achieved both by hand or machine.

Engraving Among the oldest of all the arts, engraving ranges from a few scratched lines of graffito on a cave wall to the exquisite draughtsmanship achieved by such artist-craftsmen as Simon Gribelin or William Hogarth, or the dozens of unidentified craftsmen who have drawn such fine cartouches for armorials or lettered such elegant inscriptions on presentation silver.

First of all the design – essentially linear – is drawn on the surface by transferring a black impression from a waxed paper. The outlines are then sketched in with a scriber, and the waxy black design can be cleaned off, leaving the engraver with a lightly scratched-on guide. As with chasing, the work is brought to the tool and is supported on a bed of pitch and held against a sandbag, to be turned clockwise to the graver as required. Again, several sizes and types of engraving tool may be required, the tool being held firmly between the thumb and the palm of the hand, so that a noticeably spatulate thumb soon becomes a typical sign of the engraver. The linear technique of engraving means that the engraver has to exercise considerable skill to achieve distinctions of light and shade – one false move and the cut may become coarse or jagged. Above all, he needs great patience, for the work must copy the original exactly. Indeed, though a high degree of competence is achieved by some modern engravers, armorials and engraved inscriptions purporting to be of early date can usually be detected not only because the recent engraving is a little too sharp at the edges, but also because the outlines are broader and coarser than is usual in 18th-century work.

Engraving today can, of course, also be done by machine, and for such silver as sports trophies and many other presentation pieces this is often adequate. The finer finish of hand-engraved work is preferable for hand-made or other fine silver.

Bright-cut engraving is a variation of ordinary linear engraving first used about 1765. Its exceptionally brilliant appearance is achieved by varying the depth of the cuts using highly polished tools, which polish the cut as the tool is drawn out after gouging the metal from the surface. By the 1800s, the standard of bright-cut engraving was often less high, the patterns often deteriorating into simple wrigglework borders. At its best, during the early neoclassical period from about 1770 to 1790, it was superbly crisp and lively and one of the most effective of all surface decorations.

Piercing It surprises many collectors to learn that until the second half of the 18th century, piercing was done using fine chisels. In the hands of the best craftsmen, very fine piercing could be achieved by this method, the design, as with engraving, being traced on to the surface. The small sharp cutting tool would be placed where the cut was required and tapped smartly with the hammer. Careful examination of pierced work – baskets, caster tops, orange strainers and the like – before 1760 shows how the metal has been cut-stamped into shape, the edges of the cut revealing the outer skin of the silver pushed over the edge.

The introduction of the piercing saw, with its fine blade set in a three-sided frame exactly like a fret-saw, somewhat mechanised the technique, which remains, however, a highly skilled aspect of the silver decorator's craft. The design, as before, is indicated on the surface of the silver, then a small hole punched in (dot piercing using simple tools such as the bow-drill has been practised since ancient times). Holding the saw exactly vertical, the piercer then enlarges the hole to the required shape, making small vertical cuts. Any deviation from the vertical is likely to break the saw. Saw-piercing can be detected because it leaves tiny ridged teeth-marks along the edges.

Complete mechanisation of piercing was developed in Sheffield with the fly-press, in effect a mechanical version of the original chisel-and-hammer method of piercing. Fine effects were achieved by the early Sheffield silversmiths and platers using the fly-press, but later fly-press work generally shows a coarseness and is readily distinguishable from hand-pierced work of any kind.

Etching Acid-etching as a decorative technique on silver was a Victorian development. Generally used to contrast plain and matted or satin-finished surfaces, it tends to have a rather 'cold' appearance. The etched surface, which has to be constantly cleaned by taking away the tiny scraps of silver eaten into by the nitric acid applied, has a roughened appearance and feel. A recent development for intricately etched patterns is photographic etching, the design being transferred photographically to a flat or only very slight curved surface.

CHAPTER THREE

Objects

Apostle spoons Certainly among the most popular of all medieval and 16th-century finials were the figures representing the Twelve Apostles. A few complete sets are known, including the Master (and omitting Judas Iscariot). More often spoons were made individually, some no doubt as Christening gifts. The styles of the finials varied from time to time and place to place; some have the nimbus, or halo, pierced, most are gilded, and some Saints are shown with an emblem related to their history. The finial is usually soldered into a v-joint in the tapering hexagonal stem and the fig-shaped bowl has a triangular pip on the back at the junction. The town mark was struck in the bowl near the stem on most 16th-century examples, though any form of marking prior to that appears rare. The maker's mark and, after 1478, the date letter was struck, if at all, near the base of the stem, the Lion Passant being added after 1544.

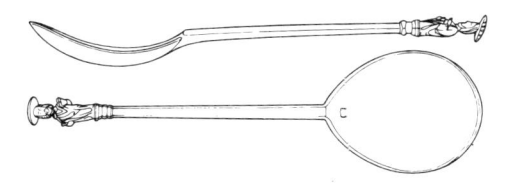

13 Apostle spoons pre-*c*. 1630.

Apple corers A popular pocket piece in the 18th century, a few early corers of late-17th-century date are known (with a cylindrical handle about the same length as the hollow blade of the corer). By the end of the 18th century, the Birmingham smallworkers in particular had introduced apple peelers-cum-corers with blades that unscrewed so that they could be inverted and screwed into the handle-sheath, which was of silver, ivory or bone. After 1790 apple corers were fully marked.

Argand lamps Patent oil lamps invented by a Swiss, Aimé Argand, with the oil chamber in a central reservoir and two 'chimneys' with wicks. The lamps were originally made up for Argand by Matthew Boulton of Soho, Birmingham, who continued to make them in large quantity, mostly in fused plate and in ormolu after the patent was revoked in 1784. Some were hung with cut-glass drops or mounted with Wedgwood jasperware plaques. They were extremely popular in America, where good examples can be seen at Winterthur, Mount Vernon and Monticello.

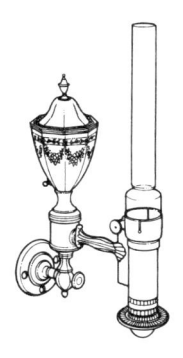

14 Argand lamp *c.* 1785.

Argyles (or Argylls) Spouted pots fitted with an inner jacket to contain hot water or with a compartment to hold a heated iron for keeping gravy hot. Made in silver and in fused (Sheffield) plate,

15 Argyle *c.* 1780.

argyles are said to have been named for the Duke of Argyll. The earliest date from the middle of the 18th century; they were especially popular between about 1770 and 1820. Early examples were usually vase- or baluster-shaped, with a few, especially plated examples, of a tapered straight-sided pattern rather like feeding cups. The spout, often rather narrow in section and curving, was generally set close to the body, and at right angles to the handle, near which was the hinged flap cover of the water container. By the 1780s, oval or drum-shaped argyles with straight tapered spouts were hardly distinguishable from teapots of the period, except for the hot-water container. By the Regency period they were largely superseded by covered tureens.

Asparagus dishes Oval or oblong serving dishes of entrée-dish form fitted with a strainer or wirework rack and sometimes also incorporating a frame for the tongs and a butter boat. They were a late-19th-century item chiefly made in electroplated ware.

OBJECTS

Asparagus tongs and servers Large scissor-like tongs with flattened ridged terminals were made from about 1745 onwards. By the mid-19th century a U-shaped pattern with broad pierced shaped oblong blades, held by a retaining bar to prevent their springing apart, gradually replaced the older tong form.

Baskets Circular baskets for fruit, bread and cakes were made from Tudor times onwards. With slightly everted sides pierced in a variety of patterns, the style changed little until about 1700, when oval shapes with end handles were preferred and many table baskets closely imitated wickerwork. About 1725, corded or flat fixed handles were introduced, followed about 1730 by the more familiar swing handle. By the mid-1730s, much more elaborate pierced designs came into fashion, often with heavily and richly cast and chased rim mounts and elaborate cast terminals to the handles. By about 1739 the pierced foot conforming to the shape of the basket was often elaborated into a cast and chased openwork apron support.

About 1768 the invention of Sheffield-plated wire brought openwork baskets made in all sizes, often copied in silver. Smaller baskets for sweetmeats, and with glass liners, for sugar and cream, generally followed the design of cake and bread baskets, which by the 1780s were usually of boat shape on a pierced oval foot, styles both hand-made and mass-produced from standard parts in Birmingham and Sheffield.

By the end of the century unpierced boat-shaped and oblong baskets catered for the middle market. But about 1800 expensive and elaborate baskets, often with glass liners, were in the form of heavy, cast and chased stands with pierced vine and grape designs being the favourite decorative motifs. About 1820 there was a revival of the heavy rococo-style basket. Most Victorian baskets were also based on earlier styles. (*See* CREAM PAILS, EPERGNES, SWEETMEAT BASKETS.)

Beakers In its simplest form, a beaker is a truncated horn, a shape that underlies even the most elaborate silver beakers in medieval and Tudor times. The beaker's practical shape made it very popular in the later 16th century and throughout the 17th century until the advent of Ravenscroft's flint glass. Late-16th- to early-17th century beakers were usually some 6 in. high, with a slightly flared body engraved near the rim with a band of stylised strapwork and arabesques, standing on a narrow spreading foot stamped with ovolos or other simple repeat ornament.

Smaller late-16th-century beakers, with a moulded rib just below the narrow, usually engraved rim, are sometimes known as Magdalen cups and were provided with covers. Their direct descendants were the smaller beakers of the 17th century, about $3\frac{1}{2}$ to $4\frac{1}{2}$ in. high, on a rim foot. (Care should be taken that such beakers are not made from old Communion cups – the placing of the engraved strapwork round the centre rather than at the top of the bowl may betray that.) From about 1660 beakers were sometimes chased with foliage and flowers, often arranged in three groups below a chased 'corded' band. Others were perfectly plain, or engraved with a crest, arms, initials, an inscription, or between 1675 and 1690, decorated with chinoiseries. A rare set of 13 beakers, one with a cover, was made in 1688 for the Corporation of Newark-on-Trent. Most 18th-century beakers were footless for use with canteens or for nesting. A few of bell-shape were specifically made for members of the English College at Douai about 1688 onwards.

There was a revival of the tapering cylindrical beaker about 1795, and occasionally octagonal or flared-pattern beakers were made, but generally speaking later beakers are replicas and reproductions of earlier types. Many later 19th century beakers appear to have been part of travelling toilet services.

Double-beakers are a variant adapted from German originals in the 17th century; the double-beaker or double-cup, is formed of two footless circular cups with a small flange, one fitting over its partner. About 1765 the fashion was revived for pairs of 'barrel' beakers fitting together, often reeded to simulate staving. In

OBJECTS

16 Beakers TOP ROW, FROM LEFT *c.* 1600; 1680; double beaker *c.* 1770.
BOTTOM ROW *c.* 1570; *c.* 1670.

Chester in particular, small versions with tapering straight-sided halves were similarly decorated with 'staving'. The fashion seems to have lasted until about 1815.

Beer jugs Usually applied to the baluster-shaped jugs of the 18th century of which at least one pair is known, engraved respectively 'Beer' and 'Ale'. Obviously ewers and flagons would also all have

17 Beer jugs FROM LEFT 1733, 1715.

been used for serving beer, wine and other beverages. It is frequently suggested that covered jugs were more often used for wine, lidless examples for beer, but this is far from conclusive. Nineteenth-century lidless jugs were often listed in catalogues as lemonade jugs, some being of pottery or glass with silver rim mounts.

Bells Small bells in silver used to summon servants were made from early times, though existing English examples do not appear to date before the second quarter of the 17th century. By the end of the century, bells were first used on the new style of inkstand, slightly smaller versions of the table bell. Handles were usually of baluster or knopped form, the bells themselves usually quite plain, occasionally with a gadrooned rim or with a rib near the shoulder. Table bells were made in novelty versions during the 19th century – as crinolined ladies, a fairy on an inverted bellflower (designed in 1848) and in a pattern with the handle forming a taperstick. (*See also* RACING BELLS.)

18 Biggins *c*. 1800.

OBJECTS

Biggins A form of coffee percolator invented some time before 1799 by George Biggin 'a man of very easy fortune . . . great chemist, mechanic, musician' from whom 'the coffee biggins take their name' (Thomas Moore, 1799). Usually cylindrical in form, with a short pouring lip, and often supplied with a lampstead, the earliest appears to date from 1796. Biggin died in 1803, but several years later, in 1817, Henry Meade Ogle of Turnham Green, Middlesex, patented 'Certain Improvements of Tea and Coffee Pots or Biggins' incorporating a strainer.

Biscuit boxes Rare until the end of the 19th century when silver, silver-plated and silver-mounted pottery or glass airtight boxes, usually cylindrical or barrel-shaped, became popular. A few earlier oval, rectangular or drum-shaped boxes have been designated biscuit boxes, in the style of large tea caddies. Rectangular examples are also sometimes termed sandwich boxes.

Blackjacks Tankards and jugs of heavy stitched leather lined and mounted with silver or other metal rims were medieval in origin, but continued to be made until about the middle of the 17th century. Few original examples remain. Silver shields or discs for arms or initials were sometimes applied to the fronts. They were also known as bombards, presumably because of their barrelled shape rather like that of early cannons.

Bleeding bowls (Fig. 34) The name commonly given in England to the shallow bowl with a single flat ear; such bowls were used by surgeons for cupping (blood-letting). In America these bowls are called porringers. The form closely relates to the two-handled *écuelle* of French silver and to the form of the quaich, or drinking cup of Scotland. The origin of the one-eared bowl as a drinking cup seems confirmed by early examples about 1630, which are often associated with skillets and caudle cups, doing duty as cover and also, inverted, as a drinking bowl.

Bottle tickets and labels The original name for what are now commonly called wine labels, the terms being used apparently interchangeably. They are small silver tags (later also made in fused plate and in electro-plate) hung on chains and engraved, pierced or applied with the name of the wine or spirit contained in the bottle or decanter. From about 1735 to 1795, they were usually cut from sheet silver and sometimes decorated with either flat-chasing or engraving, or with pierced or stamped borders. Heavier cast labels and die-struck labels were introduced at the end of the century alongside plainer oval, eye-shaped, octagonal and oblong patterns. Very small labels were also made for sauce and condiment bottles. The chief variations of design were flat escutcheons (very like key and handle plates on furniture) until about 1745, usually quite plain or flat-chased; bowed escutcheons (from about 1745 to 1765); crescent, also known at the time as half-moons, from about 1760 to 1780; shaped oblongs and ovals, sometimes with pierced borders, beaded borders or feather-edged, to about 1785. Variations on the crescent and the oblong with decorative domed panels, scrollwork and shields or urns at the top, often decorated with piercing or bright-cut engraving, preceded the cast labels of the Regency, when shells, quatrefoils, vine wreaths and other elaborate shapes, often gilded, were introduced. Vine leaves followed about 1823. A rarer style of decanter label took the form of a splayed hoop or a ring with the label suspended below. Single initials, such as 'P' for Port, 'M' for Madeira, 'C' for Claret and so on (possibly designed to confuse the servants) were made in plain and stamped decorative designs, while towards the end of the 19th century there was a fashion for the whole name to be spelled out, cut from linked letters. By then, however, the paper label for bottles had been introduced (about 1866) and gradually the variety of silver and other labels (bone, ivory, mother-of-pearl, enamel and so on) diminished, most being reproductions of earlier patterns.

Before 1790 few labels bear other than the maker's mark (usually that of a smallworker, many of whom, such as Sandilands Drinkwater, Richard Binley and his widow Margaret, and Susanna Barker very much specialised in labels), and the Lion Passant, such smallwares being exempt from full marking. From 1790, however, all but very small and light labels had to be submitted for assay and marking. Among the prominent specialist London smallworkers were Phipps and Robinson, T. and J. Phipps, John Reily, Reily and Storer, and Rawlings and Summers, while silversmiths, such as Emes and Barnard, Paul Storr, Scott and Smith and the Batemans also made many labels. The Bateman method of stamping letters individually, as well as their use of certain designs, such as that surmounted by Prince of Wales's Feathers, make their labels readily recognisable. The more important silversmiths such as Storr and Edward Farrell sometimes used applied letters for their grander labels. Provincial labels, especially those made in Scotland and Ireland, also have distinguishing characteristics. Irish labels are often well engraved with bright-cut borders. In Scotland the style of engraving names with long strokes and the taste for having matching sets of labels in sizes, with large ones for wine and small ones for spirits, often helps to identify them. By the second quarter of the 19th century huge numbers of stamped labels were made in Birmingham and the practice of buying in from firms in London, Birmingham and Sheffield spread styles quickly throughout the country and, indeed, to faraway places such as India, South Africa, and Portugal. The huge variety of labels, their often fascinating titles using half-forgotten names (though care must be taken that these have not been later engraved to make, say, a common Madeira label more attractive) and their relatively modest price makes them a favourite subject for the silver collector satisfied with a minor art of the silver smallworker.

Bowls (Fig. 33) It is difficult to distinguish bowls intended for drinks from those for various foods. Covered bowls were used for soup, stews, hot caudle, punch, as sugar bowls, race prizes and even for the toilet. Uncovered bowls were used for punch, fruit, sugar, cream, as slop basins and, indeed, for any practical or decorative purpose. No doubt their use changed even in the same household over the years – certainly large punch bowls of the late-17th to early-18th century have been known to do duty as Christening fonts. Small bowls were traditionally given as Christening gifts in the Channel Island of Jersey. (*See* BLEEDING BOWLS; CUPS; ECUELLES; PORRINGERS; SUGAR BOWLS; TOILET SERVICES; TUMBLER CUPS.)

Boxes (Fig. 59) Boxes have been made throughout the centuries for every conceivable purpose, from holding precious jewels and documents to containing snuff, cigarettes and cigars, pomade, sugar and spice, tea, aromatic sponges, patches, gaming counters, knives, medical instruments, sandwiches, biscuits, toilet things, wax tapers, pounce and sand, pens and pencils, seals, salt, soap, wafers, even canister shot extracted from a wounded officer. Some are small personal and pocket pieces, others grand presentation caskets bestowed on kings, princes and dignitaries.

Brandy saucepans Small tapered or baluster-shaped saucepans, usually with a rising turned wood handle and short lip are often called brandy saucepans – apparently a modern term. A few such small saucepans are found with spirit-lamp stands. All were probably intended for heating butter, sauce or invalid foods.

19 Brandy saucepan *c.* 1730 to 1775.

Braziers Stands on three or four feet, usually of scroll form, in which a lamp for burning spirit (more rarely charcoal) is fixed and with a rim to fit the base of the pot. The term is not much used, lampstand being more common whether applied to kettles and urns, shaving jugs, dish crosses, breakfast dishes or chafing dishes.

Breakfast dishes Shallow oval, oblong, or octagonal covered dishes fitted with lampstands, virtually indistinguishable from the objects usually referred to as chafing dishes.

Breakfast service Sometimes applied to a matched service including tea and coffee pots, condiments, egg-cups and stand, dishes and casters in the 19th century.

Buckles Buckles of all sizes were made by smallworkers in gold and silver, and in fused plate and base metals for shoes, knee-breeches, belts, hats and cravats or stocks. Silver buckles chiefly date from the late-18th to early-19th century, though dress buckles for women remained fashionable throughout the 19th century and are still worn as part of a nurse's uniform.

Butter boats Smaller than average sauceboats (cp., cream boats) for melted butter.

Butter coolers and dishes Covered bowls, usually with a fitting glass liner, and often of tub shape, especially popular in Ireland, and adopted by English silversmiths, such as John Emes, during the last decade of the 18th century. Irish examples are often pierced and chased with foliage and rural scenes. Most English examples are plain or with ribbed banding simulating staved tubs, with rising handles and often with a model of a cow for cover finial. Others were wholly of glass with silver mounts. The term 'butter cooler' appears to be a trade term introduced about the 1880s, a misnomer since it does not actually cool the butter.

Butter shells The popular term for small dishes of escallop form, with or without feet, the earliest known being a silver-gilt set of three made in 1675. Usually made in sets of three or four, they were especially popular during the first half of the 18th century, but continued to be made at least until the 1830s. Recorded in 1740 in the Wakelin Ledgers as 'Scollops for Oysters', they were

OBJECTS

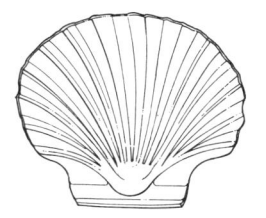

20 Butter shells c. 1730.

probably also used for serving scallops, pickles, butter, nuts, etc. The Emes & Barnard ledgers in 1824 perpetuate the original term escallop shells.

Butter spades and slices Flatware used for cutting or handing butter, with a triangular, trowel-shaped or flattish elongated blade. The earliest example appears to date from 1708. Rare until the end of the 18th century, when butter slices (miscalled butter knives) became fairly standard 'extras' in large table services. Nineteenth-century butter servers often have blades very like fish eaters, and handles of bone, ivory or mother-of-pearl, as well as in silver (filled) or in fused or electro-plate.

Buttons Gold, silver, fused plate, base metal and mounted buttons were important articles of dress ornament throughout the 17th and 18th centuries, and for livery uniforms until the end of the 19th century. Usually made in sets, often only single examples remain. Some are circular, with engraved ornament (including hunting motifs) made *en suite* with smaller cuff buttons; for livery use, silver buttons were die-struck with devices or crests or were of cone shape.

Caddies *See* TEA CADDIES.

Caddy spoons Originally a small ladle with a long handle used when the cap-style cover (used as a measure), gave way to the slide-in and hinged styles of cover in the 1730s. With the extensive growth of the Birmingham toy, or smallwares, trade, and the development of the two-division tea caddy, small shell-shaped and other styles of caddy spoon, usually with a large oval bowl and short curved handle, kept inside the caddy, became popular. Many were stamped out and simply decorated. Similar small spoons, usually given a little finer finish, such as feather-edge, beaded or bright-cut borders, were also made in London. There were innumerable variations, including novelty shapes such as hands, miniature shovels, jockey caps, and so on. Eagles' wings and filigree patterns were a speciality of some Birmingham makers.

Cagework cups A rare style with a chased and pierced sleeve of silver overlaying a plain inner body, usually gilt for greater effect. Few are fully hallmarked and some do not even bear makers' marks. Most appear to date from 1667 to 1680, and the majority are of straight-sided porringer form, with covers *en suite*, the

21 Cagework cup *c.* 1670.

sides richly chased in baroque style with flowers, foliage, birds and cherubs, and usually with foliate scroll handles and a pomegranate or open acanthus bud finial to the cover.

Candlesticks (Figs 7, 22, 56) Though silver candlesticks are recorded in early-16th-century inventories, none has survived other than a single silver and rock crystal example of about 1580. A pair with a chased bun-like base, dates from about 1610. They are close in design to a pair of 1624, chased with strapwork, in the Kremlin. Three rather curious examples on domed tripod bases, of 1615 and 1618, are of uncertain provenance, though the tripod form of support is repeated in a pair made about 1630. A pair of 1653 have trumpet bases, and so have a more decorative pair of 1663 now in Moscow; but by the Restoration the square base seems established. The broad drip pan was reduced in size and the stem became columnar.

Decoration was usually restrained. Variations included hexagonal and octagonal bases, or spreading bases of lobed or shaped outline, fashionable during the 1670s. The massive tripod form survived in mid-century designs for altar candlesticks, which were usually fitted with prickets or spikes for the candles instead of sockets. The best candles were made of wax, cheaper ones of tallow. 'Monument' or column candlesticks continued to be made until well into the 18th century, though more fashionable patrons had been quick to adopt the Huguenot cast baluster 'stick, of small size and good weight, about 6 in. or 7 in. high, and between 18 and 30 oz. the pair, according to quality. The earliest of these appear to be four of 1683 by the first immigrant silversmith to be allowed to work in London, Pierre Harache. Within months others were being cast in similar designs, with stepped octagonal bases rising to a moulding above a circular well, from which the knopped stem rises to a plain vase-shaped socket. The baluster was to remain the basic underlying form for candlesticks (and for many other domestic objects) for almost a century. Many were made by specialist makers who, from master to apprentice, continued the trade for many decades – Joseph Bird for instance, his apprentice David Green and Thomas Merry. A few years later there were the Cafes and the Goulds. In some instances these specialists may

22 Candlesticks FROM LEFT 1653, c. 1714, c. 1742, c. 1744, c. 1762.

well have provided the castings to which other craftsmen – even those such as Lamerie and Elizabeth Godfrey, Peter Archambo and Charles Kandler – put their mark, though obviously the finest, often very elaborate, examples were the work of these master craftsmen.

A variant of the octagonal baluster 'stick from about 1710 was a faceted pattern without a central well and sometimes exaggerated into an umbrella-like outline. Another, from about 1718 onwards, had incurved sides. Some were square-based with cut or incurved corners, but decoration was the exception until about 1730, when ornament began to overlay the basic octagonal shape with shells and scalework in the new French style. The vase-shaped decorated stem provided a rich alternative to the commoner basically simple table candlestick, while two- or three-light branches afforded an instance of practical ingenuity. With the advent of Sheffield plating, the branches were often more inexpensively made of fused plate.

The rococo taste revived the fashion for figure candlesticks, first made rarely in the 1690s and now often in oriental taste. Even so, many candlesticks remained simple in style, with square gadrooned bases and gadrooned and fluted vase-shaped stems. The advent of the stamped candlestick, built up from sections and loaded to give it stability, was a skill very much associated with Sheffield. The technique was used both for silver and plated candlesticks, and meant that decoration in relief could be achieved at low cost, providing that really good dies were initially made. It was a technique that coincided with the new taste for classicism. From about 1765 onwards Sheffield vied with the London makers of cast candlesticks producing fashionable fluted, vase-shaped, beaded and festooned patterns. These skills were not a little resented by London makers who frequently overstruck their own maker's mark on them, obliterating that of the Sheffield firm, and even on occasion sending them to the London Assay Office to be overstruck with London hallmarks as well.

By the end of the century, the tapering vase-shaped patterns that were watered-down versions of the original Adam and Wyatt designs gradually began to give way to much more elaborate – and costly – Regency patterns, enriched with applied detail, caryatid figures, laurel wreaths, sphinxes and other relief decoration. A host of grandiose designs poured forth from the workshops of Scott and Smith and of Paul Storr, all of whom worked exclusively for Rundell & Bridge in the early years of the new century. Most candlesticks were by now as much as 12 or 14 in. high. Many more candelabra were made, often of gargantuan proportions, set on huge incurving triangular pedestals and rising two feet or more to five, six, seven or more lights.

Such grandeur was not, of course, available to the more modest households, and Sheffield continued to supply quantities of plainer candlesticks in both stamped silver and in fused plate, while in Birmingham Matthew Boulton capitalised on the new lighting by oil and produced a variety of special lamps burning oil.

Candlesticks and candelabra (Fig. 7) continued to be made throughout the 19th century. There was a revival of the rococo, essays in the Gothic, a taste for naturalism, for medieval and Tudor styles and for wholly Victorian versions of what they fondly called 'Queen Anne' or 'Adam' without in fact reproducing any known original. By the time the colourful and odourless paraffin wax candle was introduced in 1854, however, the age of the candle was fast waning, except perhaps for the chamber candlestick. Gas and electricity were already becoming commercial propositions.

Chamber candlesticks Candleholders on dished stands with a ring handle or a longer spoon-like handle were set out in the hall to light the way to the bedroom as well as in the room itself. Many large houses had quantities of such chamber candlesticks to judge from the numbers sometimes found scratched on the bases. One early example of about 1685 has No. 17 on the base, and surviving sets of twos, fours and tens made in the first half of the 19th century are recorded. Basically the design changed little over the years, though the flat pierced and long tubular style of handle was replaced by a short one by the 1720s. Ten years later

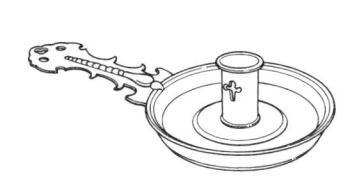

23 Chamber candlesticks *c.* 1685, *c.* 1775.

OBJECTS

the ring handle or open scroll was usual. The simple dish base – in at least one instance extremely large, as though the owner greatly feared fire – either plain, or with a moulded, beaded, reeded or gadrooned border remained almost standard until the 1880s and the arrival of gas and electric lighting. There were, of course, a few elaborate examples made, presumably to special commission.

A number of chamber candlesticks of early date, and most of those made from about 1770 onwards, also incorporate snuffers which fit in a slot below the candle-holder and a conical extinguisher which fits into a slot in the top of the handle; later snuffers were frequently Sheffield-made and close-plated.

Cans The old term for drinking pots and mugs, and still used in America for children's cups. (*See* MUGS.)

Canteens A necessity for the traveller as well as for officers in the Army and Navy, since most inns provided little in the way of suitable silver for eating or drinking. From at least the 17th century, shagreen, fishskin or wooden cases fitted with one or two beakers, sometimes oval in section, and with a block containing

24 Canteen *c.* 1800.

knife, fork and spoon with screw-on handles, a spice and salt box, a nutmeg grater and corkscrew, perhaps also a toothpick and napkin hooks provided a compact canteen. Later transposed to the large wooden chest containing a complete table service of flatware and cutlery.

Card cases The formality of making and repaying visits brought the visiting card into use by the end of the 18th century and within a few years cases to hold the rather large pieces of engraved card were made in silver and other materials such as tortoiseshell and ivory. The first silver card cases date from about 1820 and the Birmingham toymen dominated the market until about 1870. Cases varied from finely stamped and chased examples in silvergilt to those that were souvenirs of famous houses, cathedrals and other monuments, from Waverley in Edinburgh to the Crystal Palace in London. From about 1875 to 1885 the Aesthetic Movement with its passion for all things Japanese brought some very fine work from firms such as Barnard Bros., whose card cases at the time were often of satin-finished silver inlaid with gold, and decorated with butterflies, fans and plants.

Casters (Castors) Sprinkler boxes for sugar, pepper and other spices made their first sporadic appearance in the late 16th century. The idea of combining casters for pepper or other spice with the salt was used in bell salts. But it was the mid-17th-century sugar-and-spice demands of the increasingly wealthy households that introduced matching sets of individual casters.

Between 1665 and the end of the century imports of sugar, for example, rose from a mere 800 tons to more than 10,000 tons a year, while mustard, home grown in Tewkesbury and Durham, pepper from Jamaica (black) and Cayenne (red), nutmeg, cloves, cinnamon and many other spices, both fragrant and pungent, were sold by the grocer who specialised in such dry goods. The earliest casters were cylindrical, on a corded or a spreading rim foot. The body was often strengthened and decorated with one or two moulded ribs, the upper one notched so that the deep-

25 Casters FROM LEFT c. 1680, c. 1720, c. 1740, c. 1795.

domed pierced cover could be secured by a slip-lock or bayonet joint. Suggesting not very finely ground contents, early caster tops were usually quite coarsely pierced with quatrefoils, scrolls, hearts or other simple designs. The foot was sometimes also pierced. Almost all early examples feature a calyx of cut-card ornament round the baluster or acorn-shaped finial. The earliest known sets date from the late 1660s but it was between 1680 and the end of the century that certain London goldsmiths were beginning to specialise, founding firms that were to continue in business, master to apprentice, for decades. One line can be traced from William Brett (whose mark is probably **WB** over a mullet) who in 1680 took Thomas Brydon as an apprentice. The line continues through Robert Keble, Samuel Welder apprenticed in 1707, and Charles Alchorne. Another long line was initiated by Jacob Harris to whom Francis Archbold was apprenticed in 1671. Free in 1678, Archbold's mark may be **FA**, fleur-de-lis below; he was a fellow apprentice of Charles Adam. The prolific caster maker of the Britannia period, his apprentices included Thomas Bamford (1703) himself master of Samuel Wood, one of the best-known caster and cruet makers of the 18th century, who between 1733 and his death at the advanced age of 90 in 1794, made hundreds of casters and cruets. His apprentices included specialist makers Robert Piercy, free in 1757, Jabez Daniell (1747), whose son Thomas and apprentice James Mince also followed the same trade. Many others combined caster-making with making salts and other small silver, while fine examples were also made by craftsmen wuch as Willaume, Lamerie and Archambo.

By 1700, the relatively large cylindrical sugar caster and its smaller pair of matching spice boxes – known by the ungainly name of 'lighthouse' casters – assumed a graceful shape under the influence of the Huguenots. The pear-shape or baluster, on a spreading stepped foot, was rapidly adopted and by 1705 the straight-sided caster was out of fashion except for the small spice dredgers with ring handles, popularly known as kitchen peppers. Piercing generally became much finer. Though still achieved with hammer and chisel, vases of flowers, flowing scrollwork and formal foliage, often picked out with engraved detail, combined the practical with the ornamental, the conical sugar loaf presumably being ground down more finely in the kitchen. Pierced designs must have been derived from pattern-books, for many are repetitive, though in the hands of masters such as David Willaume, Pierre Harache, Anthony Nelme and George Garthorne, the piercing often showed great delicacy incorporating naturalistic flowers, birds, scrolls and figures. Experiments were made to replace the rather clumsy and not very elegant bayonet joint or slip-lock fastening, and gradually the sprung-in top took over so that by about 1710 the bayonet joint was virtually obsolete.

About 1708, the first octagonal casters appeared, sometimes pear-shaped, sometimes of baluster form broader at shoulder than base. Sometimes one caster of the trio was left unpierced, or blind, for dry mustard, which at the time was mixed with wine or water individually at the table. From the same period date the first ring-frames or cruets to hold a set of casters and oil and vinegar bottles. Throughout the 1720s the octagonal vase form remained the most popular, to be followed by the plain vase. Even at the height of the rococo this remained in fashion, the shape modified only to accommodate chased or applied ornament strapwork. The practical generally outweighted fashion, the only concession to ornament being confined to swirl-fluting, a festoon of chased flowers and foliage, to variant panels of piercing on the covers, and to wrythen or flame finials.

The advent of neoclassicism in the 1760s, revived the vase, though in a manner closer to classical urns. Trios of vases, either with rising loop handles or with short side handles, the bodies chased with flutes at the base and with sturdy gadrooned rims and borders, (once thought to be tea caddies) have been reassigned as condiment vases. Their reattribution does much to fill the gap in the number of casters made between about 1749 and 1785, when elongated versions, often with a pronouncedly pear-shaped base, revived the long-popular vase shape. By the end of the century, almost all sugar casters and condiment vases were assembled together in cruet frames. Smaller casters, singly or in pairs and of vase form were usually known as muffineers. (*See also* Cruets.)

Caudle cups Caudle was a warm, spiced drink of gruel mixed with wine or ale, served chiefly, it would appear, in the covered cups generally known as porringers. Since the drink was traditionally given to nursing mothers (and to her guests) Clayton has suggested that the cups used were small, though Irish assay office records refer to these as dram cups. The variety of covered cups made between about 1650 and 1700 is legion, from ogee-shaped (with or without engraved, flat-chased, repoussé-chased, applied or cagework decoration) to almost straight-sided. Covers are usually of low-domed form with a decorative finial – a snake-like coil, an acanthus bud, a pomegranate, or sometimes an acorn, baluster, disc top, or a truly baroque type with masks on either side of Tragedy and Comedy. More rarely the knop takes the form of the owner's crest. Handles are either of scroll or double-scroll form, often with heads at the top so stylised as to appear as foliate knops; others are rather emaciated cast caryatids. Most such cups are on a plain skirt, spreading or narrow rim foot, though a few on individual cast feet are known.

Cayenne scoops Also known as kyan scoops, miniature round bowled, often gilt, long-handled spoons used for red pepper; sometimes attached to the bottle-cork of cruet bottles.

Chafing dishes Lampstands fitted with arm-like supports above used for keeping plates or dishes warm introduced in the mid-17th century, their purpose recorded by Samuel Pepys in 1666 when he purchased one. However, they were also employed, according to Isaac Walton, as they are today, as braziers for heating and even for cooking certain foods, so that saucepans with stands and lamps may also be understood by the term. By the 1770s such dishes – the flame protected from draughts by a shield so that the dish resembled a bottomless saucepan – were generally being superseded by heater bases to entrée dishes, and by dish crosses with extendible arms.

Chamber pots Not uncommon in silver, from the late 17th century onwards in the pattern conventional in pottery and porcelain. Eight dating between 1714 and 1743 were rather coyly described as 'bowls' when they were sold from the Foley-Grey collection at Christies in 1921. Chamber pots were used in the dining-room rather than the bedroom, and one unusual example of 1818, by Robert Garrard, fitted with a cover and having two handles, is traditionally said to have been made for use in a coach. Ladies reputedly took a portable pot, or bourdaloue, to church, concealed under their skirts, if the preacher was known to be a long-winded gentleman. One such, by Robert Garrard, dated 1845, was recently presented to Trinity Hall, Cambridge, to celebrate the admission of women to Fellowship.

Chandeliers Inevitably extremely rare in silver, surviving English examples number fewer than a dozen. Of those two, by Paul de Lamerie, 1734, hang in the Kremlin in Moscow. A third, of about

1695, is at Colonial Williamsburg, U.S.A. There are records of 'Tenne hanging candelsticks' in the inventory of Queen Elizabeth I's plate, but these might be sconces. By the following century there were several in the Royal palaces, often described as 'branches' – a confusing term further compounded by the French word 'chandelier' used for candelabrum.

A very fine chandelier of 1752 was made for Fishmongers' Hall in London, while in 1836 Robert Garrard made a huge tiered example for 18 lights, for the Duke of Abercorn. Glass was more usual from about 1760 onwards. Some very creditable copies of the Hampton Court chandelier of about 1690 were made in electro-plate during the 1930s, adapted for electricity.

Cheese scoops An implement with a long and sturdy scoop set in a wooden, bone or ivory handle used by cheese tasters. Many early-19th-century scoops were fitted with patent devices so that the cheese can be slid off the blade.

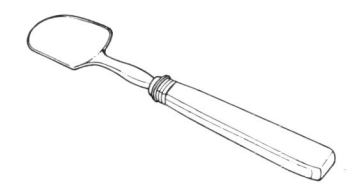

26 Cheese scoop *c.* 1790 to 1810.

Cheese stands Until the Wakelin Ledgers were found the oblong pierced stand now known to be a cheese stand was generally called a 'jardinière' or cache-pot. At least two of these oblong pierced stands have now been identified, presumably designed to hold a half-cheese, and dating from 1760 and 1764. Substantial footed salvers are also thought to be cheese stands. Several of late-17th-century date are included in this category, while another of 1809 by Paul Storr has been described as a cheese dish – the theory being that their great weight and size were suitable for supporting an English cheese.

Chocolate cups Small cups, with or without handles and sometimes with matching saucers in silver or silver-gilt are sometimes designated as cups for tea, coffee or chocolate, though they were quickly superseded by similar cups in porcelain. Silver is not, of course, really suitable for hot drinks; a compromise was a silver frame to hold the delicate handleless porcelain cups used in the early years of the 18th century. Such silver cups or frames are exceptionally rare.

Chocolate pots As early as 1657, 'that excelent West India drink' could be purchased in Queens Head Alley off Bishopsgate, at, perhaps significantly, the house of a Frenchman. 'Jocalette' soon became the fashionable drink of London; though it never quite acquired the popularity it did in France, the club and chocolate house known as The Cocoa Tree survived until well into the middle of the 18th century. The original hot chocolate was a rich frothy beverage not at all like modern cocoa, which was not introduced until the 1820s when the Van Houtens deprived it of the fatty cocoa butter.

Chocolate pots are distinguishable from those for coffee primarily by the aperture in the lid through which a stirring rod or 'molionet' could be inserted. Very few of these whisks have survived, one notable exception being that with a rather bottle-shaped pot of 1738 by Paul Crespin (now in the Ashmolean Museum).

The earliest chocolate pots that have survived date from the 1680s. They were of baluster shape on a reeded rim foot, with a fairly short curved spout at right angles to the wooden scroll handle. By 1700 chocolate pots sometimes showed more fanciful spouts, silver strapwork applied to the handles, or sometimes handles set horizontally, stepped domed covers and occasionally they were supported on three scroll feet in the French style. These characteristics suggest they were specially commissioned. More usually they conformed in design to coffee pots (*q.v.*) of the period with tapering straight-sided bodies and high-domed, often fluted, covers. Occasionally pots definitely designed for chocolate with baluster bodies and short lips were made during the 1730s, and it is possible that many smaller covered jugs with leather-covered, wickered or other insulated handles were intended for the drink, the broader bases making the whisking of the thick liquid easier. The vase-shapes revived during the neoclassical period were also suited to chocolate, but by the end of the century the drink had generally fallen into disfavour.

Cigar lighters Small spirit lamps usually in the form of a Roman or Aladdin's lamp appeared in the early years of the 19th century, as the fashion for smoking cigars rather than pipes increased. They provided a safer flame than the open brazier sometimes associated with pipe-smoking.

Claret jugs Covered jugs and flagons for serving beer, ale and wine date back at least to the 16th century, but the so-called claret jug was very much a 19th-century development of the late-18th-century neoclassical ewer. Among the earliest that can properly be called 'claret jugs' are a pair of covered ewers (with

27 Claret jugs LEFT *c.* 1820, RIGHT *c.* 1860.

matching goblets) by Andrew Fogelburg, 1780, with pear-shaped bodies set on a domed foot. It is usually very difficult to differentiate these from jugs for water, beer, chocolate, coffee or hot water, though the three last are often fitted with insulated handles.

A design by John Flaxman and made up by Paul Storr in the early 1800s is a replica of a Roman original with everted rim and a rising curved spout. Most early 19th-century covered jugs are, however, basically of vase shape, often half-fluted and with a border of anthemion, shells, Greek key pattern or other neoclassical motifs at the shoulder. A much repeated design for Rundell, Bridge & Rundell in the 1820s was a jug with melon-shaped body and tall neck, applied at the shoulder with bacchanalian masks and vines rising to a vine-stem handle.

Charles Fox, William Elliott (or Eaton) and the Barnards varied the theme with other foliate and vine-chased designs. Elliott was the first to reproduce the so-called 'Cellini' ewer in the late 1820s, the vase-shaped body intersected by narrow mouldings, the whole richly chased with masks, scrolling foliage, applied masks in oval medallion, scrolls and strapwork which were fondly considered to be in the manner of the Renaissance. It was a design that continued to be made in silver, and later in electro-plate, throughout the century.

By the 1830s highly elaborate cast and chased ornament, often reminiscent of 17th-century North German tankards, was making its appearance, with groups of bacchantes amid vines chased in high relief on the sides of otherwise simple baluster jugs. Most had vine or grape finials, but one design made up by Storr from a Wedgwood pattern by Lady Diana Beauclerk features a rather incongruous winged cherub finial. Storr's jugs also included matted versions based on the Greek *ascos*, a kidney shape that was also made up in frosted glass, white or coloured, with silver or silver-gilt mounts. Glass jugs mounted in silver became increasingly fashionable, often attractively applied with cageworks of vine foliage rising to tendril and vine-branch handles. A few were made with stands to match. Very much the same designs were also made in all silver, while there was also a taste for decorative straight-sided flagons.

By 1845 there was, however, some reaction against the over-ornamented, and many glass-mounted examples make use of simple flask shapes with plain silver bands and handles, the only concession to decoration being masks or flower chasing on the deep neck-band. This pattern was made first by J. W. Figg about 1845 and still in his catalogues nearly forty years later; it was much exploited by the growing trade for such wares in Birmingham. It is interesting that the ascetically simple mounted claret jugs designed by Christopher Dresser for the Birmingham firm of Hukin & Heath in the early 1880s were really unadorned versions of Figg's basic design. There was also a demand for mounted wares of novelty design – blown glass shapes mounted in silver to provide wine jugs in the form of magnum Champagne bottles, squirrels, sea monsters, and so on, also found in silver, such as wyvern pattern jugs (based on a Vienna porcelain original) by Charles Fox. Pottery originals were also exploited by the Barnards, who made copies of Wedgwood's Flaxman-designed ewers with figures grasping the necks to represent Wine and Water. Others appeared to imitate glass decanters in silver, and besides the 'Cellini' pattern there was a long and continuous demand for 'Armada' ewers, for others in Near-Eastern taste and for a host of reproduction styles – in contrast to the simple Lotus and other jugs that represented the 'aesthetic' taste.

Coffee pots (Figs 3, 28) 'Coffee and Commonwealth came in together' runs the old adage. Within a few years of the opening of the first coffee-house in Oxford in 1651, John Evelyn reported that coffee drinking had 'become a common entertainment all over the nation'. The habit had spread from the Near East and it is said that the first coffee pots were shaped like Turkish wine ewers – rather like the bulbous-bodied wine pots of the Tudor period.

OBJECTS

None has, however, survived and the earliest known English silver coffee pot dates from 1681. It is of a tapering cylindrical shape that must have been derived from a tankard or flagon of the period, the silversmith George Garthorne adding a conical cover and a rather narrow straight spout set opposite the handle (and in fact almost identical to the earliest recorded teapot made in 1670). Pasqua Rosee, the former servant of a Turkey merchant, opened the first London coffee-house in St Martin's Alley, off Cornhill in 1652. By the beginning of Queen Anne's reign, there were some 450 coffee-houses in London providing a centre for social, political and business life. A man would select his coffee-house as carefully as his friends and, in later days, his West End club.

Much the same styles of silver coffee pot were made for private use as for the coffee-houses, early examples usually having the

28 Coffee pots FROM LEFT *c.* 1732, *c.* 1742, *c.* 1759.

handles at right angles to the spout for pouring by a servant. After about 1700, spouts were usually curved, and sometimes fitted with a small hinged cover; the cover of the pot itself was domed and surmounted by a finial, usually vase-shaped and sometimes surrounded by cut-card work *en suite* with similar applied decoration around the spout and handle sockets. A few early pots were of elongated baluster form, but generally the baluster did not supersede the straight-sided until about 1730. A variation from about 1712 onwards was the faceted or panelled style, generally octagonal in outline. Soon the spout was placed opposite the handle. By about 1730 the tuck-in base became fashionable; the cover was now usually of compressed shape with a vase-shaped, baluster or acorn knop.

By the end of the 1730s, more decorative styles paid homage to the rococo, though often coffee pots received no more ornament than a rococo cartouche for the owner's armorials; a great many repoussé-chased pots have suffered later and often ill-conceived ornament, though, at their best, contemporarily ornamented pots are exceptionally fine. Similarly, plain pots vary considerably in quality, and may weigh anything from about 18 oz. to as much as 35 oz. (all in). One or two rare examples include the probably unique square pot made in 1745 by George Wickes – and another of 1704 fitted with a tap instead of a spout. Generally speaking, however, the standard form was followed of a relatively plain elongated body with a tuck-in base. More decorative versions were fluted, chased with scrolls and foliage (usually at top and base, leaving space in the centre for the owner's engraved armorials).

By about 1753 the even taller and more curvaceous baluster overtook the type with tuck-in base. Still the greater proportion of pots were left undecorated, though patrons who could afford it favoured the richer rococo-chased styles, with scrollwork, foliage, chinoiseries and, towards the end of the 1750s, swirl fluting. On plain pots a gadrooned foot, scrollwork beneath the spout, a cone or flame finial and a gadrooned rim and foot were often the only concessions to ornament.

Though the true neoclassical designs did not take a firm hold on coffee-pot design until the 1790s, and even then had to compete with the large pear-shaped pots made throughout the 1780s, the first evidence of the new classicism appeared in the early 1770s. There were vase-shaped bodies in the manner of wine ewers set on circular or pedestal bases. Short spouts, like those used for wine, chocolate and hot water jugs, suited the style better than curved spouts but sometimes make accurate definition of the actual nature of the pot difficult; though often described as coffee jugs it seems unlikely that those with metal handles, unless wickered, were for hot beverages. Ornament usually consisted of festoons of draperies and foliage chased on the body, applied laurel swags, paterae, chased leafage or, more rarely, of plain and matted vertical panels in the manner of Wedgwood basalt wares. For plain pots, beading (or pearling) superseded gadrooning. By the end of the century threaded or reeded edges proved a variant, especially for those with borders of bright-cut engraving. Vase-shaped pots with the base of the body fluted and with long narrow spouts began to be made *en suite* with tea-table wares of the turn of the century.

The early 19th century saw a distinctive change of design of coffee-pots: the addition of a spirit-lamp stand. Most early examples were made by Paul Storr for Rundell & Bridge. These vase-shaped pots had more or less decoration at the shoulder – perhaps a simple band of basketwork or a more ornamental border of anthemion, with narrow applied detail below the upper handle socket and round the rim of the lampstead, which was invariably supported on three incurving feet; the burner was sometimes set on a triangular base. Nearly all the Storr jugs had wood or ivory handles with classical scroll terminals and a mask below the upper part, opposite a short case and chased lip, and with a low domed cover with ornamental bud finial. Half-fluted, baluster and other vase-shaped coffee pots of the first twenty years of the 19th century were also often supplied with heater stands, though a few customers still ordered more conventional tall vase- or baluster-shaped coffee pots, usually as part of a tea and coffee service. (*See also* BIGGINS; TEA AND COFFEE MACHINES; TEA AND COFFEE URNS; TEA SERVICES.)

Coffee urns (*See* TEA AND COFFEE URNS.)

Compasses Pocket compasses in silver cases have survived from the late 17th century onwards, the small slim box enclosing the compass also often engraved with details of towns and cities throughout Europe that might have conceivably proved helpful to the young men on their Grand Tour.

Counter dishes The name by which small fluted dishes are known in Ireland, for holding the counters and coins for playing cards, etc. In England these counters, often of ivory or bone, were known as 'fish' and a silver 'basket for fish' recorded in the 1740s was presumably for these.

Cordial pots Small spouted pots chiefly dating from the mid- to late-17th century are believed to have been used for serving cordials, a term applied to various soothing drinks, medicinal, spirituous, herbal or other waters used as cures and remedies for minor ailments. Often quite decorative, suggesting their use by the ladies of the household, the earliest show a basic form very like a small two-handled porringer with a curved spout. Towards the end of the century they approximate to the wine-shaped teapot; differentiation between cordial pots, spout pots, early teapots and later saffron or tisane pots is not always possible. (*See also* SAFFRON POTS.) During the 18th century cordials were more often served from small glass decanters and jugs.

Corkscrews or **Bottle screws** are recorded from the middle of the 17th century onwards. The basic spiral screw is common to all types, which show ingenuity in making patterns suitable for packing into travelling canteens – the shaped open ring handle, for instance, with a screw that folds, or the small T-shape. By the end of the 18th century, corkscrews were fitted into the base of mace-shaped nutmeg graters; others were of the kind which extract the cork with a continuous turning motion. From the early part of the 19th century dozens of different patterns were made, very often of registered design.

Cow creamers (Fig. 31) A curiosity of the late 1750s and 1760s was the cream or milk vessel in the form of a cow, a pad of flowers on its back with a knop formed as a fly or a bee, and the tail curled as the handle. Most were made by John Schuppe, who was probably of Dutch origin. An earlier example in the Victoria and Albert Museum is by David Willaume and another by Edward Aldridge is recorded. Many not by Schuppe are, however, of doubtful provenance.

Cream boats (Fig. 30) Smaller versions of the sauceboat used for cream made their appearance about 1730. On three scroll supports or a central foot, they had a broad lip at one end and a scroll- or flying-scroll handle. During the rococo period, many were cast and of heavy gauge silver; later, plainer versions were often almost flimsy and did not even feature a rim mount but had a simple everted, cut edge. This feature was more sturdily interpreted in the typical everted and often engraved rims of such boats made in Scotland and the North of England. In the West of England a local variation was the circular boat with a short lip at right angles to the handle. The boat-shape, abandoned during the neoclassical period, was revived during the early 19th century. Then compressed shapes were favoured for cream ewers and a few fine cast examples were made in revived rococo style such as a series by John Tapley in the late 1830s and 1840s formed as overlapping oak leaves in imitation of early Wedgwood and Chelsea patterns.

Cream jugs (Fig. 29) The fashion for taking cream (often warmed) with tea or coffee – said to have been introduced by Mme de Sévigné's daughter 'because she liked it' – was only just established when the first baluster cream jugs were made in England about

OBJECTS

29 TOP ROW, FROM LEFT **Cream boat** c. 1750. **30 Cream jug** c. 1735.
BOTTOM ROW **Cream jug** c. 1715. **31 Cow creamer** c. 1764.

1705. It was really another fifteen years or so before they were made in any quantity; they were elegant and very small on a moulded foot, conforming in outline to the circular or octagonal shape of the jug. Circular examples with small lips are sometimes called 'sparrow-beak' jugs. By the 1730s, bellied jugs on three scroll supports set the style for about the next thirty years, relatively plain or richly rococo according to taste or pocket.

The huge popularity of tea-drinking during the second half of the 18th century no doubt increased demand for cream jugs and many were often of quite flimsy gauge, weighing a mere 2 or 3 ounces. The country themes of the cream pail and the cow creamer (*q.v.*) may have inspired the simple chased decoration of some of the light pear-shaped and bellied jugs of the 1760s and later, which were embellished with farmyard scenes, milkmaids, cottages and the like. Some of these chased scenes are patently of later date, but others are probably contemporary.

By then, however, taste was rapidly changing and from about 1765 to 1770 fashion was demanding the new classicism and the helmet-shaped ewer jug on a square pedestal base with high reeded or beaded loop handle was firmly in fashion. Again, some were of good gauge, and decorated with beaded or thread-edge mounts and with attractive well-executed bright-cut engraving; others were lighter, even the beaded motif interpreted with punched, instead of applied, mounts. One rare example of 1797 by Robert and David Hennell has a hinged cover.

By the 19th century most cream or milk jugs were incorporated in the tea service. They became progressively larger and were more often used for milk than for cream, the compressed circular shape conforming to the design of the teapot and sugar basin.

Cream pails Small pail-shaped pots appear to have been used for whipped or clotted cream from about 1735 onwards. The earliest were of straight-sided piggin shape, soon followed by everted shapes, the sides ridged to simulate wood staving, and usually with swing handles. By about 1760, pierced cream pails with blue glass liners made a charming variation, and during the neo-classical period these were paired with matching sugar baskets, often of much larger size than the earlier cream pails which rarely exceeded about 3 in. in height. There was a revival of the small cream pail about 1850, generally in reproduction styles, though occasionally imitating Irish butter tubs in miniature.

Cream skimmers Rare flexible pieces of silver, usually circular, with a thumb ring or handle, the centre of the slightly dished circle pierced with fine holes, so that the solids are retained on the skimmer and the liquid drains away.

Cruets Frames containing either oil and vinegar bottles or complete with casters in sizes as well as bottles. The first were usually of double circle or octagonal outline, and appeared from about 1720 onwards. Larger cruets including casters are usually called Warwick cruets, though examples are known before that of 1715 at Warwick Castle. Shaped stands, of varying sizes, with ring frames to hold the various bottles and casters, were followed from about 1770 by boat-shaped stands; a central handle replaced the earlier back-handle type. Smaller cruets of the early 19th century are often known as breakfast cruets. By then glass-mounted bottles for all the condiments, sometimes as many as ten in number, were common. Frames for sauces and spices known as soy frames were also made, fitted with various containers for oil, vinegar, soy, ketchup, mustard, salt, pepper, lemon and a variety of other sauces, usually indicated by small silver tickets. These have now often become separated from the cruets, and are generally in styles associated with other wine and spirit labels. (*See* BOTTLE TICKETS AND LABELS.) Other glass-mounted bottles in ring frames were intended for sauces and chutneys. (*See also* CASTERS.)

Cucumber slices Efficient slicers of ivory with adjustable silver blades were made from about 1770 onwards. Two flat slices of ivory, with a simple handle end to one were linked with a single blade held between two springy pieces of silver clamped by a screw. A variant known in a rare example of fused plate was a cylinder with a handle turned to cut the vegetable. Small ivory-handled saws of the later 19th century with serrated silver blades are also believed to have been used to slice cucumbers.

Cups (Figs 32, 40, 58) Standing cups were the most important of medieval and later plate until the mid-17th century; they were replaced by the two-handled cup. Early inventories and wills show cups to have been in even modest households, but 'my best cup' is often the closest description one finds. It is possible, just, to build up a picture of styles from the few surviving examples that have escaped the melting-pot over the centuries, from the elegantly tall and enamelled cup known as King John's Cup made about 1325 at King's Lynn to the squat Gothic font-shaped cups that preceded the Renaissance styles of the 16th century. The most usual type of 15th-century cup had a hemispherical chalice-like bowl set on a trumpet-shaped stem, and with a domed cover

OBJECTS

32 Cups TOP ROW *c.* 1660, *c.* 1735, *c.* 1670. BOTTOM ROW
33 Covered bowl *c.* 1640. **34 Bleeding bowl** *c.* 1635 to 1700.
35 Cup *c.* 1645.

surmounted by a bold knop or finial. Some were plain, with chased and pierced borders, others more decorative, like the Richmond Cup of the Armourers' and Brasiers' Company.

During the early 16th century there was a fashion for shallow font-shaped cups, often much more elaborately decorated with embossing and chasing. From about 1535, the new classically inspired Renaissance styles began to infiltrate English silver, and the variety of designs for cups multiplied; there were fluted bowls of inverted conical shape, waisted cups, cups with everted cylindrical bowls, shallow-bowled drinking cups now known as tazze, goblet-like cups, and others more fanciful and mannered in design shaped as gourds, pineapples, melons, even as birds and beasts. Most important examples (except the shallow-bowled types), had covers with ever increasingly taller finials, sometimes of baluster form, sometimes with warriors or 'mannikins' standing on spool-like and bracketed pedestals. Not a few incorporated bowls of rock crystal, nautilus shells, ivory and other rare and costly materials. (*See* MOUNTED WARES.)

One way of creating height was the steeple finial, a fashion found on 150 such cups from 1599 to 1646. On a waisted trumpet-shaped foot, most had deep bell-shaped bowls supported on a bracketed stem, and low-domed covers with the steeple rising from a spool-shaped pedestal. Decoration consisted of repoussé-chased strapwork, flowers, shells, bunches of grapes, sea monsters and wave ornament, and other almost standard motifs. The Civil Wars and Commonwealth interrupted the development of the standing cup, though at the Restoration in 1660 there was some attempt at its revival, usually with a cylindrical-bowled cup and cover on a tall baluster stem; a few more elaborate versions were made, notably the Royal Oak Cup given by the King to the Barber-Surgeons in 1676, which is chased overall and hung with pendant acorns. The heyday of the standing cup was over, replaced by the two-handled cup, and few were made after about 1670; the last known were the silver-gilt cups of 1720 to 1721 by Benjamin Pyne now in the Mansion House, London.

The two-handled cup and cover began to replace the standing cup as the principal item of domestic display plate about 1650, and within about fifteen years had virtually abolished it to the back of the plate-cupboard. There is some controversy about its nomenclature, and the term porringer (*q.v.*) is still mostly applied

OBJECTS

to it, at least until the 18th-century taller cup and cover was introduced. The first two-handled cups (porringers, caudle cups) were broad and bell-shaped, on a circular spreading or skirt foot, later a rim foot, with a low-domed cover with a finial, usually of baluster form. Scroll handles were usually plain, very occasionally of cast scroll form with caryatid terminals or even grotesque in style. A few early examples were of lobed form. About 1660 bombé shapes chased with baroque flowers and animals in the Dutch manner brought Continental fashions to England with the return of the exiled courtiers; such cups and covers were frequently accompanied by standing salvers to match. (*See* SALVERS AND WAITERS.) Others were plainer, with almost vertical sides, sometimes matted or with chased acanthus foliage or applied cut-card ornament round the base and on the cover. By the mid-1670s, the lower part of the bowl was sometimes fluted, introducing the more formal styles that were to be ubiquitous by the end of the century. Then, too, came the fashion for taller cups, often encircled by a moulded girdle, and with bold scroll handles: a style presaged by two of the largest known cups and covers of their time, those of 1685 now in the British Museum that were heirlooms of the Croft family.

Within a few years, the impact of Huguenot design had generally turned the two-handled cup into a tall bell-shaped piece, often with harp-shaped handles accentuating its height, and with a stepped domed cover with formal finial, the body and cover often applied with formal strapwork. As the decorative taste of the second quarter of the 18th century became more and more pronounced, so the applied detail – alternate plain and pierced strapwork, chased and engraved borders, leaf-caps to the handles – became more elaborate; finally even the formal baluster shape was turned and twisted into exotic rococo shapes, mounted on rocky coral-encrusted bases. Formality returned with the neo-classical period about 1700, with half-fluting, applied festoons and oval medallions surrounded by laurel wreaths, pine-cone finials, and reeded loop handles to vase-shaped bodies set on high pedestal supports. The cups of the period were also generally larger, from about 9 to 20 in. high, and by now were as often given as race prizes as used for domestic display.

The Napoleonic Wars at the end of the century furthered the taste for great cups, and sea captains benefited from the decision of a committee at Lloyd's to reward prowess with a Trafalgar Vase, specially designed by John Flaxman and made by Scott & Smith; one side shows Britannia, the other Hercules slaying the Hydra, while the cover features a lion between two upcurving handles terminating in classical paterae. Classicism was also emulated in the Warwick Vases, made from about 1811 onwards, chiefly by Paul Storr; they were miniatures of the great marble vase formerly at Warwick Castle (now in Glasgow Museum); its campana shape was also used for innumerable wine coolers (*q.v.*), bowls and vases from about 1800 to 1850. The early-19th-century skill at modelling was perhaps unsurpassed, but it did tend to endow later cups and covers with a mass of often unrelated ornament: allegorical figures, horse-and-jockey reliefs and finials, even handles formed as figures, especially cupids, caryatids and tritons. Cups and vases became *tours de force* of the modeller's craft, centrepieces rather than race-cups.

Inevitably, by the end of the century, there was a revival of older styles, so that reproductions and replicas became more tasteful than the extravaganza of the artists. As yet for the racegoer the finer points of art nouveau and other crafts styles were too avant-garde; in fact it is only in recent years that designer-silversmiths have in any numbers been entrusted with the trophies given for sports of all kinds.

Cutlery *See* KNIVES.

Decanter labels *See* BOTTLE TICKETS AND LABELS.

Decanter stands (Fig. 60) *See* WINE COASTERS.

Decanter trolleys Double stands on wheels for a pair of bottles or decanters. (*See* WINE COASTERS.)

Dessert dishes and stands Relatively more decorative versions of dishes and plates, or of silver-gilt, used primarily for serving desserts and fruits. The earliest surviving examples, dating from the early 17th century, are usually chased, engraved or pierced circular dishes. They are supported on a central trumpet-shaped foot, the shallow dishes often with everted rims, and presumably originally made in pairs or larger sets. Early illustrations occasionally show such footed dishes (miscalled tazze by many writers) used for fruits or sweetmeats. By the beginning of the 17th century, shallow fluted dishes, without feet, often called strawberry dishes, became popular; their actual use is not certain. Small versions were known to have been used for gaming counters in Ireland. English versions of the 1630s have been ascribed as saucers (i.e., sauce or mustard dishes). Usage is often determined by personal choice. By the 1740s, table services included circular, oval, rectangular and rarely fan-shaped dishes, often gilded, which appear to have been specially for dessert, accompanied by similar footed dishes or matching those incorporated in épergnes. By the early 19th century, silver-gilt dishes, plates and standing bowls were usually made in sets. They are not always, unless gilt, readily distinguishable from the more decorative styles of dinner service.

Dinner service Though plates and dishes were made from early times in silver, the complete banqueting service was exceptional until the second half of the eighteenth century. A full suite would include meat and fish dishes, soup plates, meat plates, entrée dishes, vegetable dishes, soup and sauce tureens and probably also dessert plates and baskets. Royal and other opulent services included table centrepieces, candelabra and other table silver.

Dishes and plates Serving dishes and plates, and dinner, soup and dessert plates of all shapes and sizes are known, though from late Tudor times seldom in sets until the mid-18th century. Most early examples have plain moulded borders, the borders fairly broad and with engraved arms or crest; a few very rare ones have stamped armorials in the early part of the 17th century. A variation of the plain or moulded rim from about 1680 was the thread edge, followed about 1720 by the gadroon and the guilloche rim. By the middle of the century combination patterns – gadroon and shell, shaped gadroon with leaf, and from about 1760, reed and ribbon and other composite mounts – gave variety.

Dish covers Domed covers for oval and circular dishes have been recorded from the 18th century; but as a rule dish covers were made in fused plate or silver from about 1800 onwards, usually *en suite* with large dinner services. (*See also* ENTREE DISHES.)

Dish crosses A gadget formed of two sliding arms extending from a central pivot to hold a circular or oval dish above the table top. In England they first made their appearance about 1730, but were most popular about 1755 to 1770, when many also incorporated a small spirit lamp at the intersection. The feet, at first of scroll form, were subsequently often of shell or pierced pattern, the upper terminals with flanges to accommodate the edge of the dish. Since dishes were often quite heavy and the dish crosses not always of very heavy gauge, especially during the 1760s, many appear to have sustained damage; repairs should be carefully looked for.

Dish rings While dish crosses appear first to have been made in Ireland, the dish rings, later to be considered typical Irish pieces of silver, were first used in England at the end of the 17th century, though in rather a different form. They consisted of a vertical pierced band or even a simple frame of silver wire supported on three or four feet, of greater or lesser distinction. The Irish variety, first made about 1760, are spool-shaped and pierced, often with scrolling foliage and sometimes with pastoral scenes; they were intended to hold a silver, glass or wooden bowl. The term 'potato ring' familiarly applied to these dish rings appears to have originated no earlier than the 1890s.

Dish wedges Triangular ridged or stepped stands first made during the second half of the 18th century, often in fused plate, close-plated and, later, electro-plated, to support meat dishes and plates.

Douters *See* SNUFFERS.

Dram cups A highly suitable name used in Ireland for the small two-handled cups that were such a feature of silver from about 1635 to 1710. Usually known as porringers in modern parlance. (*See* PORRINGER.)

Dredgers *See* CASTERS, CRUETS, INKSTANDS, MUFFINEERS.

Ecuelles Far from common in English silver, two-eared shallow bowls with covers were a traditional French gift to a nursing Mother; it is perhaps significant that most known English-made examples are the work of Huguenot silversmiths. Later examples are sometimes known as broth bowls or, in one instance at least, as porage bowls, or individual soup bowls.

Egg coddlers Egg boilers or coddlers are silver saucepans fitted on a spirit-lamp stand and fitted with an internal rack for four or six eggs. Most date after about 1790. At least one is recorded with an egg timer fitted to the lid.

Egg cups Small cups on trumpet-shaped feet of a size to hold an egg have been recorded from the early part of the 18th century. Usually gilt inside to help obviate corrosion, most are plain, though during the later 18th century many were decorated with bright-cut engraving; many have neat gadrooned or beaded borders. Frames to hold egg-cups have been known for as long as the cups themselves, and vary from rather flimsy wire frames to grander cast and chased examples for four, six or eight cups, sometimes also incorporating a central salt and racks for the egg spoons. A basket for egg-cups has also been recorded as dating from 1770.

A form of double egg-cup, one end of standard form, the other so that the egg can be laid on its side (said to have been favoured by Count Bernadotte in Sweden as he ate nothing but eggs for fear of being poisoned), has been alternatively described as a medicine cup and an eye bath. The unmarked examples of double egg cups of about 1800 noted are perhaps of Continental origin.

Egg spoons Of similar size to tea spoons, they are recorded as early as 1668, but do not appear to have survived or, at least, to have been recognised as such. Most egg spoons have rather elongated bowls, which are usually gilded for protection.

Entrée dishes Shallow-shaped circular, oval, oblong or octagonal dishes with or without covers (sometimes accompanied by heater stands) appeared at the table from about the middle of the 18th century. They soon became a feature of the matched dinner and breakfast services of the day. By the 19th century, entrée dishes and their heater stands were often of massive proportions, so stands were frequently of fused plate. Many from this period had stands of similar outline to the dishes contrived to hold hot water; others were pierced for use with spirit or charcoal burners. As with tureens for soup and sauce, vegetable and other covered dishes, the handles of entrée-dish covers were sometimes formed as the crest of the owner.

Epergnes Said to have derived from the French *épargner* (to be thrifty), the name 'épergne' for a table centrepiece crept into the language to be used, to judge from early contextual use, for the 'Pyramid of dry'd Sweet meats' and other dessert and for all sorts of savoury titbits, such as pickled cucumber and walnuts, mushrooms and lemons. At their simplest, they were a series of three or more dishes supported on a decorative frame; at their largest they held as many as ten or a dozen baskets and dishes, towering above the table. Others incorporated sets of casters for sugar and condiments, oil and vinegar bottles and, often interchangeable with dishes or other tablewares, candleholders as well.

The age of the rococo produced some of the most spectacular épergnes of all, among them a magnificent canopied example of 1745 made by George Wickes to designs by William Kent, now in the Royal Collection at Windsor. The taste for rococo chinoiseries introduced épergnes with canopies, often hung with bells; they gained their effect with intricate piercing of canopy, baskets and central dessert dish. Probably the most prolific maker of épergnes was Thomas Pitts, who must have registered his mark about 1758 and who supplied Wakelin with large numbers of baskets and épergnes. Other important makers were Butty & Dumee and Norwegian-born Emmick Romer. In the 1780s, there were William Pitts, James Young, Orlando Jackson and Robert Hennell, all of whom managed to adapt the table centre into a neoclassical stand with oval dishes and baskets, often restricting the pierced work to Vitruvian scroll of anthemion pattern borders and using bright-cut engraving to fine effect. By the 1790s, the number of bowls and baskets tended to diminish, the former now often being of cut glass set on Roman-style frames, such as the 'gazebo' centrepieces made by Pitts & Preddy, who also made standing dessert dishes which were arranged on large mirror plateaux.

About 1806 there was a brief excursion into the Graeco-Egyptian style; enormous examples by Philip Cornman are supported on a triangular base with sphinxes at each corner. More often Regency épergnes were in the Grecian style with three caryatids standing back to back supporting a large central dish and flanked by two smaller similar stands. Attention to figure-work, with much casting, chasing and rich applied ornament made the épergnes of the 18th century look almost flimsy. The naturalism of the 1820s brought in centrepieces ornamented with flowers and more graceful nymphs or coy cherubs, but by the middle of the century, solidity and massiveness outdid elegance. Battling warriors, figures symbolic of Industry and Agriculture, straining Atlasses and incongruous animals and birds bore aloft the dishes that held the grapes, pomegranates, pineapples and oranges that trade and Empire brought home.

Etuis (also contemporarily written as etwees) Any small box in gold, silver, pinchbeck, wood, tortoiseshell, shagreen or other material to hold personal pocketwares such as pins, needles, bobbin, scissors, thimble, bodkin and ear-pick, toothpick, tweezers, inch rule, pen, pencil and memorandum pad, etc. Many étuis were exquisitely enamelled during the 18th century and were among the richest productions of the smallworker in gold and silver.

Ewers and basins The large ewer and basin for handing rosewater with which to rinse the hands at table was also an important piece of display plate from the beginning of the Middle Ages until at least the middle of the last century, though by then its actual use at table was virtually abandoned. Most surviving ewers and basins are now in public, university or Livery Company collections and show considerable virtuosity in their design over the centuries. In the 16th century the usual form was a bellied flagon with a broad-rimmed circular basin, though one early 17th-century ewer and dish is in the form of a mermaid with a shell for the bowl. There followed tapering cylindrical covered ewers that in turn, by about 1635, developed into the almost straight-sided ewer on a high foot and with a beaked lip. This style was revived after the Restoration, though the pronounced lip changed to a short lip or even none at all. The Huguenots developed that most elegant of ewer forms, the helmet-shape, adding a bold flying-scroll handle. That form survived throughout the rococo period, though the handle by then was frequently a richly modelled double-scroll often with a figure terminal. A few later ewers derived from the baluster jug; by the 1750s they were in any event rarities, though the historically minded 19th century did produce a few grandiose ewers and basins.

Eye baths Of the standard form still in use today, on a narrow stem with circular foot, silver eye baths are very rare until the 19th century, when they were often included in travelling toilet services.

Fish carvers A misnomer for fish servers, which part but do not cut the fish.

Fish dishes Serving dishes of rather narrower form than standard meat dishes and often fitted with a strainer-dish or mazarine; the

Fish eaters The trade term for knives and forks with silver or plated prongs and non-cutting blades, first introduced about the middle of the 19th century.

Fish servers A flat pierced implement with a long handle used to pick up fish. The blade sometimes is slightly curved, often with a shaped edge on one side to enable the fish to be separated, without breaking the flakes. In the 19th century, the idea of two servers was general. Often massive patterns were made, with a large pronged fork accompanied by a slice which was sometimes of scimitar shape though without a cutting edge.

Fish slices *See* FISH SERVERS.

Flagons Originally the term applied to large bottles or flasks, but by the mid-16th century transferred to large bellied jugs used for serving wine, or water, generally without spout or lip, but always with a cover. Also known as livery pots, there are two distinct patterns: a bellied pot on a high domed foot and a straight-sided, slightly tapering cylinder on a rim or skirt foot. After the Reformation, such flagons were widely in use in churches for refilling the Communion cups, and the straight-sided form continued to be made for Church use until recent times.

Flasks Pocket flasks for spirits, derived from the saddle flask, are very rare before the later 19th century when glass, leather-covered and silver mounted examples proliferate. Usually of flat form with a bottle-like neck and screw-on stopper, a few tall cylindrical examples are known, the base sliding off to form a drinking tumbler. (*See also* PERFUME FLASKS.)

Forks Two-tined forks are known to have been used for spearing preserved fruits at the Court of Queen Elizabeth I, but their use at table for meats and other foods was not accepted, even at noble tables, until the end of the 17th century. The rare examples of earlier forks that have survived in English silver only accentuate the insularity of the English as compared with the 'foppish' French and Italians of the time. However, three-tined forks began to appear in sets to match trefid spoons about 1680, though a hundred years later Fanny Burney complained that there was a shortage of forks even at Court. The early two-tined forks were often made to match the knife; but by the beginning of the 18th century, it was the spoon and fork which were made of similar patterns. They developed from the trefid to the dognose, then the round-ended Hanoverian pattern that continued in fashion until about 1760, when the Old English and its variations were introduced, at the same time as the four-pronged fork. From then on, spoon and fork (flatware) rather than the knife (cutlery) dominated tableware design; carving knives and forks have retained the old knife/fork association even to having two tines.

Fox mask cups and boxes *See* SNUFF BOXES, STIRRUP CUPS.

Freedom boxes Boxes of various sizes presented to those granted the Freedom of a City, Borough or Company. Usually decorated with the arms of the donor and sometimes also of the freeman, and intended to contain the document recording the occasion. Irish towns and cities between about 1780 and 1820 were particularly noted for the giving of their Freedom to officials and others.

Furniture Tables, a throne made in 1731, mirrors, tea-tables, candlesticks, clocks, even a bed made for Nell Gwyn, are among silver and silver-mounted furniture recorded in the 17th and 18th centuries. Survivals are now in museums, the Royal Collection, at Knole and in the Hermitage, Leningrad. Most are of wood, mounted with silver and sometimes exceptionally finely engraved or chased, though the rare tea-kettle stand of 1724 with its matching kettle by Simon Pantin is all of silver (now in the Metropolitan Museum, New York). Silver mounts were also made for cabinets and other wooden furniture especially during the later 18th century, while looking glasses of silver, for wall-hanging or with strut frames for dressing-tables, have survived from the 17th century onwards.

Besides silver-covered furniture, hearth fittings were sometimes made of silver, including andirons or firedogs, which stood on either side of the fireplace. The vase-like fronts were of silver, with iron frames behind to hold logs. Sometimes only the finials of these firedogs were made of silver, of baluster form or even modelled as putti or other figures. Pokers, shovels and tongs are also known in silver, all dating before about 1725. Their styles are closely reproduced in the silver toys of the period.

Ginger jars (Fig. 59) Bellied jars, sometimes associated with taller vases and large beaker-like vessels, were used during the second half of the 17th century to embellish the stepped mantelpieces of the Dutch-style hearths or to be used as sideboard display plate. Sometimes of relatively light gauge, most were richly chased with foliage, birds, cherubs and other motifs, and occasionally gilded. In size they ranged from about 10 to 14 in. high. A few rarer examples featured engraved chinoiseries rather than chasing, and were even supplied with large footed salvers. Their place was almost entirely taken as display silver after about 1700 by the two-handled cup and cover.

Goblets *See* WINE CUPS.

Grape scissors As their name implies, these scissor-like cutters were made specifically for grapes, the blade on one side with a ridge that held the bunch firmly. Early examples of about 1780 had plain rings and bows. During the 19th century vine-laden styles and patterns to match flatware such as Kings, Coburg and Hourglass, were more usual. They were often gilt to match dessert flatware and cutlery.

Honey pots Straw beehives, or skeps, were the inspiration for the charming honey pots made between the 1790s and about 1810, with a few later reproductions and variations up to about 1850. The earliest examples usually have the finial in the form of a reeded disc in which the owner's crest or monogram could be engraved. The cover lifts off about a third of the way from the top to reveal a glass pot; a reed-and-tie bordered stand was also often supplied *en suite*. Several by Paul Storr, 1799, introduce the apt

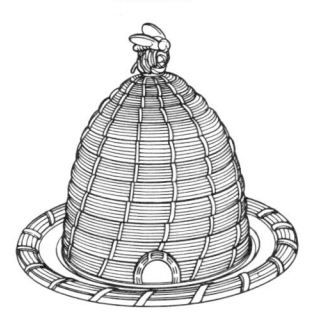

36 Honey pot *c.* 1800.

design of one or two bees forming the handle, a design also followed by John Emes by 1800. Most by these two makers were realistically tooled, but later Victorian examples are more fanciful, with Gothic and other decorative chased ornament. Many were gilded both inside and out.

Horns Not only cow and other animal horns were mounted in silver for drinking and ceremonial purposes from Anglo-Saxon times at least, but also ivory tusks, wood, bone and metal were all shaped to imitate animal horn and mounted with more or less extravagance in silver and silver-gilt. They were used for convivial occasions and as prizes for prowess at sports, for hunting and even, in medieval times, as objects of superstition; an example of the latter is the so-called gryphon's claws, usually in fact a cow or ibex horn, richly mounted in remembrance of St Cornelius who tended a wounded monster and was rewarded with one of his talons. Drinking horns are among the oldest silversmiths' work to survive in England. They are, in fact, virtually the same in design as the tenure horns, usually made to signify overlordship of an area of forest preserved for hunting. Others had civic significance, for summoning citizens to meetings

– moot horns – similar to that still used by the Watchman at Ripon in Yorkshire. From such horns derived the silver and silver-mounted examples given as prizes for sports, notably for archery, a fashion especially popular at the end of the 18th century.

Hot milk jugs Originally drunk plain, by the first decade of the century the fashion for taking milk or cream with tea was established. Sensibly, the milk was warmed and served from small lidded pots – a practice authenticated in literature by Jonathan Swift. He noted the foibles of society as early as 1709, but did not publish his *Polite Conversation* for another thirty years: Lady Smart upbraids her maid 'Why sure, Betty, you are bewitched, the cream is burnt too . . . run girl, a warm fresh cream.' The baluster jug on a stepped moulded foot followed teapot designs – plain or octagonal – replacing the oviform jug on three scroll feet. With rare exceptions it was entirely superseded by the cream or milk jug by about 1730. A few small covered jugs made later conform generally to unlidded styles.

Inkstands (Figs 11, 37) Originally known as standishes, the earliest inkstands likely developed from the box of writing implements carried by medieval scribes. Most were in the form of a silver casket fitted with ink and pounce pots (the latter containing powdered gum sandarac to re-buff the paper after erasure), a partition for wafers for sealing, and for pens, and either a taperstick or another partition for the wax. Another kind was a stand incorporating the pots and a box with a central carrying handle. By the middle of the 17th century, an oblong casket hinged in the centre set the style for the so-called Treasury inkstands, which were of a pattern issued to ambassadors and still in fact in use today.

By the end of the century, the tray-type inkstand, fitted with two or more pots, a taperstick and/or a bell initiated the style for nearly all future inkstands; obviously the style changed with different fashions. With the development of better glass in the

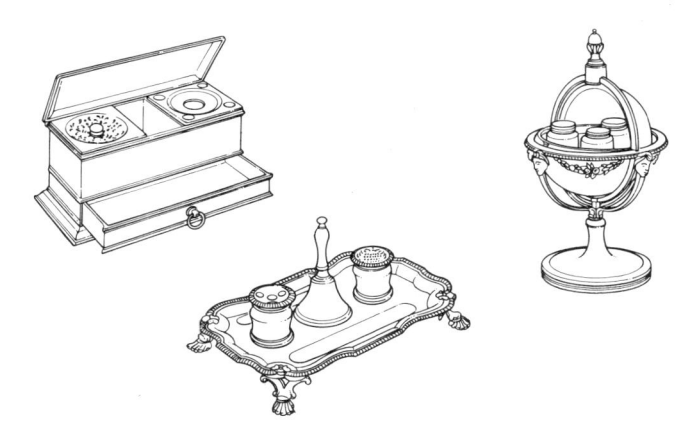

37 Inkstands TOP ROW *c.* 1680, *c.* 1792 to 1804, BOTTOM *c.* 1745 to 1755.

1760s, many inkpots were made of glass mounted in silver rather than of silver alone – a wise precaution since early inks tended to corrode. During the second quarter of the 19th century the design of the inkstand as a centrepiece for the desk rather than as a working piece of silver introduced some fanciful designs, often ornamented with allegorical figures. At the same time there was a fashion for small inkstands in naturalistic foliate styles made for lady's writing tables and bureaux. From about 1770 there was a vogue for 'globe' inkstands. The earliest was recorded in 1771, but most date between 1792 and 1810 and were a speciality of John Robins. Many actually had maps of the world engraved on them. The two hemispheres divided to reveal the tiny pots and miniature pen, ruler, tablet of ivory and penknife. Similar inkstands were also made in Sheffield plate.

Jardinières Large silver bowls are sometimes designated jardinières, though often their exact purpose is uncertain. However, references to 'a flower vase' in inventories suggest that silver examples were usually large and heavy, though some may well have been used for punch, as monteiths, or even as tureens. The famous rectangular pierced dishes now known to be cheese stands were originally thought to be jardinières.

Jugs and ewers (Figs 40, 61) Besides ceremonial ewers associated with rose-water dishes and the flagons used for replenishing the wine at Communion, jugs and ewers for all kinds of purposes are known from medieval times. Many 16th-century examples, such as tigerware jugs, have no lip, though that in no way impedes their use as pouring vessels. Many such large flagons for wine and beer were of bulbous form, and often very large. By the end of the century, however, cylindrical forms were more common; most 17th-century jugs or flagons resembled very large tankards, though taller. Later rosewater ewers retained the helmet shape, but the beer or wine jug of the beginning of the 18th century was of baluster form, with a bold scroll handle and on a circular spreading foot. Most beer and wine jugs had silver handles, but later similar jugs with wooden or wickered handles may have been used for mulled drinks or even been intended for hot water at the tea or coffee table. (*See* BEER JUGS, CLARET JUGS, CREAM JUGS, EWERS AND BASINS, HOT MILK JUGS.)

Knife boxes Wooden boxes, often of mahogany inlaid with brass or covered with fish-skin or shagreen, placed on the sideboard to hold up to a dozen knives to protect the sharpened steel blades. The interior usually was lined with baize. Very rarely these boxes had silver mounts. The sloping cover meant that the knives appeared stacked. Often a set of six picture-back tablespoons was included in the fittings of the box. Large oval silver trays with deep everted sides are also sometimes called knife trays, but are more likely to have been jardinières (*q.v.*).

Knives Until the end of the 17th century, knives were simply practical cutlery brought to the table to supplement the spoon. In rare instances they were a decorative addition to the table silver with a handle of ivory, bone, wood, or even precious materials such as agate or enamelled metal. With the advent and acceptance of the fork as a piece of table silver, the trio of knife, fork and spoon soon became recognised as a necessary adjunct to other domestic silver; suites or services were made, usually in dozens. Knife handles of silver, in simple patterns such as pistol-grip or the tapering pip-ended cannon sorted well with the Hanoverian style of flatware. They were only very slightly modified from the 1760s onwards when Old English and its variations, feather-edge, thread edge, bead, shell end and the like were introduced. It was, however, at the beginning of the 19th century, with more elaborate Regency-style patterns such as Kings, Queens, Hourglass, and Coburg that matched services really came into their own, though – with steel blades liable to rust and soft resins to fill the handles – many knives have perished, whereas the solid spoons and forks have survived. Hundreds of new patterns, some to survive, many to perish, were made during the century from about 1850 to 1950. The 20th-century examples at least had the advantage of being hard-soldered at the bolster, or junction with the handle, and, after the First World War had stainless steel blades. Larger knives, such as carving knives, remained, however, very much the province of the cutler rather than the silversmith and even now retain the old two-pronged fork. For fruit, silver forks and silver-bladed knives, often set in ivory or mother-of-pearl handles, and frequently gilded, are of dessert size or smaller.

Ladles Large serving spoons for soup and meat and for basting, and smaller round-bowled examples for serving sauces are usually known as ladles. The oldest made in any quantity date from the later 17th century and followed tablespoon design, with trefid or dognose ends, and rat-tails along the back of the ovoid bowls. Many were of very large size, as much as 15 or 16 in. in length, and proportionately heavy. Some incorporated marrow-scoops in the handles, but most followed general flatware patterns. The soup tureen, introduced in the 1720s, brought the large round-bowled soup ladle with curved handle, usually terminating in a decorative end. Smaller versions of the soup ladle were used for sauce, often being made in pairs or larger sets *en suite* with sauceboats, later for sauce tureens. From about 1765, a favourite terminal was the scroll pattern Onslow, named for Arthur Onslow, six times Speaker of the House of Commons. Others more ordinarily were made in Old English, Hanoverian and similar standard patterns. Very large ladles are usually called basting spoons, but more probably were used for serving, as smaller versions in the later 18th century were used as gravy spoons. Other small ladles were also used for cream, while in the 19th century some were pierced as sugar sifters. (*See* PUNCH LADLES, TODDY LADLES.)

Lemon strainers *See* ORANGE, LEMON AND LIME STRAINERS.

Lime presses The trade with the West Indies that introduced many spices, rum, sugar and citrus fruits to England coincided also with the taste for punch. While orange and lemon were the chief fruit

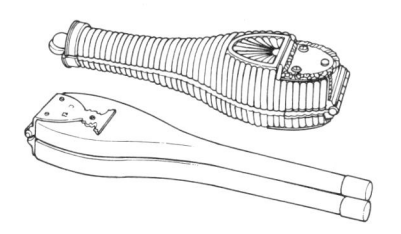

38 Lime presses TOP 1816, BOTTOM *c.* 1800.

constituents of the drink, lime was also used; wooden presses, formed of a small hemispherical depression at the hinged head of two long arms were sometimes mounted with silver. Most appear to date from about 1800 to 1830.

Livery pot (Fig. 2) The old name for a small tankard, such as those used by members of City and other Companies at feasts.

Marrow scoops Large joints with large bones provided a rich and tasty delicacy that was formerly much esteemed, though nowadays generally flavours soups and stews rather than being eaten as bone marrow itself. From about 1700 to 1800, silver scoops of sturdy gauge were found in many households, having at either end two elongated scoops in sizes. In some instances, scoops were made with spoon bowls at the other end, in all sizes from teaspoon size, through tablespoon to serving ladle proportions.

Mazarines Though the word 'mazarine' was used as long ago as 1673, its meaning appears to have changed over the centuries. It apparently originally referred to dishes or sets of dishes rather than to its present use as a strainer fitting over a fish dish. The bills for plate supplied to the Prince Regent by Rundell, Bridge & Rundell do not mention mazarines, but one of 1823 lists 'Four 22 in. dishes with shell and gadroon borders, 468 oz.' followed by '2 fish plates for ditto, 119 oz.' which suggests that the fish plates

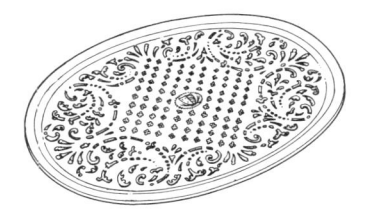

39 Mazarine *c.* 1780.

were what we call mazarines. Indeed, the modern usage seems to be of early-20th-century origin, for as late as 1908 a trade catalogue illustrates them under 'Fish Dish with Drainer'. However, the attractive term is now firmly applied to the oval or, more rarely, circular pierced strainers that have accompanied serving dishes since at least the 1740s. By far the most elaborate known are a pair of silver-gilt mazarines of 1762 in the Royal Collection, the strainer pierced with a net of fish that are so beautifully represented that the different species are actually identifiable. Stylised scrolls and foliage designs were inevitably more usual, even during the neoclassical period; an interesting highly formal circular example is that of 1769 by Boulton & Fothergill which is also exceptional in having side handles. Since most mazarines that come to the market are divorced from their dishes, a practice has grown up of having them mounted in wooden frames as tea or coffee trays.

Mirror plateaux An effective device to give added brilliance to table centres. Very few in silver have survived intact, though there are many equivalents in ormolu and in later electro-plated ware. Two types are recognisable: a single piece of glass set in a round, oval or oblong frame, used as a support for a dessert stand, and larger versions, with several sections to run the length of a dining-table. The earliest appear to date from about 1797, as supports for dessert stands, and most examples date from between then and about 1830; some have exceedingly richly cast and chased frames with claw, shell or even eagle supports. Sir Edward Thomason of Birmingham describes in his memoirs the making of a silver plateau for the Duke of Northumberland 'thirty three feet in length'. With a frieze of strawberry leaves above an arcaded gallery, and incorporating motifs from the Percy arms, it dates from 1818. It is interesting that an identical border to an 88-inch long plateau of 1822 bears the mark of Philip Rundell, who perhaps bought it in from Thomason and had it hallmarked in London.

Mirrors Most silver-framed mirrors were components of toilet services, first made in extensive numbers in England after the Restoration. Most early mirrors, of easel-type, have a richly chased border with a decorative cresting at the top with scrolls, foliage and amorini enclosing the arms or initials of the owner.

OBJECTS

About 1680 flat-chased chinoiseries became a favourite ornament for toilet silver of all kinds, and mirror frames were therefore much plainer, of simple rectangular form with an overlay of foliage at the angles and the cresting with a shaped moulded edge. The two types continued in fashion until about 1690; then plain moulded frames with a cresting surmounted by vases and reclining cherubs or even simple trefoil mouldings were made. Indeed, with rare exceptions, simple moulded, gadrooned or shaped mouldings applied with shells were the rule until the middle of the 18th century. Curvaceous frames of the rococo typified the last years of the great toilet services, which ended with those made for the daughters of King George III in the 1750s and 1760s, and the Williams-Wynn service of 1768. All were by Thomas Heming and the latter is now in the National Museum of Wales. A few subsequently displayed neoclassical reed-and-ribbon borders; but by the early 19th century toilet services, both for men and women, tended to be of travelling type, with a quantity of silver mounted bottles and boxes all neatly fitted into a large wooden chest.

Models A few rare silver figures are known, mostly modelled from life. The include several fine portrait models of royalty such as one by Paul Storr of George III, another of Queen Victoria, and examples of other notabilities such as the Duke of Wellington. On a more modest scale, one of the most delightful must be Kandler's milkmaid, engraved 'Nanny', made in 1766. During the 19th century there were many fine models made, both individually and as integral parts of large centrepieces; these include sets of the Seasons, of various allegorical figures and of Britannia as well as pairs of figures in the manner of those made in porcelain. Models of buildings and monuments were also made, varying from a great model of Eton College Chapel made by John Tapley in 1834 to one of Bishop Rock Lighthouse by Barnard & Co. dated 1858. Scale models of fire engines, trains and, later, cars have also been made. Indeed, today there is still a great demand for models of all kinds of animals, birds and fishes made in silver.

Monteiths (Fig. 43) 'A vessel or bason notched at the brim to let drinking vessels hang there by the foot, so that body or drinking place might hang in the water to cool them ... called a Monteigh from a fantasticall Scott who ... wore the bottom of his cloake or coate so notched.' Anthony à Wood's diary entry made in December 1683 records the proper use of the montieth bowl, a useful reminder, for all too often such bowls are now described as – and were probably once also used as – punch bowls, since within two or three years of their first being introduced, monteiths were often provided with detachable rims. If these were lost or discarded as the fashion for cooling the glasses waned, then the bowl could prove an excellently large punch bowl (*q.v.*). No monteith bowl appears to pre-date the first reference to it; indeed, the earliest known date from 1684, relatively shallow bowls some 11 or 12 in. in diameter on a moulded foot, the sides panelled to allow eight or ten notched depressions. One particularly fine and unusually heavy bowl of 48 oz. by George Garthorne is plain except for contemporary armorials; most of the period were fashionably flat-chased with chinoiseries, the rim with a simple moulding or a decorative mount. Another Garthorne bowl of 1686 incorporates probably the first ever scalloped rim, or collar; he was also the maker in 1690 of one of the first bowls to be supplied with lion mask and drop handles. Generally, however, it was the exception to find a collar or removable rim until about 1696. Most bowls, after the brief age of chinoiserie, were boldly designed, with scrolled flutes enclosing matted and plain panels alternately or even with gadrooned cartouches to match the heavily gadrooned circular foot.

By 1697, applied masks and scrolls at the rim gradually became part of the detachable collar, though both types continued to be made until the end of the century. By then greater formality, with panels of vertical fluting enclosing the scroll bordered, scalework cartouches for the armorials and drop handles at the side added dignity as well as practicality. In style the bowl was almost indistinguishable from that of the punch bowl, whether fluted or plain. Gradually fewer and fewer bowls were made with scalloped rims, and by 1730 a monteith rim was a rarity. One fine 88-ounce example of 1730 by Charles Hatfield was a 'gratuity' of a 'piece of plate not exceeding the value of thirty guineas' from the proprietors of Fulham Bridge to the builder. This plain one contrasted with the highly elaborate one of the same year by John Swift presented to a Mr Busfeild for his services. This piece was enriched with applied rococo strapwork, massive lion mask and ring handles and weighing over 112 oz. Even more elaborate was a rococo-chased monteith bowl of 1739 with an everted crown of rococo scrolls and handles formed of female busts, presented to the Corporation of Boston (sold with the rest of the regalia in 1837). It was one of the last English monteith bowls ever made, though a bowl with a fixed rim of Vitruvian scrolls by Daniel Smith and Robert Sharp, 1786, revived the old form and another, without a foot, by Wakelin & Taylor, 1790, evoked the French style. The old name was recalled in an enormous silver-gilt bowl of 1820 by Edward Farrell, probably originally commissioned by Kensington Lewis on behalf of the Duke of York. At the sale of his effects in 1827, the catalogue noted the 'superb monteith round which is represented Alexander's Battle of the Granicus in a very spirited group of about 27 figures . . .' It was not properly a monteith, for the pierced frieze that forms the rim is not designed for glasses, while the bowl itself is not only large – 17 in. in diameter – but also very deep. Weighing 230 oz., it was obviously a showpiece rather than a monteith.

Monument candlesticks A contemporary name given to column candlesticks on square bases which resembled Sir Christopher Wren's great pillar commemorating the end of the Great Fire of London. (*See* CANDLESTICKS.)

Mounted wares Since Anglo-Saxon times at least, the rare, the curious and the precious have been enhanced by the addition of

OBJECTS

40 Mounted ware Jug, *c.* 1570 to 1590; cup, *c.* 1640 to 1660.

gold and silver mounts. Beautiful shells from distant lands brought home by mariners – nautilus and conch and mother-of-pearl – fine oriental porcelain, rock crystal, amber, agate and other hardstones, and curiosities such as ivory, ostrich eggs and even polished coconut shells as well as more utilitarian materials like Rhenish stoneware and Turkish pottery, cattle horn, wood and leather were all mounted, many for display, others for everyday use. Because of the small intrinsic value of the actual objects as bullion, many survived the hazards of war and taxation, though of course many disappeared through breakage; nonetheless, mounted wares have often survived where larger and more important all-silver pieces have gone to the melting-pot. During the Renaissance especially there was highly imaginative mounting of rare objects, while stoneware, wood (especially the spotted maple) and leather continued a tradition well established during the Middle Ages for drinking vessels of all kinds. Generally speaking the custom of mounting anything other than rare hardstones dwindled during the silver-rich 18th century; about 1760 the expansion of the glass industry and the subsequent taste for richly coloured and cut glass brought a new affinity between the two. Silver-mounted toilet bottles and cruets, inkwells, tea caddies, sweetmeat bowls and decanters, and of course, blue glass liners for salts, caddies and dishes began a trade that continued on a large scale throughout the 19th and early 20th centuries. The beginning of the 19th century, with the growing taste for medievalism and historical reproductions, brought some revival of the mounting of ivory and coconuts, usually in goblet form. A few instances are known of coconut jugs, bowls and even a teapot with the nut carved in imitation of cut glass. Travellers also brought back curiosities such as emu eggs from Australia, ostrich eggs from Africa, nuts and shells from South America, while inexpensive Staffordshire pottery as well as Wedgwood wares and the like were often provided silver or plated rims to form biscuit barrels, teapots and so on. Fairings were also mounted, much as Elizabethan stoneware or tigerware jugs had been used as lottery prizes in the late 16th century, the hard German stoneware with its mottled glazed finish supplying sturdy yet decorative pots for even quite modest households.

Muffin dishes Covered dishes, usually circular, with a fairly deep well, for serving hot muffins or tea cakes. Most date from after 1800.

Muffineers A small caster for sprinkling sugar, salt or spice on muffins. Presumably so called because in the early 19th century muffins became exceptionally popular. The term is sometimes mistakenly applied to muffin dishes.

Mugs The term usually applied to an uncovered pot or tankard for drinking, and which during the reign of Charles II – when it was first made – came soon to oust the small beaker. The earliest examples in fact approximate to a beaker. They were either of tapering cylindrical type or slightly bellied and applied with straps, to which a single handle, usually of scroll form, had been added. It became especially popular for children's silver, but was

OBJECTS

41 Mugs TOP ROW *c.* 1700, *c.* 1690, BOTTOM *c.* 1710.

also widely used in larger sizes for beer and ale. Since 17th-century mugs are rare, collectors should be wary in case simple ribbon handles have been unscrupulously added to beakers or even tumbler cups. There can be small doubt about the mug with a narrow foot reeded or otherwise decorated to match the lip and handle, or the globular style with a deep reeded neck. Both patterns were popular until the 1690s. Meanwhile the baluster form made its first appearance for mugs. One early example of 1688 has a swirl-fluted base and a rib near the top; it is unexpectedly fitted with a gadrooned cover, perhaps for use by an invalid. In simpler form, without a cover, it was repeated by several makers during the next decade, along with a few mugs of plain thistle shape. This pattern was especially popular in the north, where the thistle mug with applied strapwork round the base became almost a national style. Like tankards, mugs remained very much the province of the native-born silversmiths, though some Huguenots did imitate the tapered straight-sided mugs with their simple moulded foot, scroll handle and rib round the body. By 1720 the simple type was varied by that with a tuck-in base, the baluster proper seldom being made before 1725. Mugs generally were kept very simple, with only occasionally applied strapwork, engraved borders or decoration other than a crest, initials or coat of arms being used. Most mugs held either half-a-pint or a pint, and were usually sturdy. About the middle of the century pairs are sometimes met with, but the straight-sided and the baluster forms remained standard designs as they still are today.

The Regency and later had, of course, grander variations with foliate chasing and borders of flowers in high relief. In one superb gilt mug by Benjamin Smith, 1827, the thistle is naturalistically adapted so that the foliage sweeps over the base and rises to form the handle. There were, indeed, many rather grandiose designs created, unbelievably, as Christening mugs; they were usually complete with equally ponderous knife, fork and spoon; many were far beyond the strength of children to lift, and so remained cased and unused.

Mustard pots First introduced into England by the Romans and much valued for its pungency – often to conceal the taste of long-stored meat – mustard was usually served dry at table, each diner mixing his own. It has been suggested that small saucer dishes were in fact used for that. With the introduction of casters, one pot was often for mustard, in which case the top was left unpierced, or blind. The first known pot for 'wet' mustard dates from 1724, a small covered baluster pot. A few vase-shaped pots were made in the 1750s, followed by cylindrical examples fitted with blue glass liners which helped to prevent the vinegar with which the herb was mixed from corroding the silver. It was an attractive style when the pots were pierced. Vase-shapes predominated from the 1770s; but most early-19th-century pots

42 Mustard pots TOP ROW *c.* 1725, *c.* 1775, BOTTOM *c.* 1785.

reverted to the drum shape, often quite plain except for gadrooned rims. During the middle part of the century the Victorian taste for humorous silver produced such pots as a barrel with a monkey aghast at the pungent sauce, a creel, military drums and so on.

Mustard spoons Small spoons with elongated bowls. Occasionally, made in special designs to go with novelty pots.

Napkin rings Circles of silver, plain or waisted, circular, oval or, more recently, oblong or square, to hold the table napkin. None is known before 1836. Earlier examples are suspect, probably made up from good gauge spoons or skewers.

Nutmeg graters Nutmeg was an important spice to ameliorate the taste of rough ales, to flavour foods and drinks and as an ingredient of punch. Nutmeg graters were widely made throughout the 17th and 18th centuries. The earliest examples are generally of box form with an inset steel grater and room within the box to hold the nut. Late-17th-century examples are also cylindrical, with a cylindrical silver or steel grater. Among the hundreds of trifles made by the smallworker during the second half of the 18th century and well into the 19th were egg shapes, mace-like cases (a pun on the outer covering of the nutmeg) frequently with a corkscrew concealed in a long tubular base, oval, rectangular, octagonal and other little boxes, often with the base hinged to hold the nut, the grater fixed below the cover. By then there was also a fashion for silver graters in the form of sconces, with a hanging section above a hemispherical or cylindrical steel grater, in the manner of those of base metal used in the kitchen. Nutmeg graters were also sometimes incorporated in spice boxes and in travelling sets.

Oil and vinegar frames *See* CRUETS.

Orange, lemon and lime strainers Citrus fruit was an essential ingredient of punch, the concoction of spirits, hot water, sugar, spice and fruit juice that was drunk in England as early as 1632 and rapidly became the drinking man's favourite drink. Oranges and lemons were imported into England soon after the discovery of the West Indies. For many years they were rarities enjoyed chiefly at Court, such as those afforded by James I who ate 'Portynggales', or oranges from Portugal, on fast days. Half a century later, however, Nell Gwyn put them firmly on the map, soon followed by the Government who decided to tax the fruit that men such as John Locke so greatly enjoyed – he hastened down to the docks whenever a shipment came into London. Many delicacies soon appeared in the recipe books, from orange water to lemon sauce. Silver was the only known ware other than glazed pottery and porcelain that could be used without taint; from about 1680 strainers with long tubular handles began to appear, the holes generally simply dot-pierced. By the early 18th century, more intricate scroll and flowerhead piercing became fashionable, with two handles cut and pierced in similarly scrolling designs. Many were made by specialist smallworkers such as John Albright, William Fleming and James Goodwin. Curiously, one or two by silversmiths such as Paul de Lamerie show simpler piercing and often had cast scroll handles instead of the pierced ear-like type more usual until the 1730s. The use of many of these strainers with punch bowls is attested to by their dimensions – the handles long enough to sit comfortably on a small punch bowl. From the middle of the century geometrical pierced dot patterns were usual. From these evolved the later tea strainers of the 19th and 20th centuries.

Ox-eye cups The ring handles on either side of the compressed circular bodies of cups traditionally used at Oxford Colleges give these small heavy cups their curious but appropriate name. Early examples date from the beginning of the 17th century. They have been made for students' use continually ever since, and also been much copied, especially at the turn of the century, to celebrate centenaries such as that of Merton College.

Pap boats Small boat-shaped dishes with a pronounced lip at one end, used as feeding bowls for children's pap. In use from about 1700 to 1830, most were practical and plain, though from about 1750 some had notched 'James pattern' or cut edges. From about 1800 a rim wire was often applied and, on occasion, a narrow band of bright-cut or other engraving.

Pastille burners *See* PERFUME BURNERS.

Patch boxes The fashion for applying patches or beauty spots was a vanity much in evidence from the Restoration onwards. The black silk patches, cut in a variety of shapes – circles, stars, even representational patches – served not only as 'coquet' patches but to conceal blemishes, pimples and pock marks. Little silver and silver-gilt boxes, a mere inch or two inches long, oval, oblong or circular, were made in large numbers from about 1650 onwards. They were simple or rich according to taste and pocket, from plain cylinders with slip-top covers merely matted or engraved with stylised motifs to such little gems as Queen Mary's gold and enamel patch box complete with a tiny mirror within the lid. The fashion for patches disappeared with the wig about 1790.

Patty pans Now recognised as a small version of the fluted dessert dish (the so-called strawberry dish) about 5 in. in diameter. Similar small dishes in Ireland are recorded as counter dishes for use at the card-table, paralleled by small baskets inventoried in England as 'baskets for fish' (i.e., bone or ivory gaming counters).

Peg measures Rare until recent times, in the form of small double cups, one cup of larger capacity than its counterpart, the rim slightly lipped for pouring. The earliest appears to be a silver-gilt measure of 1780.

Peg tankards Tankards and, more rarely, mugs with a series of pegs set inside, used as wager cups, the bet being to drink no more nor no less than one 'peg measure'.

Penners Travelling inkwell, pen holder and seal, usually of cylindrical form in the 17th century, though sometimes designed as a small casket for pen, ink, pounce and penknife used chiefly by travellers and army and navy officers.

Pen trays Very like spoon trays (*q.v.*) and some of the later plain oblong and long-oval snuffer trays (*q.v.*) these first appear about 1770 though are more usually incorporated in the furnishing of an inkstand. (*See* INKSTANDS.)

Pepper pots Originally called pepper boxes, one of the casters specifically used for ground pepper, the top pierced, often fairly coarsely. Smaller casters, dredgers and muffineers were often used as much for spices as for pepper. (*See* CASTERS, CRUETS, MUFFINEERS.)

Perfume burners Recorded from medieval times, burners used to burn sweet-smelling incense have not survived before the 17th century and resemble the charcoal braziers used with teapots and kettles at the end of the century. Several are known dating between about 1670 and 1690. By the mid-18th century, pot-pourri vases were more usual, though silver examples remain rare. Matthew Boulton's range of silver and ormolu wares included cassolets in which perfumed pastilles were burned, and small vases on stands with lamps below were made by Andrew Fogelburg in the 1780s.

Perfume flasks Small phials for perfume were first made fairly extensively at the end of the 17th century, though few were fully marked until after 1790. Later examples are often of glass contained within a silver case.

Perfume funnels Small funnels, first made in the 1670s, are sometimes found in association with toilet services and dressing cases, and were most likely used for perfume or toilet water.

Pincushions Usually included in 17th century and early 18th century toilet services, a few have become divorced from their fellows. They are either free-standing, mounted on rectangular frames, or incorporated in the lids of toilet caskets. Smaller examples were included in sewing sets. By the 19th century they were also used for hat-pins, provided with a frame to keep the long pins from scattering.

Pipes Silver pipes in the manner of clay pipes were made from quite early times but are seldom found before the early 1800s, when they were made, often in sections, by several Birmingham smallworkers. Miniature silver pipes, some with tampers and stoppers and cased up together, were also made during the 19th century and later.

Plaques Plaques of early date were usually of Continental origin, embossed and chased in relief or engraved with scriptural and classical subjects. They were often incorporated in caskets and boxes. Others were framed as pictures, while miniature examples were used for snuff-boxes and other personal smallwares. In the later 19th century larger wall plaques in silver and electro-plate were made in quantity by Elkington's of Birmingham, often by electrotyping metal, ivory or other originals. (*See* SHIELDS.)

Plates *See* DISHES AND PLATES.

Plummets A pear-shaped bob with a hook at the end, occasionally found with toilet plate, suggesting that it was perhaps used for

OBJECTS

tightening stays. It could also, perhaps, have been used to draw the curtain over the easel mirror, though it is not clear if that custom survived into the 18th century.

Porringers There has long been speculation about the correct term for the ubiquitous two-handled cups with or without covers, some with stands, made in every shape, size and style. They were also made throughout the 17th century and in small versions surviving until the end of the 18th, before being revived about 1880. Caudle cups, posset pots, porringers, broth bowls and, for the smaller uncovered versions, dram cups, children's cups, Christening cups, all have their adherents. In America, porringer is applied, not to the two-handled cup but to the single-eared bowl known in England as a bleeding bowl. The term 'porringer', which is a derivative of 'pottager' or vessel for pottage of stew, by way of pottinger and altered to its familiar form on the analogy of porridge (itself also a corruption of pottage), should perhaps only be applied to bowls known to have been used for food rather than drink. Many of those 17th-century two-handled cups were certainly intended for liquid refreshments and are so inscribed. But for children no doubt they could equally be used for food and drink, easy to hold and even accompanied by a small spoon. Unfortunately, when Pepys put some spoons and a porringer into his pocket to go to a Christening, he did not describe the piece specifically. Other larger versions with covers were probably intended for display as much as for drinking, and by the end of the 17th century refinement of their design by the Huguenots brought in the most fashionable of all silver for display and presentation. Generally simply listed as cups, one tantalising entry in the Wakelin Ledgers records the sale to Lord North in 1741 of 'A porrenger and cover 32 = 11' – its weight concomitant with the larger two-handled cups and covers of the late 17th century. (*See* CUPS; BLEEDING BOWLS; DRAM CUPS; ECUELLES.)

Posset pots Probably a two-handled cup and cover used for the hot spiced drink which was fashionable in the 17th century.

OBJECTS

Perhaps also served from spout pots when taken by invalids.

Potato rings Misnomer for dish rings (*q.v.*).

Pounce boxes Cylindrical or baluster-shaped containers with sprinkler top for pounce, a fine powder such as gum sandarac, used to smooth the surface of paper after erasure and prevent ink from spreading. Usually part of the fittings of an inkstand or standish (*q.v.*).

Powder flasks Both military and sporting flasks for powder were made from at least the 17th century, the earliest usually of complete carapaces of tortoises, more rarely of mother-of-pearl. The later 18th century saw the development of patented methods of dispensing exact quantities of powder. Sporting flasks are sometimes decorated with chased hunting scenes.

Punch bowls The first recorded reference to punch in England appears to date from 1632. Between 1658 and the end of the century references proliferate just as the fashion for the eastern spirituous concoction – the ingredients varied according to taste – spread into convivial society. The origin of the word is obscure, but probably derives from the Middle Eastern word for 'five' referring to the spirits, spices, fruit, sugar and milk or water that composed the drink. Despite the evidence of punch and punch parties some twenty years before, no identifiable silver punch bowl exists before an example of 1680. From then on until about

43 LEFT **Monteith** *c.* 1700. **44** RIGHT **Punch bowl**, *c.* 1775.

1710 it is often very difficult to distinguish a rimless monteith from a bowl specifically made for punch. Punch bowls are often a little smaller and lighter than the glass-coolers and in rare instances are fitted with covers.

Several flat-fluted bowls about 9 in. in diameter, dating between 1700 and 1710 are usually ascribed as punch bowls. By then, plain bowls, about 10 to 12 in. in diameter can fairly confidently be so termed, though missing monteith collars can sometimes be suspected as in a 9-in. bowl of 1706 which has a vertical 'neck' below the moulded rim. The plain circular bowl on a stepped moulded foot was fully established by 1715. They were often of impressive size and weight, such as the superb 1722 bowl with short side handles by Thomas Farrer weighing 161 oz., with which are associated a contemporary ladle, a mixing rod and a pair of silver-mounted fruit crushers. The following year Lamerie's famous Treby punch bowl, now in the Ashmolean Museum, features a procession of gentlemen and the words '*Amicitia Perpetua* and Prosperity to Hooks and Lines' – engraving that is attributed to William Hogarth. Another superb Lamerie bowl with lion mask and drop handles is enriched with applied strapwork enclosing scalework. Generally speaking, punch bowls were plain with no other decoration than the owner's crest or armorials. They were often given as racing plate, one of the earliest known dating from 1718 and won at Newcastle. By 1762 such bowls were an established prize from the City of Chester for the local Westchester Races, many of them in a bombé shape not otherwise usual. A magnificent silver-gilt bowl by Thomas Heming, 1771, now in the National Museum of Wales, is in neoclassical style, applied with festoons, anthemion borders, guilloches and rams' heads, and a few others in neoclassical style are recorded. The bombé shape on a high stepped foot typified most of the bowls of the turn of the century, though one unusual example by Scott and Smith, 1803, rests on three lions couchant on an incurved triangular pediment. The 1820s saw the demise of the silver punch bowl, though its form was revived during the second half of the century for racing trophies.

Punch ladles A long-handled ladle with a circular or oval bowl was an obvious serving spoon for punch, and a few punch bowls with associated ladles have remained together over the centuries. The earliest appears to be that of about 1685 presented to Stamford Corporation, with an almost hemispherical bowl fluted at the base, *en suite* with the punch bowl. More usually, however, the punch ladle was plain, sometimes with a lip and with a turned wood handle, or, more rarely a tubular silver one. By about 1740, a shaped oval bowl with a lip to the side, and fluted into shell-like pattern set the style for the next twenty years or so. There were a few more elaborate ladles, notably made by Phillips Garden, in rococo style with the bowl, plain or richly chased, in the form of a deep conch shell. Plainer styles were revived during the neo-classical period, and there was also a fashion for simple oval ladles, sometimes with turned-over edge, often without a lip, but set in the centre with an old silver coin. This was sometimes gilded to suggest a gold insertion. It has been suggested that many of these were intended as Jacobite mementoes. In Scotland from about 1770 onwards, many smaller ladles were made for serving hot toddy. (*See* LADLES.)

Punch whisks Long-handled devices with silver flanges to whisk up the ingredients of punch.

Racing bells At Carlisle two enclosed bells of 1509 and 1599 are rare survivors of prizes in this form for horse-matches. Presumably a northern form, they gave rise to the phrase 'to bear away the bell' or prize. The type is perpetuated in the small bells hung about children's rattles.

Rattles (Fig. 57) Delightful portraits from the 16th century show young children with rattles, or corals and bells as they were sometimes known. Hung to the girdle by a long chain, the usual form was a piece of coral, about 3 in. long, for teething, set in a silver or silver-gilt holder which was hung with six or eight

OBJECTS

enclosed bells and which had a whistle in the end. A variant was a ball-shaped pierced head containing a pea or other rattling device, and with a whistle at the end of a long pipe-like handle.

Razor sets Cased sets of razors with silver mounts and tortoiseshell handles were made at least from the first half of the 17th century, though rare until the middle of the 18th century. Such sets were sometimes called 'Field Companions' though used, no doubt, by travellers and in the home as well. They comprised four or more folding razors, one or two strops, a pair of tweezers, scissors, button hook, lotion bottles, even a pair of curling tongs, shaving brush, soap box and so on. The typical cases of the 18th century were wedge-shaped, rather like knife boxes, with a hinged cover, made of fine wood such as mahogany or of wood covered with leather or shagreen, sometimes edged with silver mounts and with a silver escutcheon key-plate. Inside the case was usually fitted and lined with velvet, each implement fitting into its own slot. By the end of the century it was usually replaced by a larger travelling dressing case.

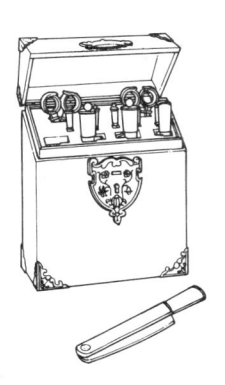

45 Razor set *c.* 1750.

Ring stands (or trees) Much more common in porcelain, a few silver ring stands are known, most of 19th-century date and later. As their name implies, they are usually of trunk shape with hooks or branches on which rings can be placed.

Rose bowls A modern term describing a circular or oval bowl derived in style from the punch bowl and the monteith, adapted for flowers by the addition of a mesh or 'net'. Much used for presentation pieces and race prizes in the later 19th century, the rose bowl proper only appeared during the late 1940s. The cover is pierced decoratively and often has a central finial or other decorative device so that it could also be used as a centrepiece when not filled with flowers.

Rosewater ewers and basins It is, of course, by no means certain that rosewater was always used for rinsing the hands at meals, but the name has generally become accepted. (*See* EWERS AND BASINS.)

Saffron pots Miniature versions of teapots, and following similar patterns, dating between about 1720 and 1790, thought to have been used for serving saffron and other herbal teas used medicinally. A few, however, may have been intended simply as doll's-house silver. (*See* TOYS AND MINIATURES.)

Salad dishes Deep bowls, often with scalloped or fluted sides, and on a central foot of three or four cast supports, were, it is known, described as 'sallad dishes' in 1744. In fact, as today, any bowl or dish may well have been used for the food. Dishes of a truncated fan shape, included in 'supper sets' may have been used for salads.

Salts (Figs 1, 56) Small, or trencher salts, have been in use since at least the 16th century, although common salt tends to corrode silver; the small well carved in the corner of a wooden trencher was really a more practical method of holding the salt that was considered not only vital for health but also played its part in ceremony at table. By the middle of the 17th century, sets of small circular, oblong or shaped salts, generally called trencher salts, were being made in fair numbers, usually quite without decoration, though by the 1680s gadrooned sides were not uncommon. A few of these early salts were almost spool-shaped and miniatures of some of the larger standing salts still being made; but about 1700 the typical trencher salt was a waisted octagonal bowl or of oval shape with a spreading foot.

About 1725 a rather taller style came in, a plain circular bowl supported on a stepped foot or pedestal. These were soon followed by salts with applied leafage or other formal ornament round the base of the bowls and on the foot.

About 1735 the rococo saw some fine virtuoso salts in the form of shells and other exotic shapes, but most were based on the compressed circular form supported on three or four feet, the style more or less elaborate as taste and pocket dictated. This was also the period of the first specialist makers: the Hennells, Edward Wood and later N. Appleton and A. Smith, and the Batemans who possibly provided the equivalent of parish patterns for other makers who finished or otherwise embellished the basic shapes. The neoclassical fashion introduced the pierced oval salt, also on four legs, with a blue glass liner, followed about 1780 by the boat-shape, very like miniature soup tureens without covers, with high loop handles and oval or oblong pedestal supports. The compressed oval developed from that, and by the beginning of the 19th century there was a more pronounced trend towards making salts, sauceboats, tureens and entrée dishes *en suite*. The caster for salt was never very practical; interior gilding, a late-19th-century development, was virtually essential, and often used for open salts. (*See also* CRUETS, STANDING SALTS.)

Salvers and waiters (Figs 56, 57) The making of salvers, waiters and trays is the supreme test of a good silversmith. A single mistake and days, even weeks, of work can be lost. Yet they remain among the most plentiful of silverwares over 300 years, in a variety of shapes, styles and sizes. They first appear in general use about the mid-17th century as serving dishes and as stands for tankards, caudle cups and even, in one instance, for a monteith bowl. The word salver is said to derive, through French, from the Spanish word to assay or test. But by the time it was adopted in England, it had acquired the meaning given by Thomas Blount in 1661: 'a new fashioned peece of wrought silver plate, broad and flat with a foot underneath, and it is used in giving Beer, or other liquid things, to save the Carpit [i.e., the tablecloth] or the Cloathes from drops.' Its use is, in fact, better expressed by the term 'waiters' which was applied to small salvers at least from 1739 onwards – the similar term 'presenter' was also occasionally used. Nowadays the terms are usually arbitrarily divided as salvers for larger trays, waiters for small examples (often in pairs or larger sets) and trays for those with handles. (Tea-table or tea board was more usual for these during the 18th century.) The use of the word *tazza* for footed salvers is to be deprecated: a tazza is properly a shallow drinking bowl on a high foot.

The first salvers were really a development of the broad-rimmed dish of the mid-17th century, with depressed circular centre and capstan-shaped foot. The border was often chased with baroque foliage, flowers and animals. Later, about 1665 to 1670, restrained gadrooned borders and plain moulded rims made their appearance, and the junction of foot and underside were often applied with cut-card ornament. Sometimes the foot was unscrewable. By the end of the century, plain moulded rims were usual; occasionally octagonal or square shapes replaced the usual circular styles. By about 1715, the central foot gradually changed to the style with three or four scroll supports. Besides circular shapes, there were square, rectangular, octafoil, hexafoil and multifoil shapes, some with upturned rims in the manner of dessert dishes. Salver-makers often ran specialist workshops: among them John Tuite who hailed from Ireland, and worked in London for twenty years from 1721; Robert Abercromby, probably from Newcastle who specialised at salver-making in London in the 1730s; George Hindmarsh, and others whose mantle was later taken over by Hannam and Crouch, Timothy Renou and other later specialists. Many of the most distinguished silversmiths also made salvers, of course, among them David Willaume, Paul de Lamerie, Paul Crespin, Edward Wakelin and, later, Paul Storr, Benjamin Smith and many more.

The plain salvers and waiters of the first twenty years or so of the century gave way about 1732 to more decorative designs, the borders engraved or flat-chased in addition to the engraved arms of the owner. Later more elaborate chasing and richly chased borders added rococo distinction to more important examples. The practical need of the salver was never completely neglected, even at times of high decoration many remaining substantially plain.

By the 1770s, oval salvers took precedence, though some continued to be made in circular and octagonal shapes, with bright-cut borders and beaded mounts predominating. These supplemented the chased chinoiserie ornament and the pierced and chased rims that had been favoured in the 1750s and 1760s. In a way, the banishing of the decorative style for salvers and waiters sounded the end of the age of the salver. Though some gilded and ornamental salvers were made in the 19th century, the salver-maker was more often engaged in making enormous two-handled trays, footed dessert stands and sideboard dishes. Waiters that were made were generally reproductions of earlier styles.

Sandboxes Small cylindrical, baluster or vase-shaped pots with perforated cover included in many standishes to hold sand for drying ink. (*See* INKSTANDS.)

Sauceboats and tureens The earliest known pair of sauceboats date from 1717, of oval outline with scroll handles on either side and a lip at either end, the rims slightly waved. This form of double-lipped sauceboat remained in fashion until about 1740; a variant form of serving vessel for sauce and gravy was first introduced in about 1726, the rather more practical shape with a single lip at the end opposite the handle. Generally made in pairs, sauceboats of this latter kind were usually oval, and plain except

OBJECTS

46 Sauceboats c. 1740, c. 1720, c. 1750.

perhaps for a border of flat-chased ornament round the slightly everted shaped rim. About 1733, rather more decorative patterns began to emerge, some on four scroll supports instead of a central collet foot. Ornament, such as applied festoons, fluted or shell-shaped bodies and lion mask or other decorative knuckles above the feet and cast chased scroll handles, was used in more or less

47 Tureens LEFT 1771, RIGHT 1813.

profusion to accord with the new taste for the rococo. Even so, many sauceboats were still made with plain and practical simplicity, and decoration, if any, was chiefly confined to the handles, bases and feet. By the 1750s, three feet, a rim strengthened with a gadrooned wire, and flying or double scroll handles were usual, though the advent of the neoclassical a dozen years later saw a return to the single collet foot on an oval base. This coincided with a new form of sauce-serving vessel, the sauce tureen, a miniature version of the soup tureen with which it was often made *en suite*. By the late 1780s few sauceboats were made, though Henry Chawner, for instance, did make some plain and elegant examples on a high central foot. From 1790 to the 1820s, however, no sauceboats at all appear to be recorded; when they were reintroduced about 1823 they were generally in revived mid-18th century styles.

Saucepans Silver saucepans, sometimes called skillets when supported on three small feet, have been known since at least the 16th century, when apothecaries often advised against using any other metal. They were made in all sizes, their use for hot caudle and other invalid foods being attested to by the form of the covers. The latter could be inverted as an eating bowl, of dished form with a single ear, in the manner of the so-called bleeding-bowl type of porringer. In the 18th century, baluster-shaped saucepans with turned wooden handles rising from silver sockets were made in all sizes, from very small ones, often called brandy saucepans, to pint-size or larger. When larger they were usually also supplied with covers, presumably used for fruit and sauces, especially those with acid ingredients. A rare straight-sided saucepan and cover, obviously one of a larger set, approximates in size and style to the standard copper pans of the day, and is dated 1773.

Saucer dishes Small shallow dishes, sometimes with flat shell-like handles, were common in the second quarter of the 17th century. They were often rather flimsy pieces that somehow seem to have survived the depredations of the Civil Wars and Commonwealth period. Usually embossed with simple lobed and stylised fruit-and-pod motifs and scrolls, most are circular though occasionally oval versions with rising cast scroll handles at the centre of the sides are found. It has been surmised that these were in fact originally dishes for sauce, hence the name saucer. They range in size from about 4 in. to 8 in. in diameter.

Scissors *See* ETUIS, GRAPE SCISSORS.

Sconces (Fig. 62) Wall sconces with a flat shaped vertical plate behind the candle-holder or candle-branches for one or two lights were made from the Restoration period. Those of the 17th century were usually richly embossed and chased with foliage, putti and scrollwork, with reflector plates of oval or shaped oblong form. A few featured a candleholder within a semicircular drip tray. Early-18th-century sconces continued generally to be highly decorated, and were often of very elongated form. Many incorporated the owner's crest or supporters in the upper cresting. One or two very plain sconces are recorded in the 1740s, and there was some revival during the early 19th century, some in rococo style, others influenced by gothicism or by French designs, though wooden or gesso sconces were more usual, often mirror-backed for greater reflectivity. Argand or oil lamps were also fitted to wall plates in the later 18th century.

Seal boxes Boxes, originally almost always of silver, more recently of other materials, in which the impression of the Great Seal or of other important documentary seals was preserved.

Seal plates Cups or salvers made from the defaced silver Seal of State, the matrix of which was frequently presented as the perquisite of the holder of such offices as Chancellor of the Exchequer, Lord Chancellor of Ireland, or of England, Keeper of the Great Seal and Lord Justice of the Court of Common Pleas. The recipient often had the silver made into a commemorative cup or, more usually from about 1727 onwards, into a large salver, suitably chased or engraved with representations of the sovereign or with the faces of the original seal. Seals were defaced on the death

OBJECTS

of the sovereign, if constant use had worn them, or if there were changes in style, such as at the Union with Scotland in 1707 and the Union with Ireland in 1801.

Shaving sets The 17th-century fashion for large silver toilet services was not restricted to my lady. Men needed shaving jugs and basins, razors and soap boxes, boxes for powder and combs and other toilet articles; though few have survived intact as services, enough items are known to be able to build up a picture of the rich man's dressing-room. The largest pieces were the shaving water jug and bowl, used by his valet who held the notched side of the basin below his master's chin as he wielded the 'cut-throat' razor, itself often mounted in silver and kept, with one or two matching strops, in a silver-mounted leather case. Being essentially functional, shaving jugs and bowls were usually plain except for the owner's armorials. While the dish, usually oval, is distinguished by its deep well and wide neck notch, the shaving jug too is of characteristic oval section, pear-shaped on a moulded foot, with a low domed cover with baluster finial, a short spout and the handle insulated, usually with wickering, sturdy and about 8 to 9 in. high. Many dishes and ewers have parted company, while the associated soap boxes and other accessories are seldom found intact with them. The most complete man's toilet service must be that of 1788 (with unmarked jug and basin) by

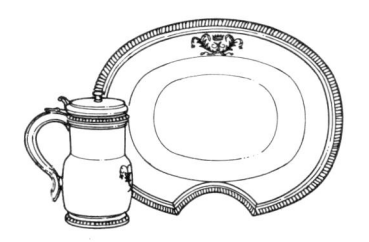

48 Shaving set *c.* 1720.

John Holloway with the crowned E cypher of Edward, fourth son of King George III; it is in a travelling case and includes boxes, silver-capped bottles, razors, strops, small objects such as toothbrush and shaving brush, and other small items as well as travelling ink and pounce pots. Such travelling sets in fitted wood cases became especially useful for young men taking the grand tour, as well as for officers on service overseas. Smaller sets comprised a cylindrical shaving pot, often with a screw-on handle that could be carried inside the pot, a spirit heater, a shaving brush in a cylindrical screw-in holder, a small soap-box, toothbrush and tooth-powder box, plus other small items such as comb, tweezers and tongue scraper. (*See also* RAZOR SETS, TONGUE SCRAPERS.)

The contents of men's dressing cases continued much the same until the early 20th century, those of the second quarter of the 19th century and later often being engine-turned and sometimes also gilded.

Shields The idea of creating enormous presentation pieces in the form of shields seems to have been conceived by John Flaxman for a commission for a tribute to the Duke of Wellington. Designed between 1809 and 1817, the Achilles Shield shows scenes from the *Iliad*, and both silver and bronze casts were eventually made, three being for George IV and his brothers the Dukes of York and Cambridge. The first is now in the Royal Collection, hallmarked 1821 by Philip Rundell. A number of other massive presentation shields were made during the following thirty or forty years, mostly as race prizes, though sometimes simply as tours de force of silversmithing skills, as the iron example of 1855 damascened with gold and silver made by Antoine Vechte, and others by John S. Hunt decorated with classical and historical scenes in high relief.

Sideboard dishes Silver for display rather than for use, a custom born in the great hall of medieval times, was exceedingly popular throughout the 16th century and continued into the late Victorian period. Huge flagons and standing cups, pairs of vases or ginger

49 Sideboard dishes FROM LEFT *c.* 1720, *c.* 1805.

jars, and great dishes and bowls, even rosewater dishes and ewers long after they ceased to be generally used at table, satisfied the love of show. Almost any large dish or bowl, especially one with a finely engraved armorials in the centre, overall engraved or chased ornament, or otherwise patently intended for display rather than use comes under the heading of sideboard dishes or chargers, in many instances their sheer weight precluding their use as serving dishes. Several large chased and pierced dishes of the 17th century are recorded, but many more are plain basins, as much as 19 in. in diameter. A charger by Pierre Harache, with a shaped gadrooned rim divided by vase-like devices, and superbly engraved in the centre with armorials in a baroque cartouche (probably to be accredited to Simon Gribelin), introduced a style of border that was repeated several times in later years by Nelme, Mettayer, Willaume and Lamerie.

After the rococo there was a lull in the production of such large dishes until the early 19th century. The taste was extended into Islam by William Beckford when he ordered a dish in Moorish style in 1814. Storr and later Rundell concentrated on the classical, while Edward Farrell mixed naturalism with classical in a series depicting battle scenes in the centre. It was a passion for elaboration later to be produced on large scale by Elkington's when they had perfected their electro-typing techniques, when everyone could afford a plated plaque of a Pompeian Lady or a scene from Shakespeare. Meanwhile, Robert Garrard and other London silversmiths concentrated on reproducing the great Régence-style dishes of the first years of the 18th century until 20th-century economy of space drove such grandiose pieces from the home.

Skewers Tapering silver skewers were made in all sizes from large examples big enough to skewer a suckling-pig to more conventional sizes from about 10 to 12 in. long. Skewers were probably used for vegetables as well as meat, oysters and other delicacies known as 'skuets'. Very small skewers were used for game and poultry. Ring ends are the most common, but shells and even family crests are known. Skewers are often found in sets, often in different sizes for different purposes. The earliest known date from the early 18th century. Few were made after about 1860.

Snuff boxes The taking of snuff, or powdered tobacco, was prevalent in all classes of society from the late 17th century until the advent of the cigarette in the mid-19th century. Boxes, at first derived from the tobacco box, proliferated, in every size, shape and material. Some contained a rasp for grating the rappee (snuff), some had compartments for different kinds of snuff. A few had room for a small elongated spoon for handing the snuff. The main prerequisite was that the box should have a closely fitting lid. Since snuff was taken both by men and women, boxes were of many kinds and it is not always easy to differentiate between those for snuff and those for counters, patches and cachous. Larger table snuff boxes are likewise not always distinguishable from caskets and spice boxes.

Snuffers and Douters Scissor-like implements used for trimming and extinguishing candles. Snuffers have a cutting edge for trimming the candle, and a box section at the end of the blade collects the snuffed wick. Douters, which are rarer than snuffers, have flat blades and extinguish the light but do not cut the wick.

Snuffer stands and trays Snuffer scissors were kept ready to hand either in an upright stand or on a shallow oblong or oval tray. The stands, in which the scissors were placed vertically, blade down, generally followed the style of contemporary candlesticks. They often included a conical extinguisher which could be hooked onto the stand. The matchbox-like container on late-17th-century snuffer stands was a suitable place for engraving the owner's arms or crest. Shallow trays were also made and generally superseded the stand style as the 18th century wore on. Since snuffer-scissor making was a specialist trade, few bear the same makers' marks as those of the trays. The need for snuffers and stands died out with the introduction of the paraffin wax candle with its self-consuming wick.

Snuff mulls Popular in Scotland, snuff mulls for storing snuff were often made of horn, hardstones, wood or bone mounted in silver or gold as well as of all-silver. Some were of table-size, and many were of fanciful shapes, especially in the 19th century. (*See* SNUFF BOXES.)

Snuff rasps Rather like coarse-ridged nutmeg graters of 'kitchen' type, for grating tobacco down into snuff.

Soap boxes Of spherical form on a moulded circular foot, to hold a ball of soap (washball), usually dating from about 1720 to 1735; occasionally found later, sometimes in toilet services and sometimes with a companion pierced box of similar shape for holding a sponge. Oblong, octagonal or circular boxes for the same purpose, with plain or pierced lids, were later included in fitted travelling toilet services.

Soup tureens (Figs 4, 47, 61) Large circular or oval covered bowls for serving soup appeared at the same time as the sauceboat, early in the 1720s. They were the product of a French fashion that turned the broth of the invalid and the poor into a culinary art. As a large and important object on the dining-table, the soup tureen was often made in the newest fashion. One of the earliest known, made by Lamerie in 1723, is in Régence style, with chased portrait medallions between trelliswork panels, which are overlaid with husks and shells. The sheer weight of large tureens necessitated sturdy collet supports or four massive cast scroll feet, and silversmiths veered between one and the other. During the rococo, the tureen as centrepiece reached a heydey, often supplied with an elaborate stand and incorporating all the massive themes of rococo art. About 1750 many silver tureens were in styles resembling those used in porcelain (or vice-versa) giving them a light appearance, with shallower bowls and covers slightly domed and applied with fruit, flower or vegetable finials. With neoclassicism, heavily chased vase shapes based on marble originals brought a new formality. That was soon abandoned by most silversmiths for good gauge, but rather dully plain, oval tureens with high reeded loop handles, an oval collet foot, and a simple foliate ring handle to the cover, or sometimes a handle developed from the owner's crest. These plainer soup tureens were often made *en suite* with those for sauce (*q.v.*). The grander styles of the Regency brought first a taste for sphinxes, heavy foliage and so on. Plainer examples usually out-numbered the more expensively chased tureens, and half-fluted bodies, oval or oblong, became fairly common; revived rococo and even tureens based on the Warwick vase added a grand distinction to many early-19th-century dinner services.

Soy frames *See* CRUETS.

Spice boxes Shell-shaped and other small boxes of Tudor and 17th-century date may well have been used for spice, though equally possibly for sugar. In the 1720s, small caskets certainly used for spice were made with two compartments and often with a small nutmeg grater included in the centre. Later examples of sarcophagus form are also known. (*See* SUGAR BOXES.)

Sponge boxes *See* SOAP BOXES.

Spoon trays Shallow fluted oval dishes or oblong trays dating chiefly from about 1700 to 1760, to take teaspoons after use, the teacup not at that time usually being supplied with a saucer. The tops of some sugar bowls had covers that could be inverted for the same purpose. (*See* SUGAR BOWLS.)

Spoons The most important piece of personal silver in medieval and later times, spoons made before about 1630 invariably have fig-shaped bowls, the tapering hexagonal stem terminating in a cast, often gilded device. The earliest known terminals include the diamond point, acorn knops, wrythen knops and various seal-like devices which by the early 16th century gave way to the baluster seal-top, the top not really a seal but a flat disc on which the owner's initials were usually engraved or pricked. A favourite late-medieval terminal was the Apostle, made singly or in sets and often given at Christenings. Other saints were represented as well as the Maidenhead, the head and shoulders of a young woman usually with flowing hair, probably intended for the Virgin. A few animal heads are known, the most charming being the Lion Sejant, and a few buds or flower heads. Plain stemmed spoons with sliced-off ends were known as slip-top. This probably inspired the so-called Puritan spoons introduced about 1630 with flattened stems and oval bowls, the tops cut straight across or with small notches cut into them. During the middle years of the 17th century these gradually developed into the trefids with cloven terminals. At the same time the small triangular pip at the junction of stem and bowl was elongated into the rat-tail, which remained a feature of the back of bowl, plain or decorated (the latter usually termed laceback) until well into the 18th century. By then the terminal trefid had become rounded into the dognose and then into a plain curve with upturned end, known as Hanoverian. By about 1700 spoons began to be made in various sizes: the standard table size, slightly smaller for dessert, and of teaspoon size. Earlier small spoons have usually been considered to be children's spoons or used for sweetmeats or suckets, sometimes then supplied with a forked end.

OBJECTS

From about 1720 to 1760 the Hanoverian pattern predominated, though by the 1740s the rat-tail diminished into a double-drop, and finally about 1760 into a single drop when the pattern was largely superseded by Old English, with the rounded end downturned. Variants of Old English included the filed edge known as feather-edge, a form of fluted border which coincided with the revival of gadrooned rims on plates and dishes. A pattern used chiefly on serving spoons and ladles made from about 1760 onwards is Onslow (named for Sir Arthur Onslow, six times Speaker of the House of Commons), which has a curled scroll or

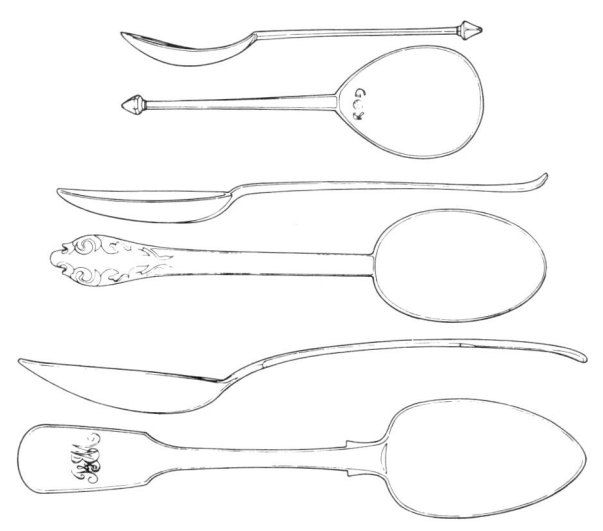

50 Spoons TOP PAIR diamond point, *c.* 1500; MIDDLE PAIR trefid, *c.* 1680; BOTTOM PAIR fiddle, *c.* 1820.

voluted finial. Old English remained the basic pattern until the last few years of the 18th century, often plain, sometimes with beaded or thread-edge borders, occasionally with a shell terminal or a combination of shell terminal with a thread edge. More decorative patterns came into fashion towards the very end of the century, the first being a 'shaped stem known as Hourglass, followed by the far grander variants of what was originally known as French Fiddle, a design with a notched section above the bowl and a waisted stem with broad top, rather like a fiddle. Plain Fiddle, Fiddle and Thread, Fiddle Thread and Shell were made in huge quantities, along with more elaborate variations such as Kings, Queens, Princes and Coburg, the shells, anthemion, scrolls and thread edges squeezed onto a blank by striking the pattern on either side of the stem and onto the back of the bowl.

By the early 1800s flatware and cutlery – knives, forks and spoons – in table and dessert sizes, the latter often gilded, along with teaspoons, serving spoons and ladles and other 'canteen extras' such as grape scissors, began to be made in complete sets. This eventually gave rise to the use of the word canteen for a case of these. During the period from about 1830 patterns proliferated, some becoming well-established, others short-lived, so that by the 1950s there were about 140 different flatware patterns in production, a number however that fast dwindled with the onset of stainless-steel flatware and a depression in the silver and plated trades. Most patterns were in effect variations either of Old English or of Fiddle. An interesting detail about the making of flatware is that before 1781, spoons were always bottom-marked, that is, near the bowl. Since the marks were struck before the final finishing and polishing of the piece, they often appear squashed. From 1781 the marks appear on the upper back of the back of the stem, and struck in a line from a single multiple punch adjacent to the maker's or sponsor's mark. (*See also* APOSTLE SPOONS, EGG SPOONS, FORKS, LADLES, TEASPOONS.)

Spout cups Small cups with a handle, rather like a mug, but with a curved spout set at right angles or opposite to the handle, used for feeding invalids or children. Made from the mid-17th century onwards, most have covers, for use with warmed semi-liquid foods, and resemble miniature tankards, though fixed lids are in fact rare.

Standing salts (Fig. 1) The pre-eminent part played by salt in medieval ceremony required suitably embellished cellars to place before the host and his chief guests. By quite early in the Middle Ages standing salts, more accurately, small cellars set in great pieces of silver, were exercising the skill of silversmiths. Few have survived from before the late 15th to the early 16th century, the earliest being the famous Huntsman or Giant Salt at All Souls' College, Oxford, and a small group of hexagonal salts. The Renaissance introduced the architectural style of salt. This often incorporated rock crystal or other precious materials, the small well for the salt placed within a pedimented stand, or in the top of a drum-shaped or rectangular column. By the end of the 16th century the rather smaller bell salt was introduced, unscrewing into three parts with the uppermost often providing a small caster. A few vase-shaped and even steeple-covered salts continued to be made, but by the 1630s were out of favour, replaced by the last style of great salt, the capstan or spool shape, often with bracket arms above believed to have supported a dish-like cover or a napkin, though one of a set of waisted salts made for the Coronation Banquet of Charles II has a domed cover surmounted by a figure of St George. The ceremonial salt was virtually a thing of the past, however, though one or two more were made in the 1670s and 1680, and a few later rarities also survive: a centrepiece of triangular form with pyramid corners made for the Upholders' Company in 1697 and the salt of 1730 with bellied bowl and scroll brackets above in the London Corporation plate.

Standishes Old name for inkstands (*q.v.*).

Stirrup cups Properly the drink offered on parting, it has been transferred to the cup used at hunt meetings, and often given as a prize for horse matches, greyhound races and so on. Nearly all the earliest recorded 18th-century stirrup cups took the form of fox heads, a few actually made of fox skulls mounted in silver. A prolific maker was Thomas Pitts who made large numbers between 1769 and 1775, though each maker tended to use his own distinctive models. Smaller versions, especially from about 1800, were sometimes made as snuff boxes. Nineteenth-century cups were often intended for coursing meetings and heads of hares, wolfhounds, setters, bulldogs and whippets were also made, as well as boars, deer, stags and horses.

Strainer spoons Spoons with pierced bowls about the size of tea spoons, but with long tapered handles usually ending in a diamond-point, used for freeing leaves from the teapot spout and probably also for removing leaves from the tea after pouring, since tea-strainers were not used until the early 19th century. Curiously called by the wholly modern name 'mote-spoon' but more properly termed strainer spoons, these chiefly date from the first half of the 18th century. The bowls were often dot pierced, but many were more elaborately cut into scroll or diaper designs; a few are related to mid-century teaspoons with attractive 'picture-backs'.

Strawberry dishes A form of dessert dish of plain shallow bowl form, the sides fluted and scalloped in a variety of patterns. (*See* DESSERT DISHES AND STANDS.) In Ireland very small fluted dishes are recorded as being counter dishes for cards and other games.

Sugar bowls Small circular bowls on a moulded central foot, with or without covers, are usually designated sugar bowls and first appeared about 1690. Some relatively large examples should not be confused with the covered bowls included in toilet services, while others were perhaps used as slop bowls. Many sugar bowls have covers with a rim foot so that it can be inverted and used as a spoon tray, saucers for teacups not being usual at the time. About 1740 rather taller bowls were made, while others are associated with tea-caddy sets, though more properly the bowl included in these, often of glass, was a blending bowl for the tea. In Scotland large bowls with everted rims, often engraved, were included in tea services. As tea services became more usual in the second half of the century, sugar-bowl patterns conformed to those of teapot and hot-water jug, but there were also many other small bowls, designated sugar or sweetmeat bowls, often with swing handles and sometimes with pierced sides necessitating glass liners, often attractively made of blue or ruby glass. The fashion for covered sugar bowls was revived for early-19th-century tea services, and were often of quite massive proportions. Large sugar vases and covers were also made for use at the dinner table. (*See also* SUGAR BOXES, SWEETMEAT BASKETS.)

Sugar boxes Indistinguishable in early times from spice boxes or sweetmeat boxes, the earliest were shell-shaped caskets, with vertical sides conforming in outline to the scallop-shell shape of the cover, apparently actually cast from a natural shell (one rare example has an actual scallop-shell cover). Small hoof spoons exactly fit into these boxes and were probably serving spoons. Shell boxes date from about 1598 to 1627. A variant was an oblong or oval casket – the earliest known is of late-16th-century date – sometimes with a central division. These, with simple latch fastenings, continued to be made even during the Commonwealth period. Lobed boxes decorated with repoussé chasing and often with cut-card ornament round a coiled snake ring handle were made during the 1670s and 1680s, and may have been what Pepys called a 'drageoir'.

Sugar crushers Sturdy silver devices with a circular disc end and plain stem terminating in a ring handle were used presumably to crush more finely sugar that had been coarsely cut from the sugar loaf. Most date from the late 18th to early 19th century.

Sugar nippers and tongs By the second quarter of the 18th century taking sugar with tea was firmly established. Early tongs appear to have been copied from the steel nippers used to cut up the sugar loaf in the kitchen; the type shown in tea-table paintings with slender arms pivoted at the top have occasionally survived despite their inherent weaknesses. About 1720 the scissor-type with looped bows, scroll shanks and shell grips ousted the 'fire-tong' style. Most date from about 1740 to 1760, and were usually quite small, about 4 in. long, with a box-like section over the joint on which the owner's initials or crest were often engraved. Few were fully marked, the maker's mark and Lion Passant usually appearing within the bow. By the 1760s the national passion for tea taking brought the less easily damaged U-shaped tong of springy silver. Early examples of the mid-1760s were often cast and pierced; by 1780 plain or shaped blades with spoon-like scoops became commonplace, the sides often bright-cut engraved, or occasionally with a stamped shell motif or a thread, beaded or feather-edge in the manner of contemporary flatware. After 1790 most tongs were fully marked, though often the Leopard's Head was omitted from London tongs. The large sugar bowls of the 19th-century tea service introduced ever larger tongs, many measuring as much as $5\frac{3}{4}$ in. long and weighing over an ounce. From about 1815 they were often in the standard patterns of the flatware and cutlery service. Novelty patterns were also made.

Sugar sifters Ladles in various patterns, usually of early- to late-19th-century date, the bowl pierced for use with crushed sugar.

Supper services A late-19th-century term for a service of covered dishes, often arranged on a special stand, complete with tureen, salts, cruet and sometimes a heater stand. The term breakfast service could perhaps equally be applied.

Sweetmeat baskets Small oval or circular baskets, usually with a swing handle, hung from épergnes or free-standing and made mostly in imitation of cake and fruit baskets. Individual examples were especially popular in the last quarter of the 18th century and later. It is not always possible to determine whether a basket was originally part of an épergne except when it has a rim foot rather than a spreading foot or individual supports. From the 1830s a few small baskets incorporating stamped plaques as used for snuff boxes and vinaigrettes were made in Birmingham by Nathaniel Mills. (*See also* DESSERT DISHES AND STANDS, EPERGNES.)

Syllabub pots References in late-17th-century inventories mention such pots for sillabub (a drink or dessert made of cream curdled with wine and flavoured with lemon, orange, spices to taste). Probably of 'porringer' form with or without handles, the actual form can only be guessed at.

Tankards (Fig. 2) The term today for a lidded drinking vessel, it was originally applied to large flagons, the smaller drinking pot often being called a livery pot. The earliest known are of bellied shape on a spreading circular foot; five examples dating between 1548 and 1578 are known. By then straight-sided tapering pots were becoming more usual, made in all sizes and styles, with high-domed covers topped with elaborate baluster or figure finials. Box hinges and cast thumbpieces were often used above the bold scroll handles. Though some were decorated with engraving, heavy embossed chasing of fruit, swags and strapwork, often on matted groundwork, was popular.

Plainer styles, often without a foot and with a flat cover, began to be made about 1619; these gradually changed to the familiar pattern on a skirt foot with a low-domed or bun-like cover, the barrel sometimes matted, that were used equally for tankards and flagons between about 1630 and 1660. A few small lidded mugs of bulbous outline have survived from the 1640s.

By about 1655 the large skirt foot gradually began to shrink, until by 1660 it was reduced to a moulded rim foot. This style continued unabated until about 1690, with the exception of 'Scandinavian'-style tankards on cast pomegranate, ball, lion couchant or eagle supports, the motif often matched by a similarly modelled thumbpiece. Being a vessel almost wholly alien to the French immigrant craftsmen, tankards generally remained in the traditional English styles until the end of the century; gadrooned details on foot and cover became usual, according with the style of furniture and other silver such as salvers. A few Huguenot tankards of the early 18th century show a change of design, the sides now tapering and with a tuck-in base. The lids became domed, often with a baluster finial. This style that immediately became fashionable in Scotland, whereas other provincial centres tended to continue to make the straight-sided type with low domed cap cover and corkscrew or scroll thumbpiece.

The advent of glass tended to restrict output of tankards; though plain uncovered versions – mugs – continued to be made in sizes large and small, the old-style covered tankard became rarer. The baluster form with high domed cover gave way about 1790 to a revival of the straight-sided type, usually with bands of reeding near the top and base, and with a flat cover, or with a moulded rib round the tapering body and a domed cover. A few unusual examples in the second decade of the 19th century followed German styles, with barrels chased in relief with processions and classical scenes, often massive in gauge and size and more akin to presentation flagons. They were often, in fact, given as race prizes.

Taper stands *See* WAX JACKS.

Tapersticks Small candlesticks, sometimes known as desk candlesticks, much shorter than the usual table 'stick, are known from about 1660. They perhaps served the purpose of the later taperstick, made for the smaller tapers used for sealing. By the end of the century, these smaller tapersticks were being made, occasionally in singles or pairs to match the larger candlesticks and in similar designs. Throughout the 18th century, tapersticks followed exactly the same patterns as the larger table candlesticks, often being included as the central feature of the inkstand or standish. A fanciful design for tapersticks in the form of harlequin carrying a taper-holder on a scalloped dish above his head was made by the specialist candlestick-maker John Cafe, the earliest apparently dating from 1749. Most date from before about 1765, though reproductions were made during the early 19th century, when a number of other novelty designs were made: Gothic towers, tripod stands, Chinese figures and a variety of naturalistic or fanciful flower patterns. In addition to the taperstick with its small sconce, desk candlesticks of between $4\frac{1}{2}$ and $5\frac{1}{2}$ in. high, but with normal size candle-sconces, are known though care must be taken to check that they have not been cut down from larger broken candlesticks. (*See also* INKSTANDS, WAX JACKS.)

Tazze Shallow-bowled wine cups on stems. The name Tazza is often mistakenly applied to footed bowls and even salvers on feet.

Tea and coffee machines An elaboration of the hot-water urn, large tea and coffee machines were introduced by the Sheffield platers about 1790 as the 'Tea Equipage Compleat' and were undoubtedly the largest items ever made in fused plate. Measuring as much as 24 in. high and about 20 in. wide, they consisted of a platform on which three urns were placed, a large one in the centre, often circular or of beehive shape, between a smaller pair. In some the large urn, with a capacity of 6 quarts, was intended for tea, with the pair for coffee holding 2 quarts apiece. More often, however, the larger urn was to supply hot water to the smaller pair. A large slop bowl was often added in front. Very few machines are marked, but some can be attributed to certain firms on style and from outside documentation. More elaborate patterns were made during the early 19th century, with fluting and melon shapes predominating. With the invention of electroplating in 1840, even more variety could be achieved; one firm in Sheffield, Padley Parkin & Co., invented a new form of coffee percolator which they decorated with the Willow pattern used on contemporary china by Spode or with more formal geometrical designs. The principle of the machine, developed by a Scots engineer called Napier in 1843 was the automatic siphoning of the water over the coffee once the liquid had boiled. Not all such Victorian gadgets made good coffee, as Brunel complained of a locomotive coffee-maker installed at Swindon. Another Victorian gadget was the self-pouring teapot, invented by J. J. Royle

OBJECTS

of Manchester about 1886 and made in electro-plated Britannia metal and also in pottery. The tea is poured out by pumping the lid up and down so that it pours, like a Parish pump, into the cup without having to lift the heavy pot. (*See also* BIGGINS, TEA AND COFFEE URNS.)

Tea and coffee urns (Fig. 5) A development of the wine fountain, large urns for hot water began to appear in English silver about 1750; the earliest known, of 1749, is said to be a chocolate urn, a rococo vase-shaped urn with a swing handle and three spigots set on a plated stand. Another highly rococo urn of 1752, also with three dolphin spigots, and a third of 1760 are both, however, called tea urns. This term was almost indiscriminately applied to any urn with a heater base or any other method, such as a heated bar of iron within an aperture within the urn, whether in fact used for tea, coffee or simply as an alternative to the kettle. By the 1760s, the urn was fast overtaking the kettle at the tea-table and, more particularly, at the breakfast table of large households and in tearooms and taverns. Those of the 1760s were of vase shape, often richly chased with chinoiseries. They were much like kettles, but with taps instead of spouts. The general shape was retained in one of the first neoclassical examples known, dated 1768, though the bombé shape gave way to the vase shape, with fluted body and applied with festoons. Others took the form of true classical urns, with rising short handles, though more easily grasped high loop handles soon began to replace them. By 1790 tea and coffee urns (the latter usually thought to be the smaller variety) were plain vase-shaped urns on square pedestal supports, decoration usually limited to a band of fluting round the base and perhaps anthemion and paw feet. By the end of the century rather squatter shapes began to be made, in many instances matching teapots. About 1815 there was some return to the kettle. Gradually it again replaced the urn, so that by early Victorian times the urn had been relegated to the storeroom.

Tea caddies (Figs 51, 56, 58) The container for keeping tea at the

OBJECTS

51 Tea caddies FROM LEFT c. 1705, c. 1740, c. 1795, c. 1775.

tea-table is known by various somewhat confusing names. No one is sure what tea caddies were called before about 1710 when 'canister' came to be applied to the silver containers. Previously 'canister' had been used as a measure 'of Tea, 75 lbs. to 1 cwt. in weight'. Similarly 'caddy', first used in the 1780s, was also originally a unit of weight, derived from the Malay *kati*, about $1\frac{1}{3}$ lbs. The wide variety of different teas imported into England, chiefly from China (cultivation not being introduced in India until the 1820s), meant that hostesses would blend to their own taste at the tea-table, using tea from more than one canister and probably using a small bowl in which to mix it. Occasionally caddies are found with 'B' and 'G' for Black and Green, or even with tea names such as 'Bohea' actually engraved on the silver. The first caddies were small and usually plain, with bottle-like necks and domed covers which could be used as measures. About 1715 baluster-shaped caddies were introduced, along with the straight-sided octagonal; a few soon had stepped covers instead of bottle tops. Slide-in bases made for easier filling, and slide-in, drop-in and hinged covers soon followed.

The provision of 'small chests and trunks' to contain two or three caddies coincided with the rococo period. Tea caddies more than any other silver except baskets seem to have been endowed with rococo ornament in profusion. Most caddies were of rectangular form in the period from 1735 to 1740, followed by the bombé or double-curved shape, often decorated with chinoiserie motifs in relief. Chinoiserie inspiration also appeared in the square tea-chest caddies popular in the years between the high rococo and neoclassicism when staved linear ornament and pseudo-Chinese characters typified many fine caddies.

The vase shape that had its beginnings in the rococo was turned into the classical urn during the late 1760s to 1770s, though in many ways the caddy-makers compromised over classicism, not always favouring the rather severe lines of the vase. A few made pierced caddies with blue glass liners, or silver-mounted glass caddies, among them a few rarities chased with theatrical scenes. They even forestalled the later 'oval' period with drum-shaped and oval caddies finely decorated with engraving, though a touch of fantasy was often retained in tea-plant or Chinamen finials. Vase-like sets of caddies have recently been reattributed as condiment vases, though many appear to have been perfectly suitable for tea and sugar which were sometimes called condiments.

By the 1790s two-division caddies tended to be made, removing the need for an outer locked case, since the caddy itself could have lock and key. By about 1800 it was often little more than a sturdy silver box, made *en suite* with the sugar bowl of the tea service. But tea-making was less of a great ceremony by then and, though a few caddies were specially commissioned, the age of the caddy was over. By 1849 when the first great Clipper Race was sailed, caddies were almost forgotten. The era of afternoon tea brought into the drawing-room had come to stay.

Tea-kettles The bodies of tea-kettles of the reign of Queen Anne are often very close in style to those of tea-pots, the only distinction being a fixed or swing handle with a wooden, ivory, wickered or leather-covered grip. By the George I period a plain pyriform body of rather compressed shape was usual. Faceted shapes were not uncommon. During the 1720s, a plain spherical

52 Tea-kettles FROM LEFT 1715, 1730, 1827.

shape came into fashion, followed by the inverted pear shape that retained its popularity throughout the rococo period. The stands for the lamp were usually tripod, with scroll feet and with pierced galleries around them concealing the lamp. Pegs were sometimes attached to the kettle by chains and were slipped into sockets in the stand to secure the two parts when moving them. Tea-kettles were largely replaced by urns about 1760, though there was a revival of the kettle form, usually with a horizontal spigot and tap instead of a spout, about 1800. The kettle was sometimes included in late George III tea services, and during the 1820s there was a tendency to revive the decorative rococo forms, especially the melon-shaped kettle. (*See* TEA AND COFFEE URNS.)

Tea-kettle stands Waiters, sometimes circular, more usually triangular on which the tea kettle was placed. The style followed that of waiters in general, the decoration matching the kettle. Most such stands date between about 1725 and 1750. An exceptional kettle stand, with matching kettle, was made in 1724 in the form of a tray mounted on a heavy baluster tripod, $25\frac{1}{2}$ in. high.

OBJECTS

Teapots The introduction of tea to England in the 1660s, as of coffee, set the silversmiths a design problem. At first, tea was drunk as a novelty, often medicinally, so pots were made very small and, having no precedent, were copied from Chinese wine-pots (after one unrepeated design of coffee-pot form, only recognisable as such because of the inscription, made in 1670 and now in the Victoria and Albert Museum). The wine-pot form was basically oviform with a handle opposite a slender curved spout. Significantly, three known examples of about 1675 to 1690 are not hallmarked, but bear the maker's mark only, suggesting special commissions. By the beginning of the 18th century, in keeping with the baluster style introduced by the Huguenot craftsmen, the English teapot established itself in a squat pear-shaped form with a curved spout, often with a hinged cover, set near the base of the body. It had a 'D'-shaped or scroll wooden handle set in silver sockets opposite, though occasionally at right angles to the spout, and a domed cover with wooden finial. Decoration was the exception, though some pots featured applied strapwork usually round the finial. A variation is a pot of square outline by Anthony Nelme, 1708, at a time when the octagonal pear shape was being introduced. Pots remained very small, no more than about 5 in. high, and were originally mostly fitted with a tripod lampstand; many of these have now disappeared, though occasionally 'happy marriages' of a pot and a stand have been achieved.

By about 1715, an entirely new design came into fashion: the bullet shape, a spherical or octagonal shape tapering slightly down to the narrower rim foot and with a straight tapering spout and flush cover, sometimes with drop-in lid, otherwise with a hinge, protruding above or concealed.

The pear-shaped pot, now often with a straight tapering spout like those used on bullet pots, continued to be made until about 1723. By then, a narrow band of engraving often added a decorative touch to the shoulder of the bullet pot. Lampstands were

OBJECTS

53 Tea-pots TOP 1726, 1785, BOTTOM 1739.

now a thing of the past, the foot changing to a narrow slightly spreading pattern. Teapots remained small. Larger examples and those with a straight rim foot or with rather broad tapering straight spouts are often suspect as having been converted from tea kettles. During the 1730s the spout generally became curved, often faceted and sometimes with a scroll moulding, echoed by similar mouldings at the handle sockets. Flat-chased ornament round the shoulders gradually became more elaborate, with rococo scrolls, shells and scalework. About 1735 a few pots were made with fluted bodies, but basically the bullet shape remained until about 1745, when the inverted pear-shape began slowly to supersede it. In Scotland the globular pot, on a high foot, remained in fashion until about 1760. The inverted pear shape was a fine vehicle for rococo-chased ornament, which often covered the shoulders and spread down the body, but many pots were relatively plain. By 1760 spouts and finials almost inevitably reflected rococo taste.

Then, in 1770, a complete change of style introduced the plain drum and the straight-sided oval. Decoration was restricted, mostly to a narrow border of bright-cut engraving, though one attractive variant was overall engraving resembling damask. In the 1780s the Swedish silversmith Andrew Fogelburg, in partnership with Stephen Gilbert, was responsible for several very unusual teapots cradled in quadrangular stands, and variants of the style chased in high relief with Vitruvian scrolls in high neoclassical manner. More usual taste, however, was for shaped ovals with fluted angles, the panels decorated with bright-cut festoons, ribbon-tied ovals and neat foliage borders, the pot accompanied by a matching waiter or stand on four panel supports. By now most tea-table silver was made *en suite* (*see* TEA SERVICES) though a few teapots, especially the small so-called bachelor pots, were made and sold as individual pieces.

By 1790, somewhat larger teapots accorded with the nationwide passion of tea-drinking, still usually flat-based and with slightly incurving oval sides, a domed cover, and by the turn of the century, often with a flange of spreading form around it. The fashion for heavier styles replaced the straight-sided oval and beaded borders with bold compressed shapes and gadrooned rims. A rim foot, panel supports or ball feet raised the base of the pot, while borders of bright-cut work became broader or were replaced by stamped or chased borders of basket-work, anthemion scrolls or Greek key pattern. Half-fluting was popular for the compressed oval and oblong teapots of the second decade of the century, but there were also many retrospective glances at earlier styles – the globular on a high foot, the inverted pear shape, even a hexagonal panelled pot with chinoiseries in high relief after an original of 1682. Several silver pots imitated porcelain styles or exemplified the fashion for naturalism by shaping the pot as a gourd on a leafy base, with leaf pattern spout and cover. By the 1830s, the melon shape was perhaps the most popular, a popularity that survived for over a century. Victorian ingenuity brought style after style to the tea-table – Gothic and

Moorish, highly decorative or ascetically simple, the aesthetic and the art nouveau – in almost bewildering variety.

Tea services (Fig. 8) Although tea rapidly became the beverage of high fashion, matched services are extremely rare until the last quarter of the 18th century. Assembled earlier services occasionally appear on the market, but fewer than a dozen sets of like date and maker are recorded before 1770. It is extremely difficult to state exactly what a complete service comprised: teapot, of course, but other components were a question of taste. Milk, either hot, for which a covered jug was required, or cold were not always drunk with tea. Sugar was sometimes taken, and for this a covered sugar bowl was used. Teaspoons would also be needed, for which a spoon tray, usually of oblong form, was supplied, or the sugar bowl cover inverted and used as a stand. There was a tea-kettle and spirit lamp, a caddy or possibly a pair for blending the tea at table, occasionally a matching coffee pot, with small waiters or stands for the pots, and a tea-table or tea board, as it was known (in modern terms a tea tray), that fitted neatly on to the wooden tea-table. It is a curious fact that in Scotland services of teapot, cream boat and open sugar bowl, perhaps accompanied by waiters, spoon tray and kettle were less uncommon in the 1730s and 1740s than in England. One of the most notable early neoclassical services is a seven-piece set by Orlando Jackson and James Young, 1774, that once belonged to David Garrick and his wife and is now in the Victoria and Albert Museum: its design in the vertically ribbed manner of early Wedgwood basalt wares; it replaced the kettle with the then much more fashionable urn, and includes a pair of basins (perhaps one intended for slops instead of sugar), a hot-water jug, and both an open and a covered milk jug, suggesting that the early-18th-century taste for hot milk with tea survived for more than half a century. The 1790s saw the birth of the fashion for complete tea services that was to dominate tea-table design for more than a hundred and forty years, the standard wedding present until recent times. Many services were exceptionally large, with the addition of a coffee pot, a large tray, and often an urn as well; from about 1820 onwards the kettle began to be reinstated. However, the great majority of 19th-century tea services were four-piece, with teapot, sugar bowl, cream or milk jug, and hot-water jug, often with a long spout so that it could also be used as a coffee pot. By far the most popular design was based on the compressed melon shape, which varied from plain to lavishly enriched with flowers and foliage. Small services, usually of three pieces only, were made for early morning tea or individual use, but the usual 19th-century tea silver was capacious, with pots holding at least two pints and milk jugs and sugar bowls comparatively capacious. It was not until the interwar years that smaller services came into fashion when even reproduction styles such as the half-fluted and the oblong gadroon were scaled down to suit smaller houses and smaller families.

Teapot stands The flat-bottomed teapot, whether the early type of about 1705 to 1725 with a rim foot, or the subsequent drum type of the 1770s and later, required a small waiter to keep the hot base off the table top. Many small waiters were used for the purpose, early ones often square or circular. The late-18th-century pots were often made with oval or shaped stands to match, the stands usually supported on four panel feet. The fashion continued well into the 19th century, both for tea and coffee pots. It is likely that many early salvers of dished form were in fact tea and coffee-pot stands.

Teaspoons Small versions of the late-17th-century trefid spoon are generally agreed to have been made for tea and coffee, and until modern times differentiation in size between those for the two drinks was seldom made. Teaspoon design generally followed that of other flatware, though the smaller spoons were often more decorative. The trefid styles were often gilded and engraved overall with attractive scrolling foliage – plain small trefids are sometimes considered to be children's spoons. The trefid was followed by the dognose, the rat-tail with Hanoverian rounded terminal, the Hanoverian with a double and then a single drop, then about 1760 by Old English with upturned instead of downturned end. In the Regency period came the multitude of flatware patterns such as Kings, Queens, Coburg, Hourglass and hundreds more, many of which have survived to this day. The single-drop Hanoverian from about 1740 is often found in teaspoon size decorated with stamped ornamental designs on the back of the bowl. These so-called fancy backs were chiefly applied to teaspoons; at the height of the rococo period from about 1745 to 1770 fancy patterns of bowl (acorn, melon, shell) and highly decorated stems – intertwining foliage was a particular favourite – made the teaspoon perhaps the most feminine of all silverwares. Many of these spoons, usually made by specialist spoonmakers, are not fully marked, being either too spindly for marking or lightweight; those that are marked, usually with only the maker's mark, the Lion Passant and the date letter, have the mark obscured because they were bottom-marked until 1780 and the stem was only finished after the spoon was returned from the assay office.

Tea strainers A modern development of the orange and lemon strainer with much finer pierced bowl. (*See also* STRAINER SPOONS.)

Tea-tables The 18th-century name, also referred to as 'tea bord' for a large oblong salver or tray that fitted the top of the table at which tea was served. The earliest date from the early 18th century. Most are oblong; but, one 21-inch-long example of 1703 is octagonal and a 1726 $16\frac{3}{4}$-inch example is a shaped oblong. About 1771 the oblong was entirely superseded by the oval. Two tea-tables on silver-sheathed frames are recorded, and one other tripod table of about 1715 fitted with a later octagonal salver is known. Some silver salvers have been found in association with mahogany tripod tables. That large salvers, oblong, oval or of other shapes, were used on special tables is in little doubt, especially as until the early 1780s handles were rarely fitted: the earliest with handles appear to date from 1775. Tea-tables followed the style of the more important salvers and waiters, plain or ornamented according to current taste. They were often the work of specialist salver-makers such as John Tuite, Robert Abercromby, Richard Rugg and Hannam and Crouch, though the very finest were commissioned from craftsmen such as Simon Pantin, Robert Cooper, Paul de Lamerie, John Le Sage and Edward Wakelin. (*See* SALVERS AND WAITERS; TEA-KETTLE STANDS; TEA TRAYS.)

Tea trays The term usually applied to salvers with end handles, which came into fashion about 1780, superseding the oblong tea-table. Most late-18th-century examples, often by specialist makers, are oval, with deep bright-cut borders. With the Regency there was a return to the oblong, although considerably heavier and more elaborately decorated than previously. Massive cast, chased and pierced borders, with intertwining snake handles brought weights of 22-in. or 26-in. trays up to as much as 200 or 300 ounces. Many were by then made *en suite* with tea services. (*See* TEA-TABLES.)

Tea vases Generally nowadays used for vase-shaped tea caddies of the later 18th century, but in contemporary references used for tea urns.

Thimbles *See* ETUIS.

Toasting forks Silver toasting forks were known as early as the Tudor times, but it was not until the later 18th century that the fashion for toasting bread and cakes became really established. Most were about a foot long, with three or more prongs and a tapering socket into which was fixed a turned-wood handle. A few early-19th-century examples were telescopic.

Toast racks First appearing about 1775, they consisted of wire frames set on an oval base, with claw-and-ball or panel feet, the wires held by loops with bars under the base. About 1790 the fixed frame toast rack made its debut, oval or oblong, with five or seven wires with a central loop handle. More elaborate and heavier versions followed during the first few years of the 19th century, usually of rather large size with anthemion panel feet and often with shaped partitions.

Tobacco boxes Flat oval boxes with close-fitting slip-on lids dating mostly between about 1660 and 1720, though earlier examples are known, and later boxes of various shapes and sizes were certainly used for tobacco. Many have the owner's armorials engraved on the covers; others are plainer with perhaps an engraved name, initials, or the name of a landlord and his tavern on the base.

Toddy ladles Small ladles with hemispherical bowls and whalebone or silver handles chiefly made in Scotland or for the Scottish market from about 1790.

Toilet services Among the most important examples of silver made during the second half of the 17th century, surprisingly large numbers have survived, though many are nowadays broken up into their component parts of mirror, ewer and basin, covered bowls, candlesticks, snuffer stand, powder and ointment boxes, lotion and perfume flasks, pincushion, brushes, whisks and comb box. The standard wedding present from groom to bride, the custom of receiving morning visits in deshabille encouraged larger and larger services to include not only cosmetic aids, but also silver for chocolate or other drinks. From about 1660 to 1675 many toilet services were richly embossed and chased in baroque style, with as many as twenty or thirty components, usually made by more than one silversmith. Many are not fully hallmarked, suggesting special commissions. From about 1675, flat-chased chinoiseries were fashionable, though more formal styles with moulded borders or gadrooned decoration came in about 1690; some of the most charming feature applied cut-card ornament. One of the most famous of toilet services must be the Treby 26-piece service by Paul de Lamerie, 1728, decorated with applied strapwork, medallions and scrolls. Mid-18th-century services were much rarer, though a small series was made by Thomas

Heming for the daughters of George III. By the end of the century large fitted dressing cases were beginning a trend popular throughout the 19th century, designed for both men and women and complete with a great variety of boxes, flasks, mounted bottles and toilet implements. (*See also* PERFUME FLASKS, RAZOR SETS, SHAVING SETS, TONGUE SCRAPERS.)

Tongue scrapers Mostly of late 18th- early 19th-century date, few are fully marked, or even bear a maker's mark. They are long pieces of springy silver, sometimes hammered into a U-shape; the terminals are flattened into grips, often twisted above, otherwise mounted into turned bone or ivory handles. The type with spatulate grips have even been seen described as sugar tongs! Most survivors are associated with small toilet sets comprising toothbrush, tongue scraper, comb, toothpowder box and other such small items.

Tooth brushes Usually of small size, the bristles are mounted in wood and then inserted in a plain silver or silver-gilt head with a tapering handle, which is sometimes itself shafted into a bone or ivory one. Most date between about 1790 and 1830.

Tooth-powder boxes Long narrow boxes of small size with covers, usually hinged in the middle, and associated with pocket-size travelling toilet sets.

Tooth picks Pointed slivers of silver, occasionally shaped as miniature arrows. The earliest survivors are of late 17th-century date, found in travelling canteens. In the later 18th century some were incorporated in pen-knives.

Toys and miniatures The double meaning of 'toy' in the 18th century is perhaps confusing to the modern collector. A 'toyman' was one who dealt in all sorts of gifts and trifles, sometimes of gold or silver, or of ivory, tortoiseshell, mother-of-pearl and so on. Toys included small boxes, nutmeg graters, vinaigrettes, perfume flasks, pomanders, tobacco boxes and stoppers, toothpicks, seals, cane handles, snuff boxes and the dozens of other pocketwares and gewgaws given as tokens of affection or bought as souvenirs at the spas and resorts which became increasingly popular during the 18th century. That toymen also dealt with silver miniatures cannot be doubted – silver utensils and furniture for the dolls' houses that became immensely popular in the courts of Europe from about 1660 onwards.

It is said that those fitted with a lock and key were not, in fact, for the children, but were adult playthings, to while away a wet afternoon, though it may merely have been a precaution to keep thieving fingers of servants and others from the pretty silver and other precious contents. With few exceptions, these were made by specialist smallworkers. They were not usually greatly troubled about scale, though some tea services, complete with silver tea-tables, do more or less conform; invariably they were faithful to current styles of furniture, kitchen utensils, fire grates, candlesticks and domestic silverwares. Even unmarked silver toys can usually be dated on style – a toy porringer or monteith in chinoiserie style, for instance, is inevitably of about 1680 to 1690. By 1715 there were pear-shaped teapots and covered sugar bowls, and the rococo can be found in toys from about 1740. Many, especially earlier miniatures, are in fact fully marked, notably those of between about 1680 and 1720 by George Manjoy; David Clayton, one of the most prolific London toymakers, usually only struck his maker's mark and had the Lion standard mark put on by the assay office – a customary and cheaper style of marking for very small objects. Most toymakers in fact registered their marks as smallworkers, though some toys are found bearing marks of largeworkers, such as Nathaniel Lock, William Fleming (who seems to have made mostly porringers) and, perhaps most surprisingly, John Le Sage and on occasion Paul de Lamerie. Later in the 18th century, Samuel Meriton, Phipps and Robinson, John Reily and, in Birmingham in the early 19th century Joseph Willmore, all made miniature silver, also reflecting current taste in the helmet-shaped cream jugs, candlesticks and so on.

Travelling sets *See* CANTEENS.

Tumbler cups Small handleless straight-sided cups with rounded bases that return naturally to upright. This is due to the silver having been worked as usual towards the rim, but then, instead of the rim being thickened (the strengthening process known as caulking) the silver is worked back again to make it base-heavy. Tumbler cups were especially popular during the 17th century. Most are small, about 1¾ to 2 in. in diameter, the earliest surviving dating from the 1670s, very few post-dating about 1770; a small number of 19th-century date are known, usually larger in size. Tumblers made in East Anglia and northwards into Yorkshire often have slightly flatter bases and are shallower, while small upright examples are commoner in Chester and elsewhere. At Chester Races, a gold tumbler cup was the prize given by the Grosvenors for many years, and several of these large and fine tumblers have survived. Occasionally, double cups of tumbler form are found, the lips interlocking. Another rare type, by the Swedish-born Andrew Fogelburg, has a kick-in base.

Tumbler-cup frame A rare design of stand with ring frames on branches to hold footed glass or other cups, perhaps intended for stirrup cups at hunt meets.

Tuns A name for beakers used at Trinity Hall, Cambridge, and for ox-eye cups (*q.v.*) at Magdalen College, Oxford.

Vegetable dishes Basically entrée dishes, but chiefly in the 19th century sometimes with a fixed divider inside. They occasionally also have a heater stand, the latter usually plated.

Venison dishes Large dishes with channels converging on a well at one end to conserve the gravy. Made from the early 19th century, some have hot-water jackets in the base.

Verrières Large oval or circular bowls of monteith type occasionally found in the later 18th century and presumed to have been used for rinsing or cooling glasses.

Vinaigrettes Small boxes to hold a saturated aromatic sponge, which from about 1800 virtually ousted the earlier 'spunge-box' although the 'smelling-bottle' continued to be made at least until the end of the century. The name, first recorded in 1811, derives from the aromatic vinegar used, necessitating gilding inside the box. Though gold and gem-set vinaigrettes were made, it was the cheaper silver box that came to be sold in every spa and resort. It was the Birmingham smallworkers who dominated the market. Many of the early-19th-century vinaigrettes were tiny, no more than an inch long, with simple dot-pierced grilles and engraved tops. About 1830 bolder styles were in fashion, with engine-turning especially popular within stamped chased borders, closely followed by a whole succession of 'castle-tops' which ranged from country houses to cathedrals, ruined abbeys and favourite monuments, such as the one to Scott in Edinburgh. Besides the variety of patterns, the smallworkers achieved greatly varied interior grilles, mostly of flower-and-scroll design. Many were commemorative – in 1806 not a few showed Nelson's bust on the top and HMS *Victory* pierced out on the grille, a speciality of the Willmores in Birmingham. Others revealed the contemporary fashion for Scott and Byron, either as books with their names down the spine, or with representations of their houses at Abbotsford and Newstead respectively. Others recorded the 1851 Great Exhibition, more rarely the Dublin Exhibition of 1853. Some twenty different houses and other scenes are recorded on the huge range of Birmingham-made vinaigrettes. In London there was rather more emphasis on hand-craftsmanship, but the boxmakers must have been hard put to it to compete with Birmingham; from about 1860 they began to produce many novelty designs, often registering them at the Patent Office Design Registry. Among the foremost London makers of novelty vinaigrettes and perfume bottles were Sampson Mordan & Co., H. W. Dee and E. H. Stockwell. Sometimes their designs were bizarre – ships' lamps, champagne bottles, half-peeled walnuts, even bullets and barrels; others were more feminine, such as roses or pinks, or were incorporated in the glass or enamelled cylindrical perfume flasks known as 'ladies' companions'.

OBJECTS

Wager cups Rare in English silver, though widely imported during the late 19th to early 20th centuries from Germany and Holland, most are in the form of a woman wearing a long skirt and holding a small tumbler in gimbals above her head. The cups were used for wagers and for wedding toasts, the scheme being to drink the draught from the upturned skirt without spilling that from the upper cup. The few English examples include the Vintners' Cup of about 1680 and one or two copies made about 1827, with many more from the beginning of the present century.

Waiters *See* SALVERS AND WAITERS.

Warwick cruets *See* CRUETS. Named after the cruet of 1715 with five casters held in a shaped ring frame at Warwick Castle. Probably a later trade term.

Wax jacks A device with a central spindle round which a soft wax taper is coiled, the end being held in a clamp, so that it could be lit for sealing. Since many wax jacks were of less sturdy construction than tapersticks, they often became broken or were discarded as useless bygones when gummed envelopes came into use in the mid-19th century.

Wine cisterns Often the size of small baths and at times actually used for washing dishes and glasses at table, a cistern weighing anything from about 500 oz. to over 3,000 oz. was a feature of the great hall and dining saloon from at least the 16th century. The oldest surviving examples date from the last quarter of the 17th century. About a dozen of that period are known, and something over two dozen for the 18th century, by when the individual wine-bottle coolers, made in pairs or larger sets, generally replaced the cistern. During the early 18th century some were associated with matching wine fountains (*q.v.*).

Wine coasters (Fig. 60) Sometimes originally known as bottle slides, the name coaster is derived from the custom of passing the bottle or decanter of port or brandy round the table after dinner, the baize-based stand preventing the table top, from which the cloth was customarily removed, from being badly scratched.

The first coasters began to appear about 1763, often made by specialist makers of baskets and cruets such as Langford and Sebille, the Hennells, Herbert & Company and Edward Aldridge. With wooden bases, the coasters or stands had pierced vertical sides, usually about $1\frac{1}{2}$ to 2 in. high, with strengthening gadrooned or other wire mounts, sometimes shaped and pierced in a variety of scrolling patterns. By about 1770, neoclassical formality was fully established, and there was a fashion for vertical pales, festoons, medallions, vases, and geometrical motifs. All these patterns were quickly imitated in fused plate, the Sheffield craftsmen adept at concealing the plating layer by rubbing it over the cut edges. By the end of the century, much larger decanters had come into fashion, and slightly everted, often unpierced coasters were made, soon followed by boldly fluted and gadrooned styles. Heavy cast, chased and pierced coasters, often as much as 3 in. in depth with mahogany bases at their finest with all-silver bases and usually gilded for even greater effect, dominated coaster design from about 1804 to 1824 or so. Less extravagant later coasters tended to have fluted or everted sides, many mounted with decorative applied wire, vines, shells and reeding in particular. There was frequent revival of rococo designs, a few of gothic inspiration; but, many mid-19th century and later coasters merely imitated old styles until the advent in recent years of the textured silver so extensively used today.

Wine coolers (Figs 54, 57) The popular name for the ice bucket or pail used for individual bottles, more domestic than the massive wine cistern. They were first introduced at the turn of the 17th century, with some of the finest being the work of Huguenot goldsmiths between about 1700 and 1720. On average they were 8 or 9 in. high. Most were made in pairs, a custom continued when the fashion was revived about 1790. At first the almost straight-sided cylindrical form prevailed, with tuck-in base on a sturdy foot, but it was not long before vase and campana shapes began to predominate, with deep borders chased in relief and

54 Wine coolers FROM LEFT *c.* 1803, *c.* 1800, *c.* 1794.

massive shaped cast and chased bases, rims and side handles. Pairs were usual, though sets of four, and even more were made. The fashion virtually died out by the middle of the 19th century.

Wine cups Tall-stemmed cups, often known as grace cups, being those from which drink was taken after grace, or as a parting drink, seem to have first come into use at the end of the 16th century. Their ceremonial nature was soon replaced by smaller, plainer versions. Even during the silver-lean Commonwealth period, stemmed wine cups continued to be made in all sizes, from little dram cups to those very like modern wine-glasses; indeed, it was from silver originals that the first English-made flint glasses which gradually overtook silver as the vessel for wine were copied. There was, however, a revival of silver goblets about 1770. Such cups, often in pairs, generally gilded inside and decorated with festoons and swags of fruit and flowers, occasionally applied or chased, more often in bright-cut engraving, were made in quantity. During the 19th century goblets were often made *en suite* with jugs or ewers, often of elaborate patterns such as the 'Cellini' in imitation of early Renaissance styles.

Wine fountains Massive vase-shaped urn-like containers fitted with spigot and tap – or taps – for serving wine, first made for the Restoration Court. Even rarer than wine cisterns, with which they are sometimes associated, they chiefly date between about 1680 and 1730. Curiously they were not revived during the Regency when so much massive plate was made, being by then completely replaced by sets of wine coolers.

Wine funnels The ordinary pattern of domestic funnel with a conical bowl survives in silver from the late 17th century, made in a variety of sizes from small perfume funnels to larger examples for decanting wine. By the later 18th century, two-part funnels came into fashion, with a slightly curved terminal to the funnel section, the pierced bowl being pressure-clamped over a piece of muslin for better straining. Sometimes a small domed stand accompanied such funnels, and many had a small flange which could clip over the edge of a bowl if required. Early-19th-century strainers often reverted to the single-piece type, the bowl more elongated and fluted or with heavily chased borders. Most were about 6 in. long at most, though one massive 11¾-inch funnel of 1816 by Paul Storr has been noted.

Wine tasters Usually associated with French rather than English silver, most silver wine tasters were the property of vintners and cellarers, and many are so engraved. The 17th-century form was a small, shallow, usually two-handled bowl of relatively flimsy silver, the centre domed or decorated with a simple flower motif, the sides embossed with similarly simple lobed and floral motifs. Plainer, more conventional, examples with everted sides, plain domed centre and without handles took their place by the mid-17th century. During the 18th century silver tasters became very rare, though a few with fluted sides have been recorded between about 1770 and 1830.

Wine trolleys *See* DECANTER TROLLEYS.

CHAPTER FOUR

Glossary of Terms

Acanthus (Fig. 55) Conventional leaf pattern based on the prickly fleshy plant found in Mediterranean countries. Used on Corinthian and other classical columns, it was adopted by the Romans and then revived during the Renaissance. Popular on English silver of the second half of the 17th century and, used more formally, during the neoclassical period, from about 1765 onwards.

Adam style (more properly, neoclassical). Designs based largely on the excavations of classical sites in Asia Minor and Greece first published in the 1750s and widely promoted by the Scottish-born architect Robert Adam and his brother James, who made a point of designing appropriate silver and other furnishings for their houses. Neoclassical designs were also prepared by Adam's rival James Wyatt who must be credited with many of the best neoclassical designs; besides numbering Boulton & Fothergill of Birmingham among his customers, he probably designed for Parker & Wakelin in London as well. Neoclassicism dominated silver design from about 1765 to 1795.

All at A term formerly seen at the head of sections in saleroom catalogues offering the lot as an entity at an all-in price instead of bidding at so many shillings per oz. (*See* 'at per ounce'.)

Alloy Originally the fineness of gold or silver determined '*à la loi*' – according to the law. Later applied to the mixing of base metal with gold or silver to harden and/or colour it. Silver is alloyed with copper in the proportion of 92.5:7.5 (or 11 oz. 2 dwt. pure to 18 dwt. of copper) to produce sterling silver, the lowest legal standard allowed in Britain.

Ambassadorial plate. A grant of plate, originally on loan, from the

GLOSSARY OF TERMS

Jewel House to the monarch's Ambassadors either resident or on missions abroad. Return of the plate was often dilatory, despite its being engraved with the Royal cypher; eventually it became the perquisite of the ambassador, who was in fact unpaid for his services. Thus many examples of domestic silver may bear not only the royal cypher but the arms of the individual envoy as well.
Annealing The process of heating silver at several stages during its manufacture to soften and toughen it after hammering has distorted the crystal structure and made it brittle.

55 FROM TOP LEFT **Anthemion** border, **Arabesque**, **Acanthus**, RIGHT **Armorials**.

Anthemion (Fig. 55) A stylised flower motif based on the honeysuckle motif of Greek ornament, often effectively used in the late 18th to early 19th centuries as a running border on silver.
Apron Decorative, often cast, pierced and chased framework between the supports of a kettle stand, épergne, centrepiece or basket, especially popular during the rococo period.
Arabesque (Fig. 55) Pattern of leaves and branches, sometimes incorporating figures, intertwined in the manner of Near-Eastern

205

or Moorish decoration. Popular as an engraved banded ornament from the Renaissance period onwards.

Armorials (Fig. 55) Properly the representation of a full coat of arms including motto and supporters (if any), the shield of arms, the helmet and crest. The shield of arms is frequently engraved on one side of a piece, with the crest engraved on the opposite side or on the cover of a pot or cup. Heraldic colours were not usually distinguished in silver engraving until the 18th century. Unhappily many pieces of silver have been engraved with armorials in recent times to suggest provenance. Crisply engraved arms on an otherwise well-worn piece should be viewed with suspicion.

Assay The testing or trial of metals by touch, fire, cupellation or other means to determine their purity to ensure that they are of the requisite legal standard. There are today four assay offices in Britain – London, Edinburgh, Birmingham and Sheffield – and another in the Irish Republic in Dublin. Formerly other offices were authorised – at Chester, Exeter, Glasgow, Newcastle-upon-Tyne, Norwich and York – while simple testing was probably also undertaken by goldsmiths themselves trying to regulate the craft in minor centres of goldsmithing. Providing the tests show the metal to be of at least the minimum standard, it is struck with the hallmarks: town mark, sterling (or Britannia standard) mark, and date letter, the maker's mark having previously been struck.

Assay scrape The portion of silver scraped from the unfinished piece by the assayer, sometimes still visible on the backs of waiters and trays as a series of long gouges. Usually the marks are eliminated by the silversmith when finishing the piece when it has been returned from hallmarking. On the Continent, assay scrapes are often of zigzag pattern.

'At per ounce' An old term used in sales catalogues when the price was calculated from bidders offering so much (usually shillings) per ounce for the lot, which was then multiplied by the weight to give the final hammer price. Commonly used in the past for tableware and for run-of-the-mill lots not at that time deemed worthy of special attention.

Baluster (Fig. 56) A curved pillar form, of circular section, swelling out from a narrow neck and recurving to the base. A popular and satisfying shape for stems of wine cups and standing cups, for candlesticks, jugs, coffee and chocolate pots and tankards, and, in miniature, for the finials on the covers of pots, caddies, cups and so on.

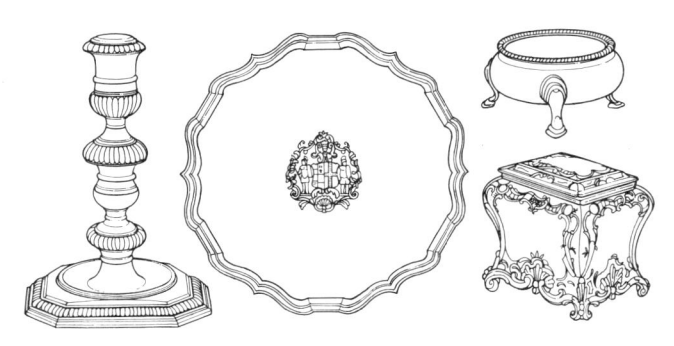

56 FROM LEFT **Baluster** candlestick; **Bath border** on salver; TOP RIGHT **Beading** border ornament on salt; BELOW **Bombé**-shaped caddy.

Bath border (Fig. 56) A moulded applied border formed of pairs of shallow curves meeting at a point intersected by short almost straight sections. Used for salvers and waiters *c.* 1725 to 1745.

Beading (Fig. 56) A border ornament composed of adjacent half-rounds; in the 18th century known as 'pearling'. Used for borders in single or double rows on salvers, waiters and trays particularly during the neoclassical period and later. Used as rim mounts at the same period; also arranged in graduated sizes and applied as outline decoration on baskets in the 1760s. Applied beaded detail of similar graduated style was also used to indicate the veins or stems of foliage on 17th-century bowls and cups, and as ribs along the spine of tankard and mug handles at the same period. At its simplest, the pattern is simply punched as conjoined domes on edges of inexpensive ware.

Billet A simple box-like moulding of alternating relief bars, usually achieved by stamping and much used on mid-16th-century plate. Also the thumbpiece (*q.v.*) on a flagon or tankard.

Bombé (Fig. 56) A baluster-like curved form but of rectangular or square basic section rather than circular, though often applied to both shapes, especially of late rococo design.

Boss *See* EMBOSSING.

Bright-cut engraving A particularly brilliant technique of engraving much used in the later 18th century. Its distinctively crisp appearance is due to the back edge of the graver burnishing the cut as the front part of the tool picks out the metal.

Britannia metal An alloy of tin, copper and regulus of antimony first made commercially by John Vickers of Sheffield about 1770. Of good weight and colour, it is often mistaken for pewter, which was, however, at that time usually cast not stamped up. Britannia metal takes a good polish, but the 'whitesmiths' of Sheffield usually plated it when the new process of electrodeposition was introduced. Most wares are stamped 'E.P.B.M'. Patterns were often in imitation of the more expensive Sheffield plate.

Britannia standard The higher standard for wrought plate obligatory from 1697 to 1720. It was introduced to prevent the use of the sterling coinage for plate-working. Marked with a figure of Britannia and a Lion's Head Erased instead of the Leopard's Head Crowned and Lion Passant, the standard is 958.4 parts per 1,000 (11 oz. 10 dwt. to the pound Troy). During the obligatory Britannia-standard period, the maker's mark had to take the form of the first two initials of the maker's surname. Some makers continued to use it after 1720, among them Paul de Lamerie who did not even re-register to work in sterling until 1732. Its use is still permitted; until 1975 the old-style Britannia marks were used. Since 1975, the Leopard's Head replaces the Lion's Head Erased in association with the figure of Britannia. (*See* pp. 242–43.)

Burnisher A tool with a very hard smooth surface, usually of agate or other hardstone, or of steel of very high grade, to give the surface of gold or silver a very high finish. (*See* p. 77.)

Campana (Fig. 57) Of Greek-vase shape, waisted like a bell. A term used to describe the neoclassical vases of the Regency period.

Cartouche (Fig. 57) Originally a scroll of paper (as in the surrounds for the names of the Pharaohs of Egypt), it was developed by silver engravers as a framework for a coat of arms or a crest. During the rococo period, cartouches were often asymmetrical, but before and since most have been of formal scrolling or shield-shape outline.

Casting Method of making silverwares using a master model and then pouring molten metal into a mould formed from it. (*See* pp. 74–5.)

Caudle A hot spiced drink much advocated in the 17th century for curing minor ills and as a recommended drink for pregnant women. It is a thin oatmeal gruel flavoured with wine or ale and sugar and spice. The term caudle cup is frequently applied to the handled bowls of various sizes which are now generally known as porringers.

Champlevé enamelling *See* ENAMELS.

Chasing Decoration in high or low relief achieved using punches of different types and sizes which are tapped with the hammer to push the metal into patterns. In chasing no metal is removed. Three forms are recognised: flat chasing, a basically linear surface decoration (sometimes confused with engraving) and matting; embossing, often further heightened by repoussé work, in which the pattern is first bumped up into domes and lobes from behind, and then given definition with punches from the front; and the loosely termed cast-chasing, which is the cleaning up and further defining of castings. (*See* p. 79.)

GLOSSARY OF TERMS

Chinoiserie (Fig. 57) Decoration inspired by oriental designs, freely interpreted. It was fashionable on English silver at different periods, the first being from about 1675 to 1690, when exotic oriental designs of trees, plants, birds, figures and temples were sometimes engraved, sometimes flat-chased, on toilet wares, footed salvers, two-handled cups or porringers and tankards. (A variant form of Chinese-style decoration is occasionally found about 1700, using a technique in high relief very like Chinese carved lacquerwork.) A second phase, chiefly used for tea-table silver, especially caddies, but also extended to épergnes and salvers, became fashionable about 1750. Caddies were repoussé-chased or cast in relief with oriental figures – including coolies,

57 TOP ROW **Campana**-shaped wine cooler; **Chippendale** mount on salver. BOTTOM ROW **Chinoiserie**, **Cartouche**, **Coral and bells** (rattle detail).

210

often in a setting of rice-fields and with straw hats, palm leaves and other non-European motifs. Epergnes were pierced and chased with similar themes, and some were enriched with bell-hung canopies. Cartouches for engraving were also sometimes of similar inspiration. The vogue was revived, though less extensively, about 1820, both in the 1750s style and the 'carved lacquer' designs.

Chippendale (Fig. 57) A moulded border of alternating long convex and short concave curves, much used for salvers and waiters from about 1730. The term 'Chinese Chippendale' is sometimes applied to the angular criss-cross pierced borders of trays and wine coasters of the second half of the 18th century, in imitation of the wood-carving patterns popularised by the furniture-maker Thomas Chippendale.

Cloisonné *See* ENAMELS.

Close-plating A method of applying a layer of silver foil to tinned steel by heat fusion and burnishing. Used from very early times, it was originally a cutler's device for plating knife-blades, scissors, spurs and the like. During the 18th century and well into the 19th century it was much used for buckles, buttons, cheese scoops, meat serving-forks, skewers, and most of all for candle snuffers. It was finally superseded by Sheffield plating and then, from about 1840 onwards, by electro-plating. The disadvantage of close-plating was that the base tended to rust and the layer of silver peel off. It was, however, a relatively simple process – close-plating can be used on virtually any metal – and was probably devised by the cutlers to 'harness' knife handles since the solder had to be of the sterling standard as enacted in 1379. It was, in fact, referred to as early as that when the Goldsmiths' Company complained that the cutlers were plating tin with silver 'so subtilely and with such sleight that the same cannot be discerned and severed from the tin'. The process is also sometimes known as French plating. Its skill lies in the laborious process of burnishing the layer of silver foil on to the tin solder spread on the steel, smoothing it perfectly. After that it is gently heated by passing an iron over the surface, causing the silver to adhere to the tin. As late as 1810 it was being used for spoons, forks, knives and other flatware made at Sir Edward Thomason's factory in Birmingham.

Coral and bells (Fig. 57) Old name for a child's rattle, usually incorporating a whistle, the coral terminal an aid to teething.

Crest The device or badge formerly worn on the helmet, and frequently used on silverwares as an indication of ownership without the expense of having a full coat of arms engraved.

Cresting An edging ornament standing proud of a horizontal surface, especially fashionable on medieval and early Renaissance silver.

Cut-card work (Fig. 11) Silver sheet of thin gauge cut into silhouettes, usually of foliage or scrollwork design, soldered on to bowls, cups, covers, coffee and chocolate pots, tankards, inkstands and other silver to produce ornament in relief. Especially popular from about 1660 onwards, the skill of the technique lies in the excellence of the soldering, so that the card appears integral with the rest of the piece. By the end of the 17th century, the Huguenot immigrant craftsmen elaborated the technique to build up applied strapwork and detail in high relief. (*See* pp. 81–2.)

Cutlery Any implement with a cutting edge, including knives, scissors, penknives, razors, but excluding fish knives, fish servers and butter knives, which are classed as flatware (*q.v.*). Silver-handled knives were made from early times, but few survive from before the end of the 17th century. Early knives were often fitted cast silver handles, of round or polygonal section broadening out to the terminal, followed early in the 18th century by various patterns of 'pistol-grip' with a voluted terminal. By the 1770s, filled knife handles became increasingly popular, the Sheffield silversmiths being especially competent at stamping out the handle in two halves, soldering it together and filling the handle with a resinous substance. Durability of the solder between blade and handle remained a problem until the advent of hard solders in recent times. Handles were also made of bone, ivory (often attractively stained green in the second half of the 18th century) mother-of-pearl and other materials. Blades were of sharpened steel, and usually of rather large size in comparison with the handles, but were of course diminished by usage and constant sharpening. Silver-bladed fruit and other dessert knives were often gilded to prevent staining. The invention of chrome-steels during the First World War resulted in stainless steel being used by the cutlery industry from 1923 onwards, while new techniques of joining handle and blade enable modern cutlery to be subjected to the greater heat of dish-washing machines. All-stainless-steel cutlery and flatware is a post-war development. (Stainless-steel knives can and should be sharpened from time to time.)

Date letter The letter of the alphabet used by assay offices to indicate the year of assay and changed annually (though until 1975 on different dates at each office). (*See* pp. 239–40.)

Diaper Ornament, often done by chasing, producing a trellised or latticed design of diamonds, squares and similar formal shapes.

Duty and Duty Drawback marks From December 1, 1784 until May 1, 1890 the sovereign's head in profile was struck to indicate that duty had been duly paid at the time of assay. For the first two years, the King's head was struck incuse, subsequently the mark was always in cameo. For nine months, from December 1784 to July 1785, goods exempted from duty because they were to be exported were struck with a standing figure of Britannia, also incuse. Possible damage to finished wares caused this rare mark to be withdrawn after only nine months, duty being recovered on invoice for exported goods. (*See* pp. 244–45.)

Egg-and-dart An edge moulding, usually stamped in sections, of ovoid shapes alternating with vertical arrow-like bars (said to have derived from shields and spears). Chiefly of 16th- and early-17th-century date, though revived by the 19th-century vogue for gothicism.

Electro-plating The technique of applying a thin layer of pure silver to a base metal by electrolysis, a method commercialised by the Elkingtons in Birmingham in the 1840s. The laws of electrolytic deposition had been formulated by Michael Faraday as early as 1833. It is interesting to note that experiments as early as 1805 to gild silver using Volta's battery resulted in the so-called Galvanic Goblet made by Paul Storr in 1814 and now in the Royal Collection.

Electro-typing An extension of the electro-plating process that allows the reproduction of intricate patterns of objects of metal or other materials by depositing a layer of metal by electrolysis on casts taken from the originals. Also known as electro-forming, the process was first demonstrated by Jacobi in 1838 and was taken up by Elkingtons, who specialised in reproducing complex designs such as shields, plaques, sculptures and carved ivory, many of which were produced for the 1862 Exhibition. In 1880 the firm were commissioned by the Ministry of Education to produce electrotypes of some of the early English silver in the Russian State collections. These faithful copies are now in the Victoria and Albert Museum.

Embossing Decoration worked from the back of a piece to bring up bosses and other relief shapes. For enclosed vessels, this is done by using a snarling-iron with a domed head, the end of the tool being tapped so that it bumps up the shape inside the piece. Usually further definition of the embossed areas is needed, and this is done from the front (repoussé work). No metal is removed by this process. (*See* pp. 79–80.)

Enamels Not extensively used on silverwares after the Middle Ages until the end of the 19th century. In medieval times, enamels were chiefly used for armorials set in the finials of covers or the prints (medallions) in the base of wooden mazer bowls and the like. More rarely they were used for decoration, as on the magnificent King John's Cup of about 1350 belonging to the Corporation of King's Lynn or the Leigh Cup of the Mercers' Company. There are several distinct types of enamelling: champlevé, in which the ground is recessed to receive the enamel; cloisonné, or cell-enamelling, in which narrow strips of metal wire are soldered to the base to form compartments into which the enamel is placed; encrusted, or enamelling in the round, applied to surfaces in high relief; painted enamels, often very much in the manner of miniature painting and used for snuff boxes, watch cases and the like; pliqué-a-jour, in which the enamel is held in a setting rather like a stained glass window; and basse-taille, akin to champlevé, using translucent enamels which cover the whole area and not only the sections between the raised edges of the work.

Engraving Probably the oldest of all decorative techniques, it is achieved by scratching or gouging out the surface with a sharp tool. The finest engraving produces a delicacy of line very akin to drawing, with considerable detail and exquisitely drawn effects of light and shade. Simpler engraving is an outline technique; even so interesting effects can be achieved by varying the width and depth of the cut. A special engraving style was developed about 1775; used extensively until the early years of the 19th century, and occasionally reproduced today, it is known as bright-cut, which has a crisp and sharp appearance due to the burnishing of the cuts. With time, engraved outlines tend slightly to blur, so that it is often possible to detect 'sharpened up' details or the misleading addition of armorials, usually of distinguished families, many of which betray the rather coarser line and sharper edges of modern gravers. (*See* pp. 83–4.)

Etching Surface decoration by which the pattern is eaten into the surface of the metal by acid. It was used during the second half of the 19th century for producing engraved styles at less cost. The article was first coated with an acid-resistant material; then the design was scribed on to uncover the areas to be exposed to the acid, which leaves a greyish area on the metal. (*See* p. 85.)

Feather-edge (Figs 6, 58) A slightly curved repeating pattern of cuts with a bright appearance due to the tool's burnishing of the sides of the cut. First used from about 1770, it was chiefly used as

GLOSSARY OF TERMS

a border (as beading and thread) to decorate plain Old English flatware and cutlery, but was also employed for edges on wine labels, small boxes and on some fused plated wares.

Festoon (Fig. 58) A garland or drapery motif arranged in pendant curves and often with a knot or ribbon at either end. Fruit and flower festoons, either repoussé-chased or engraved, were much used on late-16th-century silver; they were revived during the neo-classical period, when such details were, in the best quality work, often applied. The later 18th-century festoons often took the form of draperies.

58 TOP **Feather-edge**; FROM LEFT **Fluting** on covered cup; engraved **festoon** decoration on caddy; **Finial** on cup, c. 1570.

Filigree Probably introduced from the East, filigree work is composed of very finely drawn wires coiled and assembled into openwork panels. In Holland from the late 17th century onwards some craftsmen actually registered as filigree-workers, and there were others in Germany and in Scandinavia. Probably the few examples of tankards, candlesticks, boxes, frames and caskets made of filigree and found in English collections were by immigrant craftsmen. Most appear to date between about 1570 and 1700. After that there is little evidence of the craft in England until the early 19th century, when several filigree workers are recorded in Birmingham, making boxes, caddy spoons and other smallwares.

Finial (Fig. 58) Ornament placed on the top of a cover or as a corner decoration on the corner of a pediment such as appear on some standing salts.

Fish-skin Often called shagreen, which is properly ass-skin, it is the tanned and treated skin of the shark or the ray, which has spiny scales that are rubbed down to leave a roughened surface, the remains of the spines being slightly glossy. Much used for covering boxes, canteens and knife-cases during the 17th and 18th centuries, it is usually stained black. (*See also* SHAGREEN.)

Flatware (Fig. 6) The proper term for all flat tableware – spoons, forks, slices, scoops, sifters and so on – that does not have a cutting edge, but is used for scooping or for parting food.

Fluting (Fig. 58) Decoration imitating the vertical channelling of classical columns, resembling a musical flute split in two and placed concave side outwards. Popular for candlesticks in the mid-17th century, and slightly later with less pronounced curves (flat fluting) used to decorate porringers, bowls and so on. Also arranged obliquely and curved (swirl-fluting), and, especially in the neoclassical period, fanning out to follow tapered shapes, for appearing as 'bats'-wing fluting'.

Frosting An acid treatment giving a slightly roughened surface. It was especially popular during the 19th century.

Gadrooning (Fig. 59) A lobed border of stamped or cast convex curves, either vertical or slanting to left or right. An extremely popular border from the late 17th century (cp., similar carved gadrooning on furniture of the period), it remained in continuous and extensive use throughout later periods.

Garnish An old term for a set of dishes or plates (usually of pewter) and of services made *en suite*.

GLOSSARY OF TERMS

German silver Not silver at all, but a white alloy of nickel, copper and zinc used as a base metal for late-period fused plate and for electro-plating. Introduced from Berlin in 1830, it was almost universally adopted by the plating trades by 1845. The alloy was said to originate from China, where it had been used from very early times. It is also sometimes known by the trade name of Argentine. Bradbury gives the best and most workable alloy as 65 per cent copper, 20 per cent spelter (i.e., zinc or zinc-rich metal) and 15 per cent nickel.

Gilding Until the introduction of electrolytic gilding in the 1860s, silver was gilded to protect and embellish it by applying a mercury and gold amalgam and then driving off the mercury with heat. Volatising the mercury left a secure layer of gold, but was highly dangerous to the operator and is now unlawful. Several layers of gold can be plated in this way, but to achieve a fine finish, it is important that each layer is mirror-polished before the next is applied. Gilding should be well burnished, using an agate tool of perfect smoothness. The process is now achieved by a similar method to silver-plating. Though red golds are generally used, the more delicate and paler lemon colours, so often associated with old gilding, can in fact be achieved electrolytically. Storage tends to make gilding darker, hence the deeper tones of gilding often noticed in covered cups and the like. Parcel-gilding is part-gilding, a most effective process in which areas not to be gilded are stopped-off with shellac, varnish or other impermeable substances, unprotected sections taking the gilding. (*See* pp. 77–8.)

Gold and **White** Old terms for distinguishing not between gold and silver but between gilded and non-gilded silver. The usage gave rise to the unfounded belief that much old plate was in fact gold.

Goldsmith Originally applied without distinction to craftsmen in gold and in silver, and in modern times perpetuated by the Worshipful Company of Goldsmiths in the City of London,

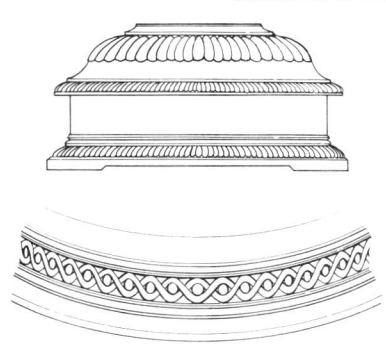

59 FROM TOP, LEFT **Gadrooning** on box; **Guilloche** ornament; RIGHT **Grotesque** decoration on ginger jar and cover.

originally the trade guild of the craftsmen. The Company is still a major force in the trade of gold, silver and jewellery-making, with responsibility for regulating the trade and for maintaining the London Assay Office. Members work to promote the craft, in education, in supporting many charities, and in being themselves great patrons of the craft.

Grotesque (Fig. 59) Fantastic human or animal forms used as decoration, engraved, chased or modelled. Often associated with intertwining scrollwork, flowers and foliage to produce bizarre or extravagant motifs.

Guilloche (Fig. 59) A running spiral ornament composed of two or more ribbons or bands twisted one over the next, sometimes enclosing small rosettes or wheel-like motifs. Used from the Renaissance, it was considerably refined by the Huguenot silversmiths in the 18th century for cast and chased borders.

Hallmark The official marks signifying that gold or silver is of the required standard of fineness and also, from 1784 to 1890, that duty had duly been paid at the time of testing. Loosely extended to include the maker's or sponsor's mark. So named from its original use at Goldsmiths' Hall in London, though of course properly used also for the marks struck at provincial assay offices.

Hanap Medieval term for a drinking cup or bowl, applied by some writers to standing cups. The term derives through Middle English from Anglo-Saxon *hnaepp*.

Hanoverian A plain flatware pattern with the terminals turning upwards towards the bowl (as opposed to Old English in which the end curves downwards). Made from about 1710 to 1775, the pattern was often engraved with crest, armorials or initials on the end, the spoons and forks being laid bowl or prongs downwards on the table.

Hob-nob To drink together. Hence the term occasionally found in 18th-century inventories applied to pairs of small waiters, presumably for handing the glasses of drink.

Hollow-ware The generic term for any metalware formed by raising, stamping, casting or spinning. It includes any form of pot or other vessel, casters, and, perhaps surprisingly, candlesticks and even trays and waiters. Other items of domestic silver, such as toast racks and dish rings cannot easily be classified under any other heading, such as flatware (spoons and forks) or boxwares.

Huguenots French Protestants of the 16th and 17th centuries bitterly persecuted in their own country, but reluctantly tolerated by the Edict of Nantes signed in 1598. Gradually many left France to settle in more congenial countries – England, Holland, Switzerland, Germany, Ireland, America. In 1685, when on October 18th Louis XIV revoked the Edict, thousands fled from France, many of them craftsmen including goldsmiths, jewellers, watchmakers and silk-weavers. Many were allowed to settle in England, and leading silversmiths of French extraction include many of the best-known Huguenot families – Willaume, Harache, Tanqueray, de Lamerie, Courtauld, Platel, Le Sage and so on. Others fled to Ireland, such as Teulon, Pantaine, Gerard and

Gervais; others went further afield, such as the Fabergés of Picardy who eventually settled in Russia in 1842, by way of Germany and the Baltic states. Throughout the 18th century Huguenot high standards of workmanship and design had a marked effect on the craft of the silversmith in England and elsewhere.

Husk (Fig. 60) Decorative motif especially popular during the neoclassical period composed of repeating bell-shapes, based on the corn-husk.

Incuse A mark simply hammered or stamped in (often simple outline letters) below the general level of the surface. Many smallworkers used such simple punches for their marks. In the assay office incuse marks were used for the King's Head duty mark from 1784 until 1786, and for the Britannia drawback mark of 1784 to 1785. Since the impression had to be cut proud of the die, such punches were easily damaged, and generally soon replaced by punches giving a cameo or relief finish, which were harder wearing and less likely to damage the piece being impressed.

Initials (Fig. 60) A 17th-century convention was to place the surname letter above the initial of husband and wife in a triangular design, the letters usually being in block capitals either engraved or pricked. During the 18th century engraved monograms became fashionable, and by the end of the century often engraved in a flowery script. A curious variation using the name split into three or four in a single line typifies most Channel Islands initials: for example Jean Le Page would appear I:L:P.

Jolly-boat (Fig. 60) Type of double wine bottle or decanter stand in the form of the shallow boat much used by the Navy. Often of red leather or wood rather than of silver or of fused plate; especially fashionable during the Napoleonic Wars.

Kitchen A tea-urn with lamp or heating iron and spigot with tap, a term used by Matthew Boulton is his catalogues to describe his plated urns.

60 TOP ROW **Husk** and ribbon tie; Lion's-head **mask**. BOTTOM ROW
Initials; **Jolly-boat** decanter stand.

Kitchen pepper A small spice dredger or caster, usually with a handle. Originally known as a pepper box.

Knife-box An upright box with sloped lid fitted with slots to accommodate knives, and sometimes also spoons and forks. Usually of wood, marquetry, shagreen, tortoiseshell or, japanned ware, a few have silver feet, lock-plates and handles.

Knop Small boss or knob protruding on the stem of a cup or candlestick, or the finial on the cover of a cup, pot, or spoon. Often of decorative design, such as a tall baluster, a vase shape, acorn, acanthus bud or, during the rococo period, as model of tea plant, Chinaman, shell or other imaginative design.

Knurl A simple ridged edge ornament, sometimes imitating ropework, used on less expensive wares instead of applied wires and mounts.

Krater Art-historical term for a two-handled vase of classical form (also crater). This design was fashionably copied in silver

by silversmiths during the neo-classical and Regency periods.
Latten Old name for brass or other yellow base metal alloy.
Maker's mark The mark officially registered at an assay office pertaining to a maker, firm or sponsor. (*See* Hallmark and pp. 235–38.)
Mask (Figs 60, 63) Decorative motif of human, bird or animal head, often grotesque, derived from the hollow head-shapes worn by Greek and Roman actors. Popular as applied decoration from the 16th century, especially for side handles with ring ends for punch bowls and so on during the later 17th century.
Magnetic plate A form of electro-plating based on Faraday's Principle of Induction and put into practice by J. Prime of Birmingham in 1844, using a magnetic machine for depositing gold, silver or copper.
Matting A series of punch marks applied evenly and close together to form an overall textured pattern, often used in contrast to polished areas, or for background effect in association with flat chasing designs.
Molinet A long stirring rod inserted through the aperture in the top of a chocolate pot to whisk the thick chocolate into a frothy beverage. Projecting flanges, usually pierced, make the lower part resemble a battle-mace. Very few survive.
Niello A black compound usually of copper, silver and lead in varying proportions, generally 1:1:2, or of sulphur, lead and mercury in equal parts, used to fill engraved detail. The niello is spread into the design, heated and excess finally polished away. Chiefly used on the Continent for enchancing scrollwork designs, especially in Russia. It was also used in early-19th-century England for blacking in names on bottle labels.
Nozzle The socket with a flange, often removable, to hold the candle firm in the 'stick and help to prevent grease from running down the stem.
Ogee A moulding, wholly of English origin, consisting of a double curve, convex above and concave below. This word has been

transferred to the curved outline of vessels as a descriptive term.
Ovolo An oval convex moulding placed vertically. Popular in 16th-century stamped work.
Parcel-gilding *See* GILDING.
Patera (Fig. 61) Circular ornament in low relief based on the classical libation dish, much used in 18th-century neoclassical silver, where it was also adapted to oval outlines. Often enriched with fluting, foliage, etc.
Patina The softened lustre of polished silver naturally resulting from usage, caused by oxidation of the surface by way of minute scratches. It can be induced artificially and should be suspect on modern pieces, or old ones that have been repaired.
Pennyweight A measure of Troy weight, the twentieth part of an ounce Troy, equivalent to 24 grains. Usually abbreviated dwt.
Piercing (Fig. 61) Cut decoration. Until about 1760, it was done using very sharp chisels, the best piercing often being extremely intricate and detailed, often enhanced by engraving. Examination of the cut edges shows how the metal has been slightly turned in as the chisel presses into the metal. Saw-piercing generally superseded chisel-piercing in the second half of the 18th century. A technique very akin to fretsaw work on wood, the method is revealed by the tiny vertical teeth-marks down the cut. Shortly afterwards, a mechanical development of chisel-piercing used on factory-made silver and fused plated wares, later on electroplated goods, was the fly-press. Simple dot punching, for small casters and the like, was done with a round cutter or the bow-drill. (*See* pp. 84–5.)
Planishing A finishing process used for hand-made silver by hammering it row by row with a slightly convex highly polished hammer to smooth and polish the surface. (*See* p. 76.)
Plate The old term for wrought gold or silver. Seldom used nowadays, because of possible confusion with plated wares.
Posset A warm sweet spiced drink of milk curdled with ale or wine. Much used as a cure-all for minor ills in the 17th century.

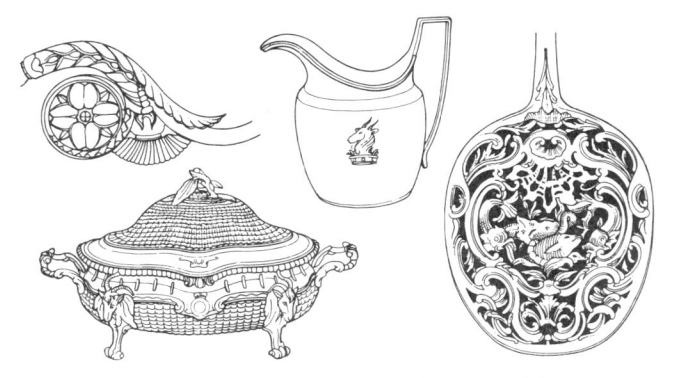

61 TOP ROW **Patera**; **Reeded** mount on jug; RIGHT **Piercing**;
BOTTOM LEFT **Quilted** ornament, on tureen *c.* 1766.

Pounce Powder of gum sandarac used to restore a smooth surface to writing paper after erasure and so prevent the ink from spreading. Not to be confused with the sand used for drying ink.

Pouncing An overall punched decoration, akin to matting but usually rather coarser, used from the early 17th century onwards. It has been suggested that it was especially popular for simple Communion cups which would be much handled but for which gilding was not considered appropriate.

Pricked A description of the dotted style used for simple initials, dates and inscriptions in the 16th and 17th centuries. Chiefly found on spoons, small cups, dishes and other pieces made for presentation at Christenings and weddings; presumably undertaken by shopkeepers not trained as engravers.

Pricket The spike on which a candle was stuck before the introduction of the socket-type candleholder. Very rare in silver other than large candlesticks made for Church use.

GLOSSARY OF TERMS

Quilting (Fig. 61) A rare form of chased ornament, resembling waves, used on tureens, candlesticks, etc., from about 1750 to 1760.

Raising The method of making silver hollow-wares by hammering and forming a sheet of silver over a raising stake. (*See* pp. 70–72.)

Reeding (Fig. 61) A moulding consisting of two or more parallel half-flutes. Sometimes combined with a ribbon-like motif traversing the reeded bands to form borders such as reed-and-tie or reed-and-ribbon.

Régence Not properly applicable to English silver, though the style was brought to England during the early years of the 18th century. Régence is a French decorative influence that made use of surface enrichment, with diaperwork, scalework, flowerheads, scrolls and masks formally arranged; often interpreted by flat-chasing or by repoussé chasing in low relief.

Regency A loose description of the taste for rather grandiose and usually gilded silver made from about 1790 until 1820 – the period of the Prince Regent's influential patronage to the London silver trade, and especially of Rundell, Bridge & Rundell. The actual Regency lasted from 1811 to 1820, when George IV succeeded.

Repoussé (Fig. 62) The process of embossing metal from the back by hammering domed punches into simple shapes, then giving definition and detail from the front by chasing. (*See* p. 80.)

Rococo Probably derived from the French *rocaille* (pebble-work) and certainly French in inspiration, the rococo style culled its motifs from shells, seaweed, coral, and other marine motifs in asymmetrical display, combined with scrolls and double curves. It was in high fashion between about 1730 and 1760. Much of the finest rococo silver was cast and richly chased.

Sconce (Fig. 62) The socket for a candle at the top of the candlestick, often with a detachable nozzle inside it. Also a branched candlestick with an oval or elongated back-plate fixed to the wall.

GLOSSARY OF TERMS

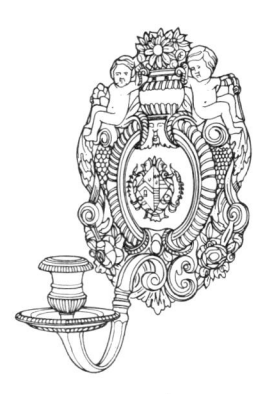

62 Repoussé sconce.

Shagreen Originally the skin of the ass (from Persian *saghari*, French *chagrin*), a leather covered with indentations formed by rubbing seeds over the moist skin and trampling them in. Much used for scabbards. In the late 17th to early 18th centuries, the term became confused with sharkskin, which has a raised pattern rather than an indented one, but was put to similar use as true shagreen. It was also used for covering boxes and caskets of all sorts. Shagreen is usually dyed green with a vegetable dye, from the inner side, a process that leaves the rubbed down spiny protrusions uncoloured. These are then sometimes rubbed down smooth so that the resultant leather is of marbled appearance.

Sheffield Plate Method invented by Thomas Boulsover of Sheffield about 1743 of fusing a layer of sterling silver over a copper core, by heating and rolling the two together. The earliest examples, used for buckles, buttons, small boxes, and the like, were plated on one side only. By the 1760s larger articles such as salvers, candlesticks, caddies and so on were being made. At this

GLOSSARY OF TERMS

time the method of plating the copper core on both sides was developed. Plated wire followed, and by the 1790s the Sheffield platers (and those such as Boulton in Birmingham and others in France) were making complete ranges of almost all the objects available in silver. The introduction of electro-plating (*q.v.*) spelled doom for the trade, however, and it was virtually extinct by 1845. Constant use and cleaning tends to wear down the silver layer, so that copper edges are often revealed. This is known as bleeding. Replating of old Sheffield plated wares by modern electrolytic methods is not usually to be recommended.

Silver-gilt Sterling silver to which a thin layer of gold has been applied, either by fire-gilding (now prohibited) or by electro-gilding, to obviate tarnishing and to enhance the appearance. Part-gilding is known as parcel-gilding.

Sinking The first stage in making a piece of silver by hand, shaping a flat piece of sheet silver by hammering over a depression to achieve a shallow bowl shape before turning the piece over the stake to raise it. (*See* p. 70.)

Spinning A very ancient method of working metal using a long-handled tool and working the metal over a shaped chuck rotating in the lathe. A useful method much used in the 18th century for casters, tea and coffee pots, jugs, bowls, and for smaller items such as egg-shaped nutmeg graters. (*See* p. 72.)

Stamping Relief ornament produced by hammering the metal from the back over dies. Especially used for sections of wire and narrow mouldings in medieval times and later. By the end of the 17th century, stamped detail was struck on the backs of spoon bowls and on their stems. This was later developed to produce straps and other decorative sections for soldering on to provide decoration in relief. About the middle of the 18th century, die-stamping was developed, especially in Sheffield and Birmingham, to produce parts for candlesticks, vases, baskets and coasters. The rather thin gauge necessary to produce ornamental stampings meant that many such wares had to be filled, or loaded, with plaster, resin or other firm substance. More modern techniques have allowed bodies of teapots, coffee pots, salvers and the like to be stamped out. Used for some factory-made silver and most electro-plated wares. (*See* pp. 73–4.)

Sterling The minimum permitted standard for silver in Britain, allowing 18 dwt. of base metal (usually copper) to the pound Troy (11 oz. 2 dwt. per 12 oz., or 925 parts per 1000 pure silver) to harden the metal. Established by ordinance in 1300, it has been the standard for wrought plate except for the period from 1697 to 1720 when the higher Britannia standard (*q.v.*) was obligatory.

Strapwork Applied ornament of elongated form, sometimes stamped, sometimes cast, and much used to decorate teapots, cups, bowls and tankards during the early part of the 18th century. Also the engraved ornament enclosed within ribbon-like borders, often interlaced, used as a border decoration on the bowls of Communion cups, beakers and wine cups from about 1560 onwards, or similar chased ornaments, often enclosing flowers, foliage or medallions, used at the period.

The term is also used for the pierced spine of silver decoration applied to the wooden or leather-covered handle of coffee and chocolate pots circa 1690 to 1710.

Swags Bunches of fruit, flowers, or foliage, often arranged as festoons or garlands, and engraved or chased. Popular on 16th-century silver, the style was revived during the rococo period and reintroduced more formally during the neoclassical.

Thumbpiece (Fig. 63) Sometimes called a billet, the cast projection above the hinge of a tankard, jug or pot by which the lid can be raised. Intricate designs include angels on Elizabethan flagons, cherubs, and so on. Later 17th-century tankards generally feature double corkscrews, acorns, and simple bifurcated shapes as well as finely modelled Lions Sejant.

Tine The prong of a fork.

Toddy A hot spirituous drink of rum or whisky mixed with water and lemon juice flavoured with sugar and sometimes spices. A

63 TOP LEFT **Vitruvian scroll** with ram's-head masks; a selection of **thumbpieces**.

popular drink in the late 18th to 19th centuries probably originally made in imitation of arrack, an eastern spirit made from coconut or date palms, and known as palm toddy.

Tolerance The permitted deviation from the standard fineness of a precious metal for which allowance was made during assay, largely because the old touchstone methods of testing were inaccurate. More accurate chemical methods of assaying silver were introduced in about 1840, though it was not until 1932 that the Gay-Lussac process of volumetric analysis was first used.

Tontines A particularly fascinating group of silverwares – and in one instance, a piece of gold – recording the names of subscribers to a loan, together with their date of death and sometimes also their ages. The last survivor inherited the whole income from an annuity based on a scheme by the Italian banker Lorenzo Tonti, who devised the scheme whereby subscribers to a loan or fund shared the proceeds among the survivors. The rarest and earliest example of a tontine is a gold tumbler cup of 1702 by Pierre Harache (now at Boston Museum of Fine Arts). Others include pairs of silver waiters, a cup and cover, a large mug, and an inkstand. Tontines should not be confused with pieces bearing memorial inscriptions.

Touch In early records, the Touch indicated the standard of fineness, with reference to the Touchstone, a black jasper or flinty slate (later replaced by Wedgwood's black pottery) used for testing gold and silver by rubbing the metal on the stone and comparing the streak with that made by needles of known fineness. Later the term came to be applied also to the marks struck on the gold or silver by the assayer.

Trefoil A three-leafed shape. Compare quatrefoil (a motif with four domed adjacent shapes converging in the centre) and cinquefoil (with five leaves). Sexfoil and octafoil are descriptive of the outlines of early 18th-century salvers and waiters with six- and eight-lobed borders respectively.

Troy weight The gold and silversmith's traditional unit of weight, a pound Troy comprising 12 ounces of 20 pennyweights each. (*See* Appendix B.)

Vermeil Gilding of silver or bronze in the French manner to achieve a reddish colour.

Vitruvian scroll (Fig. 63) A regular wave-like scroll ornament much used in neoclassical silver.

Volute A spiral scroll as used in Greek architecture, usually with two scrolls placed at either end of a flat section. Sometimes twisted.

Warwick vase The great marble Vase from Tivoli, purchased by Sir William Hamilton who then sold it to the Earl of Warwick, inspired copyists during the first half of the 19th century to make replicas in silver and bronze. One by Sir Edward Thomason of Birmingham was in bronze, and full size. Most were miniatures, between $5\frac{1}{4}$ in. and $9\frac{1}{2}$ in. high. In some cases they were mounted on plinths or adapted as wine coolers, fruit coolers, tureens

or vases. Most were made in the Rundell & Bridge workshops.
Water-leaf A stylised leaf shape especially popular as chased or applied decoration on neoclassical silver and popular well into the 19th century. Also applied to water-lily leaves.
Wickering Plaited split withies used to insulate the handles of jugs, kettles, argyles, coffee pots and other vessels used for hot liquids. The skill is now virtually extinct, though until a few years ago was still undertaken in London, where a 300-year-old firm had records showing that between 6d. and 1s. was charged to silversmiths such as Paul de Lamerie and Edward Wakelin in the mid-18th century for the service.

CHAPTER FIVE

The Marks on Silver

Silver collectors are most fortunate in that they can almost always verify the quality (standard) of the metal itself, the identity of the maker and the year of manufacture – even, on occasion, to within a few months. Such exactness is seldom afforded to the collectors of brass or glass, pewter or porcelain, furniture or fine art.

Marks for 1497, the second year of the date letter system, on the chalice at Nettlecombe Church, Somerset.

Hallmarks, so called from Goldsmiths' Hall in the City of London, where the authenticating marks on gold and silver made in London and by makers registered in London are still applied, are the official marks that indicate the standard, or quality, of the metal. The marks comprise the standard mark, the mark of the assay office where the metal has been tested and passed, and a variable annual date letter. Other official and commemorative marks have been authorised from time to time. In addition to the hallmarks proper, there is the maker's mark (now renamed the sponsor's mark) which must by law be struck on the ware before assay and marking.

The Goldsmiths' Company has since medieval times had jurisdiction over the regulation of the craft in England and Wales. Scotland had its own authority, though after the Act of Union, London-made laws affecting gold and silver applied there equally.

THE MARKS ON SILVER

In Ireland, the Dublin Goldsmiths' Company was responsible for the craft, having been granted a Royal Charter in 1637, though generally speaking the English laws applied there.

The earliest statute concerning gold and silver was an order of 1238 laying down standards of fineness and obliging the mayor and aldermen to choose 'six discreet goldsmiths' of the City of London to superintend the craft. It was not until 1300, however, that the true beginning of hallmarking was decreed when standards were redefined and 'no manner of vessel of silver depart out of the hands of the workers, until further, that it be marked with the leopard's head'. Silver was to be 'of the sterling alloy', that is, 92.5 per cent pure silver, of the same alloy as the coinage; in addition it was decreed that 'the Guardians of the craft shall go from shop to shop among the goldsmiths, to assay'. It was further enacted that 'in all the good towns of England where there are goldsmiths . . . one shall go . . . to London to seek their sure touch.' So the Guardians of the craft, the Wardens of Goldsmiths' Hall, were given responsibility for overseeing the Assay, as they still do today, where the London Assay Master still bears the title of Deputy Warden.

THE LEOPARD'S HEAD

The oldest recorded mark is that of the London goldsmiths, the Leopard's Head, which was probably originally the standard mark. It was crowned until 1820. It was also used in provincial towns as a mark of the Goldsmiths' Company's authority, alongside the marks for Exeter, York, Newcastle and Chester (though not in Birmingham and Sheffield).

THE MAKER'S MARK

In order to supervise the craft efficiently, it was obvious that some way had to be found to identify goldsmiths who were submitting sub-standard wares; in 1363 Edward III ordained that 'each Master Goldsmith shall have a mark to himself, and which mark shall be known by those who shall be assigned by the king to supervise their works'. The marks were often symbols rather than initials, many probably taken from the goldsmith's shop sign; others were often a rebus (or pun) on the goldsmith's name. It is interesting that the 1363 ordinance states that the King's Mark (the Leopard's Head) was to be applied after the Assay and finally the maker's mark – in reverse order to that obtaining nowadays.

Gradually during the 17th century, initials, usually embellished with symbols, became more usual. When the immigrant Huguenot craftsmen began to register their marks in London, they tended to follow the custom of their native France and use a fleur-de-lis and two grains (or pellets) above their initials.

In 1697, when the higher Britannia standard came into force, silversmiths were required to re-register their marks. Previous records, except for mark plates, have been lost. Originally recorded on vellum, they were probably lost during the fire at the Assay Office in 1681; so, until other evidence is forthcoming, we can not, for instance, identify who used the mark of the Hound Sejant other than the fact that he made superlative pieces at a time when much English silver was thin and sometimes clumsily made. Now and again marks can be identified with confidence – much investigation has recently been made into spoon-makers (very much a specialist craft) with several certain identifications; relationships and records have revealed at least one Elizabethan maker, Robert Taylboyes, as having the mark of a Stag's Head. Such important research has also identified the late 17th-century maker, Thomas Jenkins, whose mark TI between Escallops was for so long misattributed to the spoonmaker Thomas Issod.

After 1696, however, with a break that makes some marks of the mid-18th century attributable, but uncertain, since the large-workers' register of 1758 to 1773 is missing, marks are at least known for most makers and/or workshops in London up to the present day, and full details of marks and brief lives of the silver-smiths, and of many related trades, have been published. (Grimwade, Arthur, *London Goldsmiths, 1697 to 1837*, Faber, 1976.)

With the restoration of the sterling standard in 1720, old-style marks were re-registered, mostly now in the form of initials, though some continued to use Britannia-style marks. To reduce confusion and to try to eliminate widespread duty-dodging all goldsmiths were ordered to re-register their marks in the form of initials of a different style to those they had used previously. A partnership of two or more silversmiths often registered a cruciform mark instead of placing the initials one above the other – though the latter could be more economical as Daniel Smith and Robert Sharp proved when they simply lopped off Richard Carter's initials when they registered alone in 1780.

By the 19th century, many of the marks referred to firms and factories rather than individual makers; some were even those of retailers who bought in their silverware from the actual makers. Nowadays the workshop mark is more properly described as the

MAKER'S MARKS

Pre-1697

Symbols were common

THE MARKS ON SILVER

1697 to 1720

LEFT TO RIGHT William Fleming; Pierre Harache, Senior; Paul de Lamerie (until 1732); William Lukin; Simon Pantin; Richard Syng; David Willaume, Senior.

After 1720

LEFT TO RIGHT Barnard & Sons; Hester Bateman; Peter and William Bateman; William Bateman; Henry Chawner; Paul Crespin.

LEFT TO RIGHT John Emes; Robert Garrard; Elizabeth Godfrey; Robert and David Hennell; S. Herbert & Co.; Paul de Lamerie.

LEFT TO RIGHT Digby Scott and Benjamin Smith; Daniel Smith and Robert Sharp; Paul Storr; Aymé Videau; Whipman & Wright; David Willaume, Junior.

sponsor's mark. This may be that of a large firm manufacturing silver, the mark of a retailer or dealer or, more rarely, the actual mark of an individual maker who has been responsible for all the processes of making the piece. In fact, for many decades there have been thousands of pieces bearing a so-called maker's mark which have been the work, not of that one man but of his workmen – silversmiths, wire drawers, casters, engravers and chasers. Some, like engravers and chasers, were often outworkers; but, it was often more practicable to employ 'journeymen' silversmiths, many of whom had probably formerly been apprenticed to the master craftsmen. They would then have stayed on when they came out of their indentures, having no money or inclination, perhaps, to start up in business on their own. The master or owner of the workshop no doubt carefully supervised his workmen and imbued their products with his own particular style, making certain that everything bearing his mark was of a standard commensurate with that of his own work. Except for rare instances when an engraver or a chaser has been permitted to sign his work, or chance documentary evidence allows an attribution to a particular craftsmen, it is the master craftsman who registered his mark that receives the credit and conceals the identity of perhaps half a dozen or more craftsmen. Even of the master himself, often only the sketchiest details are known – perhaps only the date of his apprenticeship, the name of his master or masters, his parentage and place of birth, his setting up in business and perhaps the date of his death. For the rest, his and his employees' work is his only testimony. Even so, the great names – Pierre Platel, David Willaume, Paul de Lamerie, Paul Crespin, Edward Wakelin, Benjamin Smith, Paul Storr, the Hennells, the Batemans and a hundred others endowed English silver with their own special styles. Frequently, even without so much as a glance at the marks one can correctly guess not only the maker, but suggest a pretty accurate date as well: not difficult for fine and important pieces, but not impossible even for more commonplace pieces.

THE DATE LETTER

In 1478 the Wardens of the Goldsmiths' Company were faced with heavy penalties should there be any default by the Keeper of the Touch, following a Statute of 1477 which included the provision that the Company was to be liable for misdeeds in the assay office and was also to have jurisdiction over alien and stranger goldsmiths in and around London.

The Company's solution was to devise that beautifully simple and, for the collector, so invaluable a system of striking year marks, or date letters. By this means, they would be able to trace, even years later, the particular assayer of the piece. Using consecutive letters of the alphabet, starting with A when the scheme was inaugurated in December 1478, the letter was changed annually on St Dunstan's Day, May 19th, when the new Touch Warden was elected. He inspected the work of the Common Assayer once every week and had the responsibility of striking the Leopard's Head Crowned on assayed plate which replaced the old 'King's Mark'.

In London a twenty-year cycle of letters, (omitting I and V to Z inclusive) was adopted, the style of letter and/or shield being altered with each new series.

The day for bringing in the new date letter each year was changed in 1660 when the Monarchy was restored after the Commonwealth. Appropriately, the Goldsmiths chose May 29th, which was Oak-apple Day and the King's birthday. Outside London, date letters were changed on various dates and the length of cycles varied at different assay offices, several having a twenty-five-year cycle. Only twice has the twenty-year cycle been broken in 500 years: in 1696 to 1697, when the Britannia standard was introduced in March, and a new cycle of Court hand letters began; and in 1975 when all British assay offices agreed to conform, and a new cycle was begun; the new annual letters now cover a calendar year, beginning on January 1st.

THE MARKS ON SILVER

1558 Small Blackletter

1578 Roman capital

1598 Lombardic

1618 Small italic

1638 Court hand

1658 Capital Blackletter

1678 Small Blackletter

1696 This cycle terminated with 't' on Mar. 27, 1697.

1697 Until May 29

1697 Court hand

1716 Roman capital

1736 Small Roman

1756 Capital Blackletter

1776 Small Roman

1796 Capital Roman

1816 Small Roman

1836 Capital Blackletter

1856 Small Blackletter

1876 Capital Roman

1896 Small Roman

1916 Small Blackletter

1936 Capital Blackletter

1956 Small italic

The London date-letter cycles cover twenty years (omitting J, V, W, X, Y and Z). Types of letter and the shields varied with each cycle.

THE LION PASSANT

Until 1544 the maker's mark and the two hallmarks of Leopard's Head Crowned and the date letter were sufficient guarantee of the standard of silver (sterling or 92.5 per cent pure) and of gold (18 ct). The English economy was, however, in turmoil. Henry VIII had found it necessary, despite the riches won from the Dissolution of the monasteries, to debase the currency again and again. Although there is no written evidence, it seems likely that the addition of the Lion Passant Guardant to the hallmarks from 1544 onwards was intended as an indication of standard, and that the mark was crowned to signify that it was the King's standard, not necessarily the standard preferred by the Goldsmiths. The Company's declaration in that year that 'none of the Company enterprise to work any worse silver than upright sterling upon pain of being punished by the Wardens' obviously defied the King; he demanded the surrender of their Charter. Susan Hare, in her introduction to the exhibition 'Touching Gold and Silver' states that only the King's death in 1547 is thought to have saved the Company. In 1550, however, the Goldsmiths ceased to use the Crown on the Lion Passant standard mark, though it seems they did tend to mark silver of below sterling standard. In 1575 to 1576 Queen Elizabeth signed a statute that firmly re-enacted the standard for silver as being sterling and at the same time raised the gold standard to 22 ct. So the Lion Passant Guardant – walking to the left, its head turned over its shoulder – remained the standard mark for silver. It also, until 1798, remained the mark for gold, when the 18 ct was permitted and marked with a Crown. In 1822, the Leopard's Head lost its crown, the Lion Passant ceased to be Guardant (in London only).

THE BRITANNIA STANDARD

After the Restoration the demand for wrought silver became so strong that melting and clipping the silver coinage posed a serious problem. In 1696, 'An Act for encouraging the bringing of wrought plate to be coined' heralded the Great Recoinage of William III. This introduced milled coins and raised the standard of wrought plate to 11 oz. 10 dwt. or 95.8 per cent pure silver – eight pennyweights to the Troy pound higher than sterling. New hallmarks were ordered, the higher standard, or 'Better Nine' as it is colloquially known in the trade, being marked with the Lion's Head Erased; the figure 'of a woman commonly called Britannia' replaced the sterling Lion and the Leopard's Head Crowned. A new series of date letters began in March 1697 when the Act came into force with a court hand '*a*'; but, the letter was changed, as usual, on May 29th, so that the first letter of the new series lasted only just over two months.

In addition, makers were ordered to re-register their marks using the first two letters of their surname instead of the more usual practice of initials of forename and surname, of a single initial or, rarely, merely a device.

The new higher standard was obligatory throughout the kingdom, but Parliament, as so often, tended to overlook the provinces; it was not until 1700 that the anomalous position of Chester, York, Exeter and Norwich was recognised, and a year later that of Newcastle. Scotland was not then under the jurisdiction of Westminster. By a curious quirk of legislation, gold was still struck with the Lion Passant and Leopard's Head Crowned during the period of Britannia standard silver.

Since the Britannia standard silver cost more than the old sterling, makers immediately began to clamour for the reinstatement of sterling; a few, especially Huguenot-born silversmiths used to the higher standard in France, and those with a thriving export business, counter-petitioned for its retention. On June 1st,

1720, both sides had their way. The old sterling was restored, but with the imposition of a duty of 6d. an ounce on all wrought plate; for those who preferred it, there was the alternative of continuing to use the higher standard, still marked with Britannia and the Lion's Head Erased.

THE DUTY AND DUTY-DODGERS

The 6d. an ounce duty, paid at the time of assay, was equally unpopular with both silversmiths and patrons. From 1720 even otherwise reputable craftsmen were not averse to 'duty-dodging'. For special orders they usually simply struck their own mark four times, hoping that most people would not examine the piece too closely and would assume that the four marks were official. After all, it was unlikely that the special piece would be later sold over the counter. More serious were their practices of using an already hallmarked piece, or having a small and insignificant piece properly assayed and marked, and then inserting it into the new piece they were making. The edges could be concealed within the now fashionable chasing or a disc with the marks let into the foot.

The assay office took steps to try to eliminate this pernicious practice of duty-dodging, and in 1739 all goldsmiths were ordered to register new marks. These had to be in a different style than their previous sterling or Britannia standard marks. Two years later they also made some effort to use scattered marks on many wares such as salvers and candlesticks, so that marks could not easily be inserted in other larger pieces, but the assay office does not seem to have kept its own rules. Nonetheless, the duty-dodgers have caused collectors many a headache; though some are of proper standard silver and the inserted marks approximate to the date of manufacture, collectors need to exercise considerable care when purchasing part-marked pieces (such as cups and covers or coffee pots with no cover mark), as they may be later fakes rather than contemporary evasions.

DUTY MARKS

In 1757 the Government recognised that very little duty was being paid over, although the silver trade was obviously flourishing. So they temporarily abandoned the tax, and imposed instead a £2 plate licence which from 1758 onwards was payable by all who made or traded in the precious metals. It also made the counterfeiting of hallmarks a felony, punishable by death.

A quarter of a century later, when a duty on silver and gold was again proposed, the authorities avoided the 1720 trap and recorded that duty had indeed been paid on every piece of precious metal (other than the lightest and flimsiest examples) by having the Sovereign's Head mark stamped on the ware at the time of assay. At first, from December 1st, 1784, until May 1786, the head of King George III was shown incuse in an octagonal punch, facing to the left. From 1786 onwards, however, the more easily cut mark in cameo was used, the Sovereign's Head facing to the right, a practice followed under George IV and William IV as well. The head of Queen Victoria, however, faces left. The mark was also struck at all the provincial assay offices, though its introduction was delayed in Dublin until 1807.

The rate of duty imposed in 1784 was the old one of 6d. an ounce on silver, but in 1797 it was doubled (when Birmingham in particular showed this double duty by striking the King's Head mark twice, though the practice was soon discontinued). The tax was increased to 1s. 3d. in 1804 and to a top price of 1s. 6d. in 1815, calculated on 5/6th of the total weight of the assayed piece. This calculation helped to allow for usual wastage in finishing.

The £2 Plate Licence remained as a further imposition on the silversmith and silver retailer. It was recently withdrawn. The duty on silver and gold was finally removed in 1890.

THE BRITANNIA DUTY DRAWBACK MARK

For nine months, from December 1st, 1784 until July 1785, the figure of Britannia – standing and struck incuse – was used on silver and gold that was exported and therefore free of duty. Since it was struck on finished wares, the danger of damage was substantial, wares normally being finished, polished, engraved, and so on after assaying and marking. It was therefore withdrawn in 1785, and duty drawback claimed on shipping bills.

OTHER AUTHORISED MARKS

On three occasions, special marks have been permitted: in 1934 to 1935 to celebrate the Silver Jubilee of George V and Queen Mary, used voluntarily on silver only; in 1952 to 1953 for the Coronation of Elizabeth II (on both silver and gold); and in 1977 for Her Majesty's Silver Jubilee (also a voluntary mark, for silver only).

THE MARKS ON SILVER

Jan. 1934 to Dec. 1935   1952 to 1953   1977

IMPORTED WARES

From 1867, a letter F was struck to denote imported silver, which had, of course, to be at least of sterling standard. This was altered in 1904, and each Assay Office struck a special mark of its own, alongside standard marks and date letters, to authenticate the standard of imported gold and silver.

PROVINCIAL ASSAY OFFICES

Birmingham (since 1773)

Chester (closed in 1962)

Before 1701   1701 to 1779   1779 to 1962

246

THE MARKS ON SILVER

Exeter (closed in 1883)

Before 1701   1701 to 1882

Newcastle (closed in 1884)

Norwich (until about 1702)

16th century   17th century   1701

Sheffield (since 1773)

1773 to 1975   Since 1975

York (until 1856)

247

THE MARKS ON SILVER

A FEW ATTRIBUTED TOWN MARKS

England

Barnstaple

Bristol

Hull

King's Lynn

Leeds

Plymouth

Taunton

Ireland

Dublin

Cork

Limerick

Youghal

Scotland

Edinburgh

Glasgow (closed 1964)

Aberdeen

Arbroath

Banff

Canongate, Edinburgh

Dundee

Elgin

Greenock

Inverness

Montrose

Perth

THE MARKS ON SILVER

UNDERSTANDING THE HALLMARKS

It is easy enough to consult a book giving tables of hallmarks on silver and gold and to accept that because a piece bears maker's mark, standard mark, town mark, date letter (and perhaps also a duty mark or another Sovereign's Head mark such as the Coronation mark) that it is of such a date and that all is well. It should be so, but what the books cannot show is every variation of the shield, the form of the mark and the placing of the marks on an individual piece. In the assay office new punches may have to be made; identical replicas are very unlikely, so that the fringed mane, say, of the Lion Passant may differ even during a single year. In busy years several punches of the same size may be needed, appearing nice and crisp in the first months from May onwards, but gradually showing signs of wear until they are replaced. Sometimes the assayers struck a large mark on a small item, sometimes they struck one punch twice omitting, say, the date letter and using the Lion Passant twice. Nonetheless, most hallmarks are very much as the books illustrate. The Leopard's Head Crowned, for instance, was good and plump in the 17th century, but became definitely emaciated by the late 1730s; by 1756 it assumed an almost pointed chin so that a correspondent once wrote that the silver in question had 'a jester's head' alongside 'a walking dog'!

The placing of the marks is a useful guide to both date and legitimacy of many pieces: flat-topped tankards of the 17th century were usually marked to the right of the handle and in full, as well across the top of the cover. With the arrival of the domed-top in the early 18th century, the cover marks were usually reduced to a maker's mark and the Lion, inside the dome. Candlesticks received individual marks inside the cast base, usually at each corner, or scattered; when loaded 'sticks became popular in the second half of the 18th century, marks were usually struck in a line along the rim at the base.

THE MARKS ON SILVER

Not only the position but also the style of the marks, the shields in which they are contained and their depth of striking will prove a guide to the collector with a keen eye. Smallwares, such as wine labels, teaspoons and so on, that until 1790 were exempted from full marking (though not from assaying), usually carry the maker's mark and the sterling Lion only. Knowing the maker's approximate dates and the shape of the Lion in the different cycles (plus, of course, the style) helps to put the piece in context and may even suggest a pretty accurate date.

Hallmarks are usually rather heavily struck, and can often be clearly seen from the inside of the piece, even when it is quite substantial. This gives the edge of a genuine hallmark a crispness which, though it may wear down through constant use of the piece and cleaning, retains a definition that is seldom blurred or 'soft'. The latter is the case with most faked marks, which are made with cheaper and more easily cut dies than the steel ones used officially.

This is not to imply that all 'rubbed' marks are suspect or that all proper and authentic marks have no softness on occasion, though one should always immediately be suspicious of Britannia marks that are fairly crisp in association with rubbed makers' marks and date letter: often a sure sign of modern Britannia pieces being passed off as antique. (*See also* Chapter Six.)

As a rule the maker's mark does not appear as clearly nor as heavily struck as the assay office hallmarks. Originally the maker's mark was struck after the assay and marking; nowadays it is put on first.

CHAPTER SIX

Notes and Hints for the Collector

The most important attribute of the collector is his or her personal taste. However rare, however expensive, however important a piece of silver may be in other men's eyes, one's own appreciation of and liking for an object must come first. To that, however, must be added a proper judgement of quality, of the 'rightness' of the piece, not only in the context of its age but also as a work of craftsmanship, unimpaired by later alterations, added or erased engraving and chasing, and so on.

A collector's taste and liking for silver is engendered by looking at silver as silver: not as a product of the hallmarking laws, nor the opinions voiced in books and the like. Indeed, books and articles even by otherwise distinguished writers often contain more than their fair share of mistakes. They may perpetuate old gaffes, carelessly repeat old wives' tales without thinking about the process of design and making silver, and ignore the results of historical and technical research. Too much reliance on the marks, invaluable though they can be, leads to neglect of the finer points of design; accepting other peoples' opinions may lead one to overlook discrepancies that a fresh personal, critical approach better reveals.

This is not to dismiss the importance of the silver dealer. Many collectors think that they can do better by making their own bids at auction rather than paying what is often only a very modest price for the advice and expertise of a dealer who spends his working life handling, buying and selling all kinds of silver. Obviously, not all dealers are academically knowledgeable, and some are openly contemptuous of the historical approach to silver. If it does not matter to them that such a maker lived in such a place, or that such a piece is related to contemporary porcelain or was used for a certain purpose, they are nonetheless very likely to understand the metal, to recognise fakes and forgeries and to advise the serious collector. The specialist silver dealer can be both friend and mentor, his special knowledge repaying the extra outlay, often surprisingly small, which he must charge to make his profit. How far to rely on the dealer must be a question of personal choice and the collector's own accumulated knowledge. For some, the thrill of the chase, the seeking out of pieces in unsuspected places, and outbidding others in the saleroom counter-balance the sense of security that a reputable dealer can offer.

A. Fakes, Forgeries and Furbishing

There have been fakers and forgers of silver about ever since precious metals were first extracted from the earth. Over the centuries, many types of forgery have been perpetrated. A great many concern coinage, and the passing off of vessels of base metal as silver or gold. Even Greek antiquities were forged in ancient times to deceive Roman collectors; in medieval times it was ruled illegal to gild copper or latten (brass). Despite the searches made by the Goldsmiths' Company and the protection afforded by hallmarking, rogues have often succeeded: a brass cup showing traces of gilding dated to 1510 is in the Victoria and Albert Museum, no doubt once passed off as silver-gilt. In 1878, when Wilfrid Cripps wrote his pioneer work *Old English Plate* he feared that fake silver was to be had by the cab load, and thought that very little genuine English plate was available in London. Even today, despite the invaluable work of the Antique Plate Committee, fakes and forgeries can and do still slip through the net to delude the gullible and the unknowledgeable.

The hallmarking regulations have, of course, been of inestimable value in deterring forgers and detecting fakes, though it seems that there are still those prepared to risk a long term of imprisonment for forging hallmarks and passing off substandard metal as gold or silver.

There are four main types of hallmarking offence: the transposition of marks from one piece to another; the actual forging of punches and applying them to a modern, often substandard, piece and tampering with genuine marks; the copying of genuine antiques by casting or by electrotyping; and illegal additions or alterations to a hallmarked piece.

Transposition of Marks

Probably the commonest of all forgeries is the transposition of marks, which is considered just as heinous an offence as forging the marks themselves. In the past, such transposing of marks was not infrequently done by otherwise quite reputable silversmiths; this practice resulted from the imposition of duty in 1720, known as duty-dodging. To avoid paying 6d. an ounce on their finished silver, especially on large objects such as heavy cups and covers, wine cisterns and even tea-kettles, the silversmith would, while making the piece, insert the marks from another smaller object. He thus avoided sending it for assay and the heavy duty charge. On cups, such marks were often applied as a disc inserted between the body and foot. The absence of any sign of the shadow of the mark in the case, plus the fact that the cover is unlikely to be marked, is a useful guide to detecting a duty-dodger. On heavily chased pieces, the marks would usually be soldered in so that the rich decoration tended to obscure the joins – a technique also used by more modern forgers, though they are seldom prepared to spend time and money on imitating the very fine craftsmanship of the rococo period.

Until recently, duty-dodgers were not acceptable by way of

trade, and if brought to the notice of the assay offices were usually broken. The law has now been amended to allow such pieces to be sold in shops or at auction provided the metal is up to standard and the piece is submitted for re-assay and marking with a sponsor's mark and the appropriate modern hallmarks, the old duty-dodging marks being erased.

The old duty-dodgers are, on the whole, of the proper sterling standard, the silversmiths perpetuating such offences – among them leading London craftsmen such as Paul de Lamerie and George Wickes – seeking to evade the tax rather than deceive their customers. The duty payable on the massive cups and bowls of the period was, of course, considerable: some £2 on an 80 oz. cup that perhaps would have cost £20 or £30 in all.

More recent forgers, using transposed marks, frequently cut from an insignificant or a damaged piece, often greedily use substandard metal for their frauds. Because the marks are cut from wares that over the years have become worn, or from vessels of which the curve of the surface is not exactly like that of the new piece, transposed marks often show signs of distortion. Marks on spoons, often used by modern forgers, are notoriously difficult to keep true. Even before re-use they show the results of the way the spoon was made, being finished after marking, while the thicker stem needs flattening out to the gauge of the new object, likely to be a more expensive coffee pot or punch bowl. Concealing the joins is often done by electroplating the whole piece; a sharp eye and appreciation of the proper colour of old silver can help to detect such forgeries, even if the base metal is indeed of sterling silver or better. Knowledge, too, of the makers and the way they worked, and the things they made, often helps to unmask these forgeries, for, with rare exceptions, spoonmakers made flatware, salver makers often specialised in waiters and trays, and so on. To find a spoon-maker's mark on a salver, or a caster maker's on a cup and cover should sound a warning to the collector as this can be a just cause for suspicion.

NOTES AND HINTS FOR THE COLLECTOR

Forged Marks

Actual forged marks made from modern dies built up from genuine old marks are also found. Here knowing one's marks intimately is an essential safeguard, knowledge that the greedy faker usually neglects. Greed also precludes his making punches of the very high quality used by the assay offices, so that the outlines are seldom as sharp and clear, even of the maker's mark, which is as a rule less sharp than that of the official punches. For economy the forger tends to cut his dies – or cast them – in softer metal such as copper or brass. The 'soft' look of these marks is flatter and unconvincing even when compared with genuine very worn marks.

His knowledge may also fail him when it comes to the correct placing of the marks. A recent case concerning forged punches was revealed when the forger struck the marks on the base of an '18th century cast candlestick' in a row, instead of scattered at the four corners. Indeed, many fakes, especially those emanating from the Continent and from America, shown an abysmal ignorance of hallmarks as well as, often enough, of period silver.

Besides the forging of marks, defacement is also a criminal offence. Instances noted include the rubbing down of the Sovereign's Head Duty Mark to suggest that a piece is dated prior to 1784, though careful examination of the form of the shields and style of the hallmarks, plus perhaps also the maker's mark, will reveal the deception. Modern silver of the Britannia standard, which is still marked with the figure of Britannia and the Lion's Head Erased, has been fraudulently defaced, the edges of the modern punches being blurred artificially, and the date letter and maker's mark defaced so that it is unclear.

Technically, overstriking the maker's mark is an offence, though 200 years ago it was commonplace. Retailers, usually in London, but occasionally in the provinces, often overstruck the marks of the actual makers. The London silversmith John Carter was especially notorious for this practice, and apparently with the cognisance and collaboration of the London Assay Office itself; dozens of examples of Sheffield-made and marked candlesticks of the 1770s have been found bearing his marks overstriking the Sheffield makers' mark, and full London hallmarks overstriking those of the newly inaugurated Sheffield Assay Office. Earlier marks of other silversmiths, among them Paul de Lamerie and many other notable craftsmen, have been found overstriking those of other makers, presumably when they were acting as retailers.

Cast and Electro-typed Copies

Silver that has been made by casting, for example candlesticks, some cups, small jugs, tapersticks and other heavy small pieces, are sometimes used as originals for fakes made by the same method. Other pieces not normally made by casting, such as spoons, may also be forged in this way. The principle here is that a pair, or a set of four or six is worth many times two, four or six times that for a singleton.

Three warning signs help to betray the origin of these forgeries: the presence of pit marks; the lack of solder lines; and the inevitable softening of the hallmarks and any decorative detail. Pit marks may, for example, be found even as part of the punch marks, an impossibility on genuine pieces since any pitting left, if the original were cast, would be cleaned off before hallmarking. Even seemingly one-piece original cast wares are in fact made in sections; tiny, often almost imperceptible, solder lines are found on even the finest and best-finished antiques at the junction of handle and body, between cover and finial, body and foot, spoon stem and finial, and so on. All cast wares need to be cleaned up by the silversmith before finishing. Modern cast copies of antique originals are made for quick gain. The men concerned are unlikely to spend good time on such niceties, any more than they would trouble to reproduce the proper appearance of patination, even if the casting were up to standard. Spoons should also be

NOTES AND HINTS FOR THE COLLECTOR

viewed very carefully: those with finials should reveal the joint of stem and top, while sets of spoons, candlesticks or anything else made in quantity will, if genuine, reveal variations in the placing of the marks; the marks were struck individually and the chances of striking exactly the same spot even on two of a kind is unlikely. Even after 1790, when group marks were used for flatware, it is unlikely that the place of each and its relationship to the separately struck maker's mark would be identical.

The invention of Sheffield plate, especially after the introduction of silver edges, provided the contemporary rogue with a chance to delude customers into thinking that they were buying sterling silver. This was easy enough as the standard of finish on Old Sheffield was exceptionally high, and the layer of sterling thick enough to be almost indistinguishable from true silverwares. The use, too, of imitation 'hallmarks' by the Sheffield platers, was misleading. This practice was ended in 1784 when all makers were obliged to register marks quite unlike those used at the assay offices.

Though brighter-looking, because the plated layer is pure silver, not sterling, electro-plating has occasionally been employed to take in the unwary; even with individually struck marks tending to look as though they might be hallmarks, anyone accustomed to handling silver, old or new, is unlikely to be confused either by its appearance or its weight.

Electro-plating did, however, give rise to the useful, but potentially dangerous, technique of electroforming or electro-typing. In use by 1845, any material, whether metal or not, can be exactly copied by the process, reproducing either in silver or base metal every detail, and as crisply, the original. There is a danger that such copies, even if properly marked as being electro-typed, could in time lose their provenance and take in the unsuspecting. The technique was, of course, extensively used by Elkington's for some of their most popular products during the 1860s and 1870s, among them decorative shields and plaques and ivory tankards.

Illegal Additions and Alterations

It is illegal to alter the purpose of a hallmarked piece or to add metal to increase the weight. During the 19th century, lipless jugs were unpopular and short spouts were often added even though, after 1844, the additional silver needed should have been assayed and marked. Restoration can be effected to make the ware legal again, the new metal added in place of the later spout needing to be assayed and marked. Other illegal alterations include new feet or borders on salvers and waiters; silver handles and hinges on tea and coffee pots; new thumbpieces on tankards or handles on cups and bowls, all of which should bear hallmarks if they are restorations.

To alter the character of a piece of silver is another fraudulent practice, usually committed to provide a more saleable article. Hence fairly common trefid spoons are converted into rare forks, or plain 18th-century spoons are supplied with modern rat-tails to counterfeit the rarer original rat-tail pattern. Small mugs are turned into straight-sided 'lighthouse' casters, bellied ones into cream jugs; there are coffee pots that were once tankards, cream boats that were formerly punch ladles, strainers and wine tasters that were once wine funnels, teapots made from kettles, salvers and shallow dishes turned into inkstands and even candle-holders and spoons made into napkin rings and into the bases of pedestal-foot casters.

Refurbishing

Other alterations, though not strictly illegal, but inherently fraudulent since their purpose is to enhance the value of an antique, include the removal of parts such as feet and applied crests, adding or removing chasing, adding or removing armorials and crests, adding inscriptions and other similar undesirable practices.

From the early 1800s until well into the 20th century, taste for the highly decorative resulted in much early plain silver being 'improved' with rather florid repoussé chasing, usually in the rococo manner. This, besides its often rather out-of-period appearance, can often be detected by close examination of the hallmarks as the chasers were seldom careful enough to make it appear as though the work were done before marking. An interesting – and authentic – example of such 19th century 'improving' is a ewer of 1698 by Pierre Harache applied with a shell-and-scroll band, also in the Britannia standard, bearing the mark of Robert Garrard. Later chasing can legally be removed, but the need for careful hammering and annealing not only makes such restoration difficult but inevitably weakens the vessel and destroys its antique patina.

The removal of feet from salvers and caskets, and even borders from dishes and plates is not necessarily illegal, though it would probably be argued that removing a broken trumpet foot from a 17th-century salver and presenting it as a dish is unlawful. Similarly, applied crests have been removed, finials replaced and the rims of mugs reswaged.

The vexed question of engraved crests and armorials is one that causes concern. Again, the object is financial, for a worthy provenance will endow an otherwise ordinary piece of silver with a mystique that appeals to the unsophisticated or the snobbish buyer. The removal of simple or later crests and monograms and their substitution with full armorials pertaining to a noble family has become a commonplace much to be deprecated. They can often be detected by their crispness, not concomitant with wear on the rest of the piece, including the hallmarks, and by the perpetrator's keenness to show off details such as colours not always used for early armorial representations on silver. Generally speaking, the more complex the arms, the later their date. Inscriptions referring to notable people or events should be most carefully examined. Many such inscriptions are, of course, perfectly in order, but like armorials they should be closely inspected for signs of modern toolwork, including that of the 'crisper-up'.

Unwanted engravings such as modern inscriptions and crests can, of course, easily be removed and satisfactorily so if the piece is of good gauge and ungilded. But removal of engraving entails removing the surface of the silver itself and any thinness where one would expect arms to be should be treated with caution.

The detecting of fakes and forgeries relies very much on a wide knowledge of styles, makers and marks, with special attention to the placing of the marks, the period of the piece and the 'feel' of it as well. In many cases, even long experience needs the additional help of modern investigative equipment. The London Assay Office, for instance, has scientific equipment that can surely and efficiency differentiate between not only substandard and standard silver and gold, but can even determine the date and place of making. In association with the Antique Plate Committee, it helps to authenticate genuine unmarked pieces as well as to eliminate fakes and forgeries, which, through the long and stringent application of the hallmarking laws, are happily fewer than might be expected in a luxury trade.

B. The Care and Cleaning of Silver and Silver-gilt

Silver is a durable metal that takes a good polish and eventually acquires that subtle lustre known as patination. It is not, however, indestructible; rough treatment, especially of gilt or parcel-gilt pieces, can irreparably damage it. A few simple precautions not only protect the surface but can enhance the lustrous sheen that is so admired a property of old silver.

The patina on silver is a slow process acquired by long usage. It cannot be truly imitated, though it can be destroyed by over-polishing. The answer is to keep it clean with the minimum application of polishing agents. Silver that is in regular use, washed and dusted, will, even in the tarnish-inducing atmosphere of towns, keep better than silver shut away in a drawer of a cupboard. Of course occasional polishing is essential, for only in exceptional conditions – in an atmosphere free of sulphur and dampness – will untreated silver be tarnish-resistant.

Tarnish is due to sulphur combining with the silver, so that when it is removed, some of the surface of the silver also vanishes on the polishing cloth in the form of silver sulphide. The thicker the layer of tarnish, the more purplish-black the corroding layer becomes – and the more difficult to remove. The burning of coal, gas and oil all contribute to sulphur in the air, and tarnishing is aggravated by dirt and dust in general. There is also sulphur present in many foodstuffs, notably peas, eggs and Brussels sprouts. Other chemicals attacking silver are ammonia in combination with dampness, ozone and, often unsuspected, hydrogen sulphide. The latter is present in many household paints and modern household fabrics and floor coverings; emulsion paint is a notorious example. The most persistant and dangerous contaminant is salt, which quickly corrodes silver, causing black spots that are extremely difficult to remove and whose removal also entails removal of the silver itself to some depth. It has been found that common salt in association with many washing-up liquids (detergents) will cause highly resistant stains on spoons, forks and knives. Salt should always be removed from cellars after use, salt spoons should be rinsed and never left in the salt, and care should be taken not to allow salt being washed off plates, etc. to contaminate silver.

Regular washing is a deterrent to tarnish that obviates the need for frequent and harmful polishing. Warm soapy water should be stirred to a good froth. If detergents have to be used, use them very sparingly. Never wash up silver without rinsing it; then drying it gently with a soft cloth or chamois leather. The same applies to silver-gilt and parcel-gilt, and to Sheffield (fused) plate and to electro-plated wares.

The actual cleaning and polishing of silver is often considered a bugbear even by keen collectors, yet modern cleaners and polishes containing tarnish-inhibitors are far less messy and far less damaging to the silver than the abrasives used in the 18th century. Indeed, our ancestors found that gilding was often the only answer to keeping richly chased silver in good condition; until 1839 they did not have the advantage even of ordinary plate powders. There was only rouge (calcined ferrous sulphate) which is not easy to use, though safe, and whiting mixed with mercury which was not only dangerous to the user but liable to cause damage to the silver as well. The fact, too, that keeping the silver clean is now often a task for the owner rather than a weekly or monthly chore for a regiment of servants means that it is less likely to suffer from heavy hands and too much abrasive polish that give too brilliant a shine and wear away marks, patina and engraved and flat-chased details at the same time. It is a wise collector who spares the polish and keeps his thumb over the marks and finer details of decoration.

Curiously enough, it was the introduction of plating as a substitute for silver that led the way to a better and less harmful method of cleaning it. In 1839 a Midlands chemist, Joseph Goddard, took the first commercial step in the production of an easily handled effective silver polish. He realised that mercurial polishes were having a disastrous effect on the relatively thin skin of silver on fused plate and on the newly developed electro-plated wares. His Non-Mercural Plate Polish was a great step forward, though still rather messy to use and requiring patience and careful brushing to extricate traces of the powder from crevices, piercing and, indeed, from the hallmarks. Nonetheless, it was more than a century before any real improvements on his polishes were made, in the forms of creams, liquid polishes and in the revolutionary new cleaner (though not a polishing agent) called Silver Dip, made, in fact, by Goddard's own firm. This is highly effective for removing heavy tarnish and for penetrating small spaces not easily reached with polish and duster. It has immediate effect on sulphur stains on egg-spoons and forks especially, but care has to be taken since it has the disadvantage of blackening steel and does smell rather unpleasant. A non-metallic bath is useful for bulk treatment, and immediate rinsing (in a non-steel sink) is also essential. Rubbing up after thorough rinsing with a soft impregnated cloth and occasional further polishing with a gentle agent is required.

Modern liquid polishes, though still entailing some dirty manual labour, do have the advantage that they contain tarnish-inhibitors of greater or lesser efficacy, and that the excess polish can be rinsed off before the silver is gently rubbed with a soft cloth or chamois leather. A soft good quality plate brush or a very soft toothbrush are invaluable for getting polish out of undercuts, crevices, and so on. Even in smoky or urban areas, the effects of modern polishes should last several months. Washing, drying, dusting and gentle rubbing up from time to time with an impregnated polishing cloth should generally suffice to keep the silver clean and softly lustrous.

For silver on display and for domestic silver that does not come into contact with more than moderate heat or is given harder use, silicone treatments have been developed. They are considerably better in appearance than varnishes and other processes which either yellow with age and tend to crack or give the silver a harsh bright finish. Rhodium-plating, for instance, is not suitable for antique or other precious silverwares, since though almost indestructible (rhodium is one of the platinum group of metals) it has a cold brilliance and cannot easily be removed – on small objects, removal is almost impossible. The most successful and almost invisible silicone treatment used in this country is the Monarch Shield process, which can be used on silver, gilt, plated wares and on base metals alike. Though not suitable for flatware and cutlery, nor for pieces that necessarily get very hot, such as entrée dishes and ashtrays, the protective layer can be removed and the piece re-treated when required. This is usually necessary after a space of some years, provided that the silver has not been cleaned by ordinary methods or is much jostled by contact with other pieces or with abrasive materials. It can, however, be kept clean by washing and rinsing gently in the same way as untreated silver.

If silver is put away in drawers or cupboards, it should preferably be wrapped in acid-free (not ordinary) tissue paper, which is available from jewellers' sundriesmen. Tarnish-resistant treated bags and cutlery rolls are also available. Pieces should be stored separately, and not allowed to rub against their neighbours. Great care should be taken that cupboards are dry and airy, and free of noxious chemical pollutants.

When handling silver, it is a good idea to wear soft cotton gloves. Always cradle the piece in your hands – do not pick up a candlestick by the sconce at the top or a cup by its handle. Similarly, when polishing, support the silver on a soft surface or hold it against the body so that the metal does not take the pressures or weight on vulnerable parts during the process. Though bruises and dents can usually be competently removed by a silversmith, the task becomes more difficult with wares that have been loaded (i.e., filled with plaster, wood or a resinous substances to give them stability). Hinges on snuff boxes and vinaigrettes can be badly damaged by holding the box by its lid. Clumsy handling may well send the lid of a tankard crashing down on to the top of the handle, even splitting it, while the rim foot of a cup, bowl, caster, coffee pot or goblet can sustain damage from having been thumped down on a hard surface. One of the most common types of damage is caused by compressing the feet of sauceboats and cream jugs so that they dent the inside of the vessel. Prospective buyers should inspect the insides of three-legged sauceboats and similar articles most carefully. Salvers, with panel feet and those

NOTES AND HINTS FOR THE COLLECTOR

with heavier cast feet are also often impacted. They can themselves damage other pieces if packed together.

Most such defects can be repaired. Damage to gilded and plated objects is less easily rectified. Because mercurial or fire gilding is not now permissible, replacement of parcel gilding is often impossible; even matching old gilding and replacing it with electro-gilding is not always satisfactory, since the colours are difficult to repeat. Plated wares are often irreparable since the process of making fused plate by the old methods is not practised, so that the sterling silver layer of plate cannot be reproduced. Modern electro-plating is not satisfactory, though it can properly be used to repair old electro-plated wares, though of course they will cease to look their age.

Appendices

APPENDIX A
Some Useful Dates

The Sovereigns of England
1272 to 1307 Edward I
1307 to 1327 Edward II
1327 to 1377 Edward III
1377 to 1399 Richard II
1399 to 1413 Henry IV
1413 to 1422 Henry V
1422 to 1461 Henry VI
1461 to 1483 Edward IV

1483   Edward V
1483 to 1485 Richard III
1485 to 1509 Henry VII
1509 to 1547 Henry VIII
1547 to 1553 Edward VI
1553 to 1558 Mary I
1558 to 1603 Elizabeth I
1603 to 1625 James I
1625 to 1649 Charles I
1649 to 1660 Commonwealth
1660 to 1685 Charles II

1685 to 1689 James II
1689 to 1694 William and Mary
1695 to 1702 William III

APPENDIX A

1702 to 1714 Anne

1714 to 1727 George I

1727 to 1760 George II

1760 to 1820 George III
(1811 to 1820 Regency)

1820 to 1830 George IV

1830 to 1837 William IV
1837 to 1901 Victoria

1901 to 1910 Edward VII
1910 to 1936 George V

1936   Edward VIII
1936 to 1952 George VI
1952 to present Elizabeth II

APPENDIX A

Notable events

1300 First Hallmarking statute

1363 Makers' marks ordained

1423 Seven assay towns named
1478 Date letter system introduced, December 17th
Annual change made on May 19th, St Dunstan's Day

1544 Lion Passant Guardant Crowned mark first used
1550 Lion Passant Guardant no longer crowned

1660 Date letter changed annually on May 29th
(Date of King's return, also his birthday)
1685 Revocation of Edict of Nantes by Louis XIV, October 18th

1696 Statute raising standard to 11 oz. 10 dwt. put into force March 27th, 1697
1701 to 1702 Provincial assay offices re-established at Exeter, Norwich, Newcastle, Chester and York
1719 Statute restoring sterling standard in operation from June 1st, 1720. Britannia standard optional. Duty of 6d. oz. imposed on wrought silver
1739 Re-registering of all makers' marks ordered
1758 Duty rescinded, replaced by £2 Plate Licence

APPENDIX A

1773 Birmingham and Sheffield Assay Offices set up
1784 Duty reimposed and Sovereign's Head Duty Mark struck on payment (incuse until 1786, in cameo thereafter)
Incuse Britannia struck on exported wares only until July 1785
1819 Glasgow Assay Office re-established
1822 Leopard's Head loses Crown. Lion Passant no longer Guardant

1856 York Assay Office closed
1883 Exeter Assay Office closed
1884 Newcastle Assay Office closed
1890 Plate duty removed (£2 Licence remaining)

1933 to 1935 Silver Jubilee mark (profile of George V and Queen Mary) permitted on silver
1952 to 1953 Queen's Head Coronation mark (facing to right)
1962 Chester Assay Office closed
1964 Glasgow Assay Office closed
1975 New series of date letters for all four remaining British assay offices changed annually on January 1st. Mark for Sheffield changed from a Crown to the Yorkshire Rose
1977 Silver Jubilee mark (Queen's head facing to left) allowed on silver

APPENDIX B

Weights and Measures

Weights
Despite decimalisation and metrication, Troy weight is still widely used.

24 grains = 1 pennyweight (dwt.) = 1.555 grammes (g) = 0.055 oz. avoirdupois weight.

20 pennyweights = 1 ounce Troy = 31.1 grammes = 1.097 oz. avoirdupois weight.

12 ounces Troy = one pound Troy = 373.2 grammes

1 gramme = 0.032 oz. Troy = 0.643 dwt.

Measures
1 inch = 2.54 cm.
1 centimetre = 0.39 in.

APPENDIX C

The Patent Office Design Registry

The growth of industrial production in the early 19th century focussed attention on standards of design; in 1835 a 'Select Committee on Arts and Manufactures' was appointed by Parliament. Its report recommended that it 'imports us to encourage art in its loftier attributes' and added that 'the cultivation on the more exalted branches of design tends to advance the humblest pursuits of industry'. This rather self-conscious concern with design meant growing jealousy among craftsmen who until then had cheerfully borrowed one another's patterns and had had, it seems, no qualms in copying the best that was being produced.

Some protection against plagiarism was afforded by the Design Acts of 1839 and 1842. At first, manufacturers simply registered their design, and often engraved or stamped the fact on the wares. In 1842 they were further assisted by the special mark of the Patent Office Design Registry, a lozenge-shaped mark which recorded the firm's patent rights over a design for a period up to three years. From the letters and numbers shown on the mark can be determined the class of goods (metalwork was Class I), the day, month and year of registration, and the parcel number from which the manufacturer's or designer's name can be checked.

Months key

C January	**E** May	**D** September
G February	**M** June	**B** October
W March	**I** July	**K** November
H April	**R** August	**A** December

APPENDIX C

Years key (1842 to 1867)

X	1842	S	1849	L	1856	O	1862
H	1843	V	1850	K	1857	G	1863
C	1844	P	1851	B	1858	N	1864
A	1845	D	1852	M	1859	W	1865
I	1846	Y	1853	Z	1860	Q	1866
F	1847	J	1854	R	1861	T	1867
U	1848	E	1855				

Years key (1868 to 1883)

X	1868	I	1872	V	1876	J	1880
H	1869	F	1873	P	1877	E	1881
C	1870	U	1874	D	1878	L	1882
A	1871	S	1875	Y	1879	K	1883

From 1842 to 1867, the lozenge, read clockwise, gives the year, the day of the month, the parcel number, and the month.
From 1868 to 1883, the lozenge reads from the top, clockwise, the day of the month, the year, the month and parcel number.
After 1884, a series of numbers were used instead, and usually appear on good prefixed by the words *Regd.* or *Regd. No.*

A Short Critical Bibliography

In consulting books on the history of silver and of hallmarks, two major points should be taken into account: first, the history of silver is a relatively modern study, and many of the earlier books have become outdated through later researches, though they remain valuable to the student who has more than a passing knowledge of the subject; and second, that many general histories, and particularly many of the recent 'popular' books on collecting tend to repeat earlier and sometimes inaccurate material. Because a fact is stated, whether in a general history, a specialised monograph, a book of hallmarks or a saleroom catalogue, it is in fact no guarantee of accuracy.

GENERAL

Judith Banister: *Old English Silver* (1965)
Judith Banister: *English Silver* (1965)
Frederick Bradbury: *History of Old Sheffield Plate* (1912, reprinted 1968)
Michael Clayton: *The Collectors' Dictionary of Silver and Gold* (1971)
John Culme: *Nineteenth-Century Silver* (1977)
Eric Delieb: *Investing in Silver* (1967)
Eric Delieb: *Silver Boxes* (1968)
A. G. Grimwade: *Rococo Silver, 1725 to 1765* (1974)
John F. Hayward: *Huguenot Silver in England, 1688 to 1727* (1959)

Carl Hernmarck: *The Art of the European Silversmith, 1430 to 1830* (1977)
Sir Charles J. Jackson: *The Illustrated History of English Plate* (1911, reprinted 1967)
Richard Mayne: *Old Channel Islands Silver* (1969)
C. C. Oman: *Caroline Silver, 1625 to 1688* (1970)
C. C. Oman: *English Church Plate, 1597 to 1830* (1957)
C. C. Oman: *English Domestic Silver* (5th edition, 1962)
C. C. Oman: *English Engraved Silver, 1150 to 1900* (1978)
N. M. Penzer: *Paul Storr* (1954, reprinted 1971)
P. A. S. Phillips: *Paul de Lamerie* (1935)
Maurice H. Ridgway: *Chester Goldsmiths from Early Times to 1726* (1968)
Robert Rowe: *Adam Silver, 1765 to 1795* (1965)
Patricia Wardle: *Victorian Silver and Silver-Plate* (1963)

HALLMARKING

Board of Trade: *Report of The Departmental Committee on Hallmarks* (1959)
J. P. de Castro: *The Law and Practice of Hallmarking* (1926)
A. K. Crisp-Jones, ed.: *The Silversmiths of Birmingham and Their Marks, 1750 to 1980* (1981)
M. A. V. Gill: *Marks of the Newcastle Goldsmiths 1702 to 1884* (1974)
Worshipful Company of Goldsmiths: *Touching Gold and Silver, 500 Years of Hallmarks* (1977)
A. G. Grimwade: *London Goldsmiths 1697 to 1837, Their Lives and Marks* (1976)
Sir Charles J. Jackson: *English Goldsmiths and Their Marks* (1921)
T. A. Kent: *The London Silver Spoonmakers 1500 to 1697*, The Silver Society (1981)
The Church plate of nearly every county in England and Wales

is covered in a number of useful books.

For handy reference there are a number of pocket books showing town marks and date letters including –

Frederick Bradbury: *British and Irish Silver Marks*

Judith Banister: *English Silver Hallmarks* (Makers' marks, not compiled by the author, should be ignored as many are inaccurate.)

SPECIAL SUBJECTS

Many special subjects are covered by exhibition catalogues, volumes on Church plate, on making and manufacture, descriptive literature of museum and other collections. Some early catalogues provide excellent illustrations and sometimes long descriptions of silver, but attributions of marks, etc. should be viewed with great care. The illustrated catalogues issued by the major salerooms, especially those of Sotheby & Co., Christie, and Manson & Woods, are of considerable interest both to the collector and the historian. Several museums in the U.S. have compiled specialist catalogues of plate in their collections, the most prestigious being that issued by Colonial Williamsburg, giving full descriptions, provenance and identifying armorials as well as illustrating the objects and the hallmarks. In addition, there are a number of worthwhile biographies of silversmiths.

Index

N.B.: Numerals in **bold** type refer to figure numbers.

Abercromby, Robert 35, 163, 194
Achilles Shield 169
Adam, Robert 39–40, 41, 43, 47, 60, 204
— Charles 106
— James 204
Albert, Prince Consort 55, 59
Albright, John 153
Alchorne, Charles 106
Aldridge, Edward 119, 201
Queen Anne 7, 28, 115, 186
Antique Plate Committee 253, 261
Apostle spoons *see* spoons
Apple corers 86–7
Appleton, N. 162
Archambo and Meure 38, 107
Archambo, Peter 101
Archbold, Francis 106–7
Argand, Aimé 87
Argand lamps **14**, 87
Argyles **15**, 87–8
Argylles *see* Argyles
Armada ewers 114
Armada service 14
Armourers' & Braziers' Company 9, 123
Arts and Crafts Movement 7, 58, 59, 60, 62

Arts & Manufactures, Select Committee on 55, 273
Ashbee, C. R. 39
Asparagus dishes 88
— tongs and servers 89
Assay Offices: Birmingham 41, 57, 73, 206, 246, 271; Chester 41, 44, 206, 246, 270, 271; Dublin 206; Edinburgh 44, 206, 249; Exeter 41, 44, 206, 246, 270, 271; Glasgow 249, 271; London 44, 206, 219, 256, 261; Assay Master at, 234; Newcastle 41, 44, 206, 270, 271; Norwich 41, 206, 246, 270; Sheffield 41, 44, 206, 246, 258, 271; York 41, 44, 206, 246, 270, 271; *see also* pp. 248–9
Assembling 75–6

Bache, John 28
Baily, E. H. 46
Bamford, Thomas 34, 106
Barker, Susanna 94
Barnard Bros 54, 57, 105, 113
— & Co. 59, 144
— Edward & Sons 63, 237
Baskets 89
Bateman & Co. 44, 47, 95, 162, 238
— Hester 44, 237
— Jonathan 44

278

INDEX

— Peter 44, 237
— William 237
Baxendale, N. G. 65, 66
Beakers 13, **16**, 89–91; double beakers **16**, 90–1
Bernadotte, Count 129
Beauclerk, Lady Diana 113
Beaufort, Lady Margaret 9
Beer jugs **17**, 91–2
Bells 92
Benney, Gerald 66
Biggin, George 93
Biggins **18**, 93, 118
Binley, Richard 94
— Margaret 94
Bird, Joseph 100
Biscuit boxes 93
Blackjacks 93
Bleeding bowls **34**, 93, 156, 166; *see also* Porringers
Blount, Thomas 163
Bodendick, Jacob 22
Boleyn Cup, Cirencester 11
Bottle labels 93–5
— screws *see* corkscrews
— tickets 93–5
Boulsover, Thomas 227
Boulton, Andrew 41–2
— Matthew 46, 87, 103, 154–5, 221, 228
Boulton's 53–4
Boulton & Fothergill 143, 204
Bowls 8, **33**, **34**, 95–6; *see also* bleeding bowls, cups, écuelles, porringers, sugar bowls, toilet services
Boxes **59**, 96–7; Freedom 134
Bradbury, Thomas 60
Brandy saucepans **19**, 96, 166
Braziers 96–7

Breakfast dishes 97
Brett, William 106
Bridge, John Gowler 54
Britannia Duty Drawback Mark 213, 245
Britannia Standard 26, 29, 31, 206, 208–9, 229, 235, 239, 242–3, 260; *see also* sterling
British Industries Fair 64
Brydon, Thomas 106
Buckles 97
Burton, Jocelyn 66
Butter boats 97
— coolers 97
— dishes 97
— shells **20**, 97–8
— slices 98
— spades 98
Buttons 98
Butty & Dumee 131

Caddy *see* Tea caddies
— spoons 98–9
Cafe family **35**, 100
Cagework cups **21**, 99
Candelabra 7, 52, 102
Candlesticks 17, **22**, 100–4; baluster **56**; chamber **23**, 103–4; Monument 146
Cans 104
Canteens **24**, 104–5, 176
Card cases 105
Carter, Albert 63
— John 256
— Richard 236
Casters/castors **25**, 32, 105–8, 162
Casting 74–5
Caudle cups 108–9, 125, 156, 162, 209

279

INDEX

Cawdell, William 16
Cayenne scoops 109
'Cellini' pattern 114, 202
Chafing dishes 109
Chalices 12–13
Chamber pots 109
Chambers, William 45
Chandeliers 109–10
Charles I 17–18
Charles II 18–20
Chawner, Henry 47, 166, 237
Cheese scoops **26**, 110
— stands 110–11, 139
Chippendale **57**, 211
Chocolate cups 111
— pots **29**, 111–12
Christening cups 156
Cigar lighters 112
City Livery Companies 60–1
Claret jugs **27**, 112–14; Wyvern pattern 114
Clayton, David 197
Clements, Eric 66
Coffee pots **3**, **28**, 29, 114–18; spirit lamp stand 117–18
Communion cups 12–13, 133; paten covers 12
Compasses 118
Comyns, Richard 60
— William 63
Cooper,
— Francis 63
— John Paul 63
— Robert 194
Coqus, John 20
Corbridge lanx 29–30
Cordial pots 118
Corkscrews 118–19
Cornick, Edward 35
Cornman, Philip 131

Cotterill, Edmund 55
Counter dishes 118
Courtauld and Cowles 43, 220
Cow creamers **31**, 119
Crane, Walter 59
Cream boats **30**, 119
— jugs **29**, 119–21; 'sparrow-beak' 120
— pails 89, 121
— skimmers 121
Crespin, Paul 32, 37, 111, 164, 237, 238
Cressener Cup 9
Croft family 125
Cromwell, Oliver 18
Cruets 121–2
Crump, Francis 43
Cucumber slicers 122
Cups 9, 13, 22, **32**, **35**, 51, 90, 122–6, 198, 200, 202, 214; covered **58**; *see also* Cagework, Caudle, Chocolate, Christening, Communion, Standing, Stirrup, Tumbler, Wager, Wine cups
Cutlery 212–13; *see* Knives

Daniell, Jabez 107
— Thomas 107
Darwin, Dr Erasmus 41
Date letter 19, 193, 213, 239; St Dunstan's Day 19, 239; Oak-Apple Day 19, 239, 270; January 1st 19, 271
Decanter labels *see* bottle tickets/labels
— stands *see* wine coasters
— trolleys 126
Decoration *passim*: 78–85; 204–32 (for separate headings

280

INDEX

see subtitles within these sections and Glossary); **12**, **55**, **56**, **57**, **58**, **59**, **60**, **61**, **62**, **63**
Dee, H. W. 199
Design Acts 1839, 1842 273
Design Council 65
Design Registry *see* Patent Office
Dessert dishes 127
— stands 127
Devlin, Stuart 66
Dinner services 127
Dishes 11, 127-8, 198; Entrée 130, 162
— covers 128
— crosses 128
— rings 128
— wedges 128-9
Dixon, Arthur 58-9
— James 58
Douters *see* snuffers
Dram cups 21, 129, 156
Dredgers 126
Dresser, Dr Christopher 58, 59, 114
Dublin Goldsmiths' Company 234
Durbin, Leslie 65
'Duty-dodging' 35, 243-4, 254-5
— marks 244

Ecuelles 129
Edict of Nantes, Revocation of 25
Edward II 235
Egg coddlers 126
— cups 129-30
— spoons 130
electro-plating 213
Elizabeth I 9, 12, 14, 17, 133, 241

Elizabeth II Coronation 66; special mark for 245; Jubilee 65, 66; special mark for 245
Elkington & Co. 54-8, 61, 66, 78, 155, 171, 214, 258
Elliott, William 113
Elson, Anthony 66
Emes, John 97, 136, 237
— and Barnard 7, 50, 95, 98
Entrée dishes 130, 162
Epergnes 34, 89, 130-1
Etuis 131-2
Etwees *see* Etuis
Evelyn, John 20-1, 114;
Ewers *see* Jugs; Ewer & basin
Ewer and basin 16, 132, 161
Eye baths 132

Fabergé 221
Faraday, Michael 214, 223
Farrell, Edward 50, 95, 146, 170-1
Farrer, Thomas 158
Festival of Britain 64
Figg, J. W. 114
Finishing 76-8
First World War 62, 140, 213
Fish carvers *see* servers
— dishes 133-2, 142
— eaters 133
— servers 133
— slices *see* servers
Flagons 11, 133
Flasks 133
Flatware **6**, 217
Flaxman, John 46, 113, 114, 126, 169
Fleming, William 153, 197, 237
Fogelburg, Andrew 40, 113, 155, 190, 198

INDEX

Forks 16, 29, 133–4
Foundress's Cup, Christ's College, Cambridge 9
Fox, Charles 113, 114
Friend, G. T. 63
Furniture 134–5

Galvanic goblet 214
Garrard's *see also* Wakelin & Taylor 47, 55, 60
— Robert 49, 109, 110, 171, 237, 260
— & Co. 63
Garrick, David 191
Garthorne, George 107, 115, 145
Gaskin, Arthur 63
George I 27, 186
George II 47
George III 45, 46, 144, 187
George IV 7, 45; as Prince Regent 142, 226
George V Silver Jubilee 65–6; special mark for 245
German silver 218
Gilbert, Stephen 190
Gill, Eric 64
Ginger jars **59**, 135
Glastonbury Cup 51
Gleadowe, R. M. Y. 63, 64, 66
Goblets 11, 13, 135, 214; *see also* wine cups
Goddard, Joseph 263
Godfrey, Elizabeth 38, 101, 237
Goldsmiths' Company (Ancient Worshipful Company of) 9, 10, 14, 25, 28–9, 41, 64–5, 211, 233–5, 241, 253
— Hall 220, 233; *see also* Hallmarks
— Wardens 35, 234, 239, 241

Goodwin, James 153
Grape scissors 135, 176
Gravelot, Hubert François 34
Great Exhibition 1851 55, 199
— 1862 56
— of Dublin 1853 199
Great recoinage 1696 26, 242
Green, Thomas 100
Gribelin, Simon 83, 170
Grimwade, Arthur; *London Goldsmiths* 236
Goodden, Robert 65
Gould family 35, 100
Guild of Handicraft 59
Gwyn Nell 20, 134, 152

Hallmarks *passim*: 219–20, 233–51, 253–61, 270–1; lion passant 241; understanding 250–1; hallmarking offences 253–61; *see also* Britannia duty drawback mark; Britannia standard; Date letter; Duty-dodging; Leopard's Head 234; Marker's mark 235–8
Hamilton, Sir William 231
Hampton Court chandelier 110
Hannam and Crouch 163, 194
Hanoverian pattern 33, 134, 140, 141, 174–5, 193, 220
Harache, Pierre 28, 100, 107, 170, 220, 231, 237, 260
John Hardman & Co. 55
Hare, Susan 241
Harris, Sir Christopher 14
— Jacob 34, 106
Harrison, William 12
Harvey, John; *Gothic England* 8
Haseler, W. H. 59

282

INDEX

Hatfield, Charles 146
Heming, Thomas 38, 144, 158, 195–6
Hennell, David 35, 121, 162, 201, 237, 238
— Robert 121, 131, 162, 201, 237, 238
Henry VIII 10, 11, 17, 26, 241
Herbert, S. & Company 201, 237
Hill, Reginald 65, 66
Hindmarsh, George 35, 163
Hogarth, William 26–7, 83, 158
Holbein, Hans, the Younger 11
Holland, Henry 45
Honey pots **36**, 135–6
Horns 136–7
Hot milk jugs 137
Huguenots 25–6, 27–9, 32, 34, 125, 129, 132, 150, 156, 182, 188, 201, 212, 219, 220–1, 235
Hukin, J. W. and Heath, J. T. 57–8, 114
Hunt, John S. 169
Hunt & Hoskell 60

Inkstands **11**, **37**, 137–8; Globe 138; Treasury 137
Issod, Thomas 236

Jacobi 214
Jackson, Orlando 131, 191
James I 17, 152
James pattern 153
Jardinières 139
Jenkins, Thomas 22, 235–6
Jensen, George 62
Johnson, Matthey 67
Jugs **61**, 139; *see also* Beer, Claret, Cream, Ewers and basins, Hot milk

Kandler, Charles 101, 144
Keble, Robert 106
Kensington Lewis 50, 146
Kent, William 130
King John's Cup 122, 214
Knife boxes 139
Knives 29, 139–40
Kyen scoops *see* Cayenne scoops

Ladeuil, Mosel 56
Ladles 140–1
Lambert, Henry 60
de Lamerie, Paul 31, 32, 49, 60, 69, 101, 107, 109, 153, 158, 164, 170, 173, 194, 195, 197, 208, 220, 232, 237, 238, 255, 256
Langford and Sebille 201
Leigh Cup 214
Lethaby, William 59
Liberty, Arthur Lasenby 59–60
— Cymric range 55
Lime presses **38**, 141
Linwoods 53
Livery pots **2**, 142; *see also* flagons
Lock, Nathaniel 197
Locke, John 152
Louis XIV 25, 32
Louis XV 60
Lukin, William 237

Magdelen Cups 90
Manjoy, George 197
Mappins 59
Marrow scoops 59
Martin Hall & Co. 60
Mazarines **39**, 132, 142–3
Mazers 9, 13
Meissonier, Juste-Aivele 34

283

INDEX

Mellor, David 66
Meriton, Samuel 197
Merry, Thomas 100
Mettayer 170
Mills, Nathaniel 53, 181
Mince, James 107
Mirrors 143–4
Mirror plateaux 143
— electro-plated 143
— ormolu 143
Models 144–5
Monarch Shield process 264–5
Monteiths 22, 27, **43**, 139, 145–6, 161, 162
Morris, William 58, 59
Mounted wares **40**, 146–8
Muffin dishes 148
Muffineers 148
Mugs **41**, 148–50, 182
Murphy, H. G. 63
Mustard pots **42**, 150–1
— spoons 151

Napkin rings 151
Napoleonic Wars 48, 126, 221
National Museum of Wales 144, 158
Nathan and Hayes 61
Nayler Brothers 63
Nelme, Anthony 107, 170, 188
Nutmeg graters 151–2

Ogle, Henry Meade 93
Oil and vinegar frame *see* cruets
Old English pattern 134, 140, 141, 175–6, 193
Onslow, Sir Arthur 141; Onslow pattern (flatware and cutlery) 141, 175–6
Ox-eye cups 153

Padgett & Braham 63
Padley Parkin & Co. 183
le Page, Jean 221
Pantin, Simon 134, 194, 237
Pap boats 153
Parker & Wakelin 204
Pastille burners *see* perfume burners
Patch boxes 153–4
Patent Office Design Registry 54, 199, 273–4
Patty pans 154
Peg measures 154
— tankards 154
Penners 154
Pen trays 154
Pepper pots 154
Perfume burners 154–5
— flasks 155
— funnels 155
Perry, Commodore 57
Phillips Garden 159
Phipps, T. & S. 95
— & Robinson 95, 197
Piercy, Robert 107
Pincushions 155
Pipes 155
Piranesi 46
Pitts & Preddy 131
Pitts, Thomas 38, 131, 178
— William 131
Plaques 155
Plate Licence 270, 271
Platel, Pierre 29, 220, 238
Plummets 155–6
Porringers 16, 21, 93, 124–5, 156, 166, 181; *see also* bleeding bowls, cups, dram cups, ecuelles
Posset pots 156–7

INDEX

Pounce boxes 157
Powder flasks 157
Priestley, Dr Joseph 41
Prime, J. 223
Pugin, A. W. N. 54–5
Punch bowls **44**, 157–9, 161
— ladles 159
— whisks 159
Pyne, Benjamin 28, 124

Racing bells 159
Ramsden, Omar 63
Rattles **57**, 159–60, 212
Rawlings and Summers 95
Razor sets **45**, 160
Régence 32, 171, 173, 226
Regency 34, 39, 40, 45, 49, 131, 140, 150, 173, 226
Reily, John 95, 197
— and Storer 95
Revere, Paul 69
Renon, Timothy 163
Rhodium plating 264
Richmond Cup 123
Richmond, John 91
Ring stand 161
Robins, John 138
Rollos, Philip 28
Romer, Emmick 38, 131
Rose bowls 161
Rosee, Pasqua 115
Rosewater ewers and basins 161
Royal Oak Cup 124
Royle, J. J. 183–4
Rugg, Richard 194
Rundell, Philip 51, 143, 169, 170
— and Bridge 46, 47, 49, 52, 102, 117, 232
— Bridge & Rundell 113, 142, 226

Saffron pots 161
Saffron Walden mazer 9
le Sage, John 194, 197, 220
Salad dishes 161
Salts: standing 8–10, 11, 13–14, **15**, 161–2, 177; trencher 14, **15**, 32, **56**, 161–2, 177
Salvers **56**, **57**, 162–4, 182, 194; *see also* waiters
Sampson Mordan & Co. 199
Sandboxes 164; *see also* inkstands
Sandilands Drinkwater 94
Sauce tureens 141, 164–6
Sauceboats 29, 31–2, 37, **46**, 162, 164–6
Saucepans 16, 166
Saucers 16–17, 127
— dishes 166–7
Scissors *see* Etuis, Grape scissors
Schuppe, John 119
Sconce **62**, 167
Scott, Digby 46, 237
Scott and Smith 95, 102, 126, 158
Seal boxes 167
— plates 167–8
Second World War 62, 64
Sharp, Robert 146, 236, 237
Shaving sets **48**, 168–9
Sheffield plating 35, 42, 73, 138, 183, 206, 211, 227–8, 258
Shields 169
Shiner, C. J. 65
Sideboard dishes **49**, 169–71
Sinking and raising 70–2, **71**, 228
Skewers 171
Smith, A. 162
— Benjamin 46, 150, 164, 237, 238

285

INDEX

— Daniel 146, 236, 237
— James 46
Snuff boxes 171, 178
— mulls 172
— rasps 172
Snuffers 129, 171–2; stands/trays 172
Soap boxes 172
Soup tureens 31, 37, 130, 141, 166, 172–3
Soy frames *see* cruets
Spice boxes 173
Spinning 72–3, **73**, 228
Sponge boxes *see* soap boxes
Spoons 11, 16, 29, **50**, 174–6; acorn 11; Apostle 11, **13**, 16, 86, 174; diamond 11, **50**; fiddle **50**; Hanoverian 174; maidenhead 11; seal top 11; Tichborne set 16; Trefid **50**; puritan 174
Spoon trays 173–4
Sprimont, Nicholas 37
Stabler, Harold 63
Stamping and pressing 53, 73–4, 228
Standing cups 9, 11
Standishes *see* inkstands
Steeple cup 13
Sterling 31, 35, 75, 206, 229, 234, 236, 241, 243; *see also* Britannia standard
Stirrup cups 177–8
Stockwell, E. H. 199
Stone, Robert 65
Stop of the Exchequer 1672 20
Storr, Paul 46, 51, 95, 102, 110, 133, 117, 126, 135–6, 144, 164, 170, 203, 214, 237, 238
Strainers 141

— orange, lemon and lime 152–3
— spoons 178
Strawberry dishes 29, 127, 154, 178
Studley bowl and cover 8
Styles, Alex 66
Sugar bowls 178–9
— boxes 179
— crushers 179
— nippers/tongs 179–80
— sifters 180
Supper services 180
Sweetmeat baskets 89, 180–1
Syllabub pots 181
Syng, Richard 237

Tankards 11, **24**, 162, 181–2
Taper stands *see* waxjacks
Tapersticks 182–3
Tapley, John 119, 144
Tatham, Charles Heathcote 45–6, 47
Taylboyes, Robert 235
Tazze 13, 124, 127, **183**; as term to be deprecated 163
Tea and coffee machines 183–4
Tea caddies **51**, **56**, **58**, 184–6
— kettles 33, **52**, 186–7; stands 187
— pots 32–3, **53**, 188–92; stands 192
— service **8**
— strainers 193
— tables 193–4
— trays 194
— vases 194
Teaspoons 192–3
Teniers, David, the Younger 50
Thimbles *see* Etuis
Thomason, Sir Edward 143, 212, 231

INDEX

Toasting forks 194
Toast racks 194–5
Tobacco boxes 195
Toddy ladles 195
Toilet pots 16
— services 144, 195–6
Tongue scrapers 196
Tonti, Lorenzo 230
Tontines 230–1
Tooth brushes 196
— picks 196
— powder boxes 196
Touchstone 231
Toys and miniatures 196–7
Trafalgar Vase 126
Travelling sets *see* Canteens
Treby Punch Bowl 158
— Toilet Service 195
Tuite, John 35, 163, 194
Tumbler cups 198
— frame 198
Tuns 198
Tureens **4**, **47**, **61**, 139, 162, 164–6; *see also* Soup, Sauce tureens
Turning up from a Cone 72

Urns; coffee **5**, 184; tea 184

Vechte, Antoine 169
Vegetable dishes 198
Venison dishes 198
Verrières 198
van Vianen, Adam 18
— Christian, of Utrecht 18
Vickers, John 208
Queen Victoria 50, 144
Videau, Aymé 237
Vinaigrettes 198–9
Vintners' Cup 200

Wager cups 200
Waiters 162–4, 187, 192; *see also* Salvers
Wakelin, Edward 38, 60, 164, 194, 232, 238
— and Garrard 46–7
— & Taylor 55
— Ledgers 97, 110, 156
Wakely & Wheeler 63
Walpole, Horace 38, 45, 54
Walton, Isaac 109
Warwick Castle 121
— cruet 32, 121, 200
— Vase and imitations 51, 126, 173, 231–2
Watt, James 41
Waxjacks 200
Wedgwood 39, 41, 43, 113, 117, 119, 191
Weights and Measures 272
Welch, Robert 66
Welder, Samuel 106
Wellby, D. & J. 60
Wellington, Duke of 144
Whipman & Wright 237
Wickes, George 47, 60, 116, 130, 255
Willaume, David 28, 107, 119, 164, 170, 220, 237, 238
William and Mary 25, 27
William IV 52
Williams-Wynn toilet service 144
Willmore, Joseph 53, 197, 199
Wine cisterns 200
— coasters **60**, 200–1
— coolers **54**, **56**, 126, 201–2
— cups 202
— fountains 202–3
— funnels 203
— tasters 203

287

INDEX

— trolleys *see* Decanter trolleys
Wire drawing 74
à Wood, Anthony 145
Wood, Edward 35, 162
— Samuel 34, 106–7

Wren, Sir Christopher 146
Wyatt, James 40, 41, 45, 102, 204

Young James 131, 191